LIVE COMPANY

Children whose minds as well as bodies have been damaged by the intrusions of sexual abuse, violence or neglect, and others, quite different, who are handicapped by their own mysterious sensitivities to more minor deprivations, may experience a type of black despair and cynicism that require long-term treatment and test the stamina of the psychotherapist to the utmost.

In *Live Company* Anne Alvarez reflects on thirty years' experience of treating autistic, psychotic and borderline children and adolescents by the methods of psychoanalytic psychotherapy. Central to the book is the moving story of an autistic child's long struggle between sanity and madness, in which the author describes the arduous journey that she as therapist and he as patient made together towards new understanding and his partial recovery.

Modern developments in psychoanalytic theory and technique mean that such children can be treated with some success. In the book the author outlines and discusses these developments, and also describes some of the areas of convergence and divergence between organicist and psychodynamicist theories of autism. Particularly important is her integration of psychoanalytic theory with the new findings in infant development and infant psychiatry. This has enabled her to formulate some new and exciting ideas relevant to working with very disturbed children and to speculate on the need for some additions to established theory.

Anne Alvarez has produced a professionally powerful and enlightening book, drawn from her extensive experience as a child psychotherapist at the Tavistock Clinic, which will be of interest to all professionals involved with children and adolescents as well as anyone interested in madness and the growth of the mind.

LIVE COMPANY

LIVE COMPANY

Psychoanalytic psychotherapy with
autistic, borderline, deprived and
abused children

Anne Alvarez

London and New York

First published 1992
by Routledge
11 New Fetter Lane, London EC4P 4EE

Simultaneously published in the USA and Canada
by Routledge
29 West 35th Street, New York, NY 10001

Routledge is an imprint of the Taylor & Francis Group

Reprinted 1993, 1996, 1998, 1999

Typeset in 10 on 12 point Garamond by
Falcon Typographic Art Ltd, Fife, Scotland
Printed and bound in Great Britain by
Mackays of Chatham PLC, Chatham Kent

British Library Cataloguing in Publication Data
Alvarez, Anne
Live company: psychoanalytic psychotherapy with
autistic, borderline, deprived and abused children
I. Title
618.928914

Library of Congress Cataloguing in Publication Data
Alvarez, Anne 1936–
Live company: psychoanalytic psychotherapy with autistic,
borderline, deprived and abused children / Anne Alvarez.
p. cm.
1. Autism – Treatment. 2. Schizophrenia in children – Treatment.
3. Schizophrenia in adolescence – Treatment. 4. Borderline
personality disorder in children – Treatment. 5. Borderline
personality disorder in adolescence – Treatment. 6. Autism –
Treatment – Case studies. 7. Child analysis. 8. Adolescent
analysis. I. Title.
[DNLM: 1. Autism, Infantile – therapy. 2. Child Abuse – psychology.
3. Psychoanalytic Therapy – in infancy and childhood. 4. Psychotic
Disorders – in infancy and childhood. 5. Psychotic Disorders – therapy.
WS 350.2 A473L]
RJ506.A9A58 1992
618.92´89820651 – dc20
DNLM/DLC
for Library of Congress 91–40447 CIP

ISBN 0–415–06096–6
0–415–06097–4 (pbk)

To Al

How, physically, could the infant mind identify persons? What features of their behaviour are diagnostic of them? Intentional behaviour has a number of features that are not shared with inanimate things, and so an intentional agent may be equipped to respond to others like itself.... Inanimate movement runs downhill, oscillates in simple ways, bounces, but it does not surge in self-generative impulses. Anything that tends to make unprovoked bursts of rhythm, like a spot of reflected sunlight, seems alive. This rhythmical vitality of movement is the first identification of live company.

(Colwyn Trevarthen 1978)

I have no doubt whatever of the need for something in the personality to make contact with psychic quality.

(Wilfred Bion 1962)

CONTENTS

PREFACE

This book is a record of my reflections on the experience of treating autistic, psychotic and borderline children by the methods of psychoanalytic psychotherapy. Some of the children and adolescents I shall describe are psychotic patients who begin to get better, some are borderline psychotics who have been hovering on the brink; all, I hope, give an idea of the two worlds of sanity and madness, the fragility of the one and the ugly and seductive power of the other. Such patients can be helped by psychoanalytic methods, but the treatment is long, arduous, and almost always places considerable strain on the therapist. Yet there is growing consensus that this strain and burden is in some way central to the treatment. Children whose minds as well as bodies have been damaged by the intrusions of sexual abuse, violence or neglect and others, quite different, who are handicapped by their own mysterious sensitivities to more minor deprivations, may experience a type of black despair and cynicism far beyond that felt by neurotic patients. A therapist suffering from too large a dose of therapeutic zeal or of passionate belief in the therapeutic power of psychoanalytic explanation, may experience great disappointment when the child doesn't seem to feel helped by her remarkable revelations, and doesn't seem to change. I have had many such disappointments myself. The patient's terrors may be too overwhelming to be easily named, let alone explained; or his destructiveness or self-destructiveness may have developed, after perhaps years of practice, into high art. The psychotherapist has to be capable of being disturbed enough to feel for the patient, and at the same time sane enough to think with him, until the patient's own ego, his thinking self, grows enough to be able to do it for himself.

Few of these chronically ill children have remained simply desperate, or simply terrified – almost all have developed protective manoeuvres which may be as pathological as the original upset, and perhaps far more dead-end. The psychotherapist is witness to the struggle to become sane and to the draining efforts to remain so; the pull backwards into madness can be tremendous. The pull backwards for the therapist can also be very powerful. The actual process by which the child becomes more alive is often painful – a girl who has behaved like a grotesque and retarded idiot all her life may face real terror at beginning to behave with grace and intelligence. Worst of all are the children who in large part have given up, who have abandoned hope, more or less ceased to have longings, and withdrawn to a point where they are almost beyond reach. Here the therapist may have to do more than feel and think for such cut-off or hardened patients; she may have, at times, to carry – for them – the knowledge that they, and the world, exist at all. Some, of course, remain beyond reach. Yet many do get better, and in fact these psychotic and borderline psychotic children are the ones whom, more and more, child psychotherapists are being asked to treat, because they have got beyond responding to ordinary human comfort, reassurance, or to the ordinary reasonable demands of parents and teachers.

In the introduction I shall trace the modern developments in psychoanalytic theory and technique which have influenced me and which form the foundation for the work described here. In the rest of the book I try to draw out implications of these modern developments for work with psychotic and borderline psychotic children. Most of the psychotic children I refer to are autistic, but some are schizophrenic. The first part of the book involves a narrative of my treatment of a severely withdrawn and psychotic autistic boy, Robbie, and of my struggles and failures to understand him. Robbie's treatment has been exceedingly long and his improvements not dramatic. I started treating him on an infrequent basis in the late 1960s when few such children were receiving psychoanalytic therapy, and little was understood about how to help them. I have continued because, although terribly slow, his progress has been continuous and its pace has even quickened as I have come to understand him better, especially in regard to the awesome impact of his autism on the rest of his personality and development.

The rest of the book discusses issues, both theoretical and

methodological, in Robbie's treatment, and in work with other psychotic and borderline children, some of whom have been severely abused or deprived. Although the borderline psychotic children have some degree of ego development or sanity available to them, the technical problems for the therapist are often similar to those with iller, more egoless psychotic patients. On the subject of autism, I have tried to show some of the areas of convergence and divergence between the organicist and the psychodynamicist theories of autism. It is unfortunate that as yet there has been relatively little dialogue between the two groups in Britain. In this context, I should note that organic psychiatrists do not describe autistic patients as psychotic. They stress instead the element of cognitive deficit and the disorder of development, and there is no doubt that the earliness of the onset of autism makes an impact on the child's cognitive and emotional develoment which is far more devastating than that of psychiatric illnesses which emerge later in a child's life, such as schizophrenia. (see Kolvin *et al.* 1971). I have kept the term 'psychotic', however, in order to emphasize the extent of the lack of contact with reality, and the weakness in ego development.

My aim has been to try to begin to sort out the theoretical baggage that was impeding my work with Robbie and other patients from the theories and thinking that really helped. I found that the theories and psychoanalytic tools I was using were a jumble of early psychoanalytic theory – theory which for the most part was based on methods found to help neurotic patients – together with more recent conceptions developed from work with patients who were psychotic but adult. Developmental thinking more appropriate to work with a psychotic person who is also *still a child* was also needed, as was recognition of the importance of understanding how psychotic illness in childhood interferes with cognitive as well as emotional development. The problem of lifelong depression or lifelong despair in someone who is still a child raises, I believe, important issues for psychoanalytic theory and technique. Such chronic clinical depression, especially in a child whose development is going awry, poses problems very different from those posed by anxiety, even anxiety of a depressive kind. A model of the mind which concentrates on defences against anxieties may need supplementing with the understanding that a chronically depressed child may have barely developed such 'defences' in the ordinary sense at all, and that when he does, these may need, in certain instances, to be viewed as developmental achievements.

My own base is the line that flows from Freud through Klein to Bion, but I have tried to show where some of the thinking of American self psychologists was also helpful, and throughout the book I have drawn on the important new findings from research in infant development and infant psychiatry. I have also drawn on my Tavistock experience of infant observation and of psychotherapy with mothers and disturbed babies. The study of real live babies is a fascinating testing ground for the psychoanalytic theories of infant development, and I have been led to speculations of my own on the need for some additions to established theory.

ACKNOWLEDGEMENTS

This book has taken ten years to write, and the number of friends, colleagues, teachers and students who have made helpful suggestions about one or more chapters is huge. In the hope of being forgiven by those I have left out, I would like to thank: Luke Alvarez, Gabrielle Crockatt, Ricky Emanuel, Betty Joseph, Israel Kolvin, Sebastian Kraemer, Juliet Hopkins, Athol Hughes, Anita Kermode, Sheila Miller, Mary Sue Moore, Edna O'Shaughnessy, Albert Reid, Elizabeth Spillius, Cathy Urwin, and also Sue Reid, Trudy Klauber and other members of the Autism Workshop at the Tavistock Clinic, as well as many other colleagues at the Tavistock.

I owe a huge debt of gratitude to the Laidlaw Foundation of Toronto, Canada, for the generous grant which allowed me to undertake the time-consuming training in child psychotherapy at the Tavistock in the 1960s, to Harvey Brooker of the University of Toronto, who gave me my first sound lessons in the clinical and research study of madness. I am greatly indebted to Otto Weininger, also of the University of Toronto, who first suggested to me the possibility that autistic children might also be persons, and to Martha Harris of the Tavistock for teaching that children's play was full of meaning. My analysis with Dr Leslie Sohn helped me to learn that there was a life outside psychoanalysis, and Betty Joseph's inspiring teaching has kept the psychoanalytic process perpetually interesting and alive for me.

I am grateful to Edwina Welham for her wise and balanced editorial counsel, to Eleanor Morgan, Michèle Noble, Davina Pariaug, Jane Rayner and Ann Westgate for their good-humoured secretarial assistance, to Angela Haselton of the Tavistock library, and to Jennie Allen and the rest of the reception staff in the Child and Family Department.

Professor Livia Di Cagno and the staff and students of the Department of Child Neuropsychiatry at the University Hospital in Turin have allowed me to try out almost every idea in this book in lectures over the years. Their comments and independent contributions have been invaluable.

I am grateful to the following psychotherapists for permission to use material from their patients' sessions and for many lively discussions: Stella Acquarone, Paul Barrows, Eve Box-Grainger, Jonathan Bradley, Janet Bungener, Cate Carey, Carol Hanson, Sue Kegerreis, Jeanne Magagna, Ann Parr, Maria Teresa Pozzan, Sarah Randaccio, Ruth Selwyn, Valerie Sinason, Ann Thompson, Louise Whelan, Cathy Urwin.

Maria Rhode, Margaret Rustin and Valerie Sinason read the whole manuscript in an early, very messy form, made numerous detailed suggestions and helped it to begin to become a book. When it was almost finished, I was fortunate to have the suggestions and expertise of Frances Tustin made available to me; I am grateful to her for her cautionary words about the dangers of entering the autistic bullring. The book, however, would never have been finished at all without the encouragement, browbeating and sometimes savage pruning of Judith Edwards, Priscilla Roth and, above all, of my husband, Al Alvarez, who saw it and me through every stage.

The introduction was first published in 1987 in *Giorn. Neuropsich. Eta Evol.* 7,3. Some of the material from Chapters 1–5 and Chapter 13 was first published in the *J. Child Psychother.* 1977, 1980, 1985 and 1988. Chapter 6 was first published in *Psychoanalytic Inquiry* 1992. Some of the material from Chapter 7 was first read at a conference on *Apprendimento e Patologia Neuropsichiatria nei primi anni di vita*, Pisa, 1989, organized by the Societa Italiano di Neuropsichiatria Infantile, Universita di Pisa and Institute Stella Maris. Chapter 8 was first read as a Freud Memorial Lecture, University College, London, February 1991. Some of the material from Chapters 8 to 11 was first read as lectures on borderline psychosis to the Association of Child Psychotherapists in 1986. An earlier version of Chapter 11 was first published in *Prospettivi psicoanalitiche nel lavoro istituzionale*, Rome, 8, 3, Sett. 1990. An earlier version of Chapter 12 was first published in *Assoc. for Child Psychol. and Psychiat. Occasional Paper 3, The Consequences of Child Sexual Abuse*, Chapter 4, 'The need to remember and the need to forget', 1990, and reprinted by permission of ACPP, 70 Borough High Street, London, SE1 1XF. An earlier version of Chapter

13 was first read at the Margaret Lowenfeld Day Conference, University of Cambridge, November 1987. An earlier version of Chapter 14 was first published in 1990 in Bondioli, A. (ed.) *Il Bambino, Il Gioco, Gli Affetti*. Bergamo: Juvenilia. It was first read in English at the joint WAIPAD–Anna Freud–Tavistock conference, *The Effect of Relationships upon Relationships*, November 1990, London. It was first published in English in 1991 in *Psychoanalytic Psychotherapy* 5, 3.

I am grateful to the above journals for permission to reproduce copyright material. I am also grateful to Professor Michael Lewis, Chief, Institute for the Study of Child Development, Robert Wood Johnson Medical School, New Brunswick, New Jersey, for permission to reproduce the Brazelton material in Chapter 5, and in the Appendix to Chapter 5.

INTRODUCTION
Modern developments in psychoanalysis

Psychoanalysis has changed almost beyond recognition since the turn of the century. There have been several separate and independent lines of development, but I shall focus mostly on a single thread, that which leads from Freud through Melanie Klein and Wilfred Bion to some of the recent work on the clinical implications of these additions to theory. Freud, great talker and great detective that he was, had reported with growing excitement that he could relieve the symptoms of his neurotic patients by concentrating on three areas of investigation: first, their past, particularly their childhood past; second, the sexual content of the memories or phantasies connected with this past; and third, the powerful repressive forces that kept the lid on this seething pot. In the last sixty years each one of these three cardinal principles has been radically reformulated – first by Freud himself, later by others – producing changes in theory, in practice, in the range of patients accessible to treatment and, for that matter, in the meta-theoretical assumptions that underlie the whole enterprise. There is now room in psychoanalysis for what pre-Freudian thinkers could take for granted, the mentalness of mind.

THE PAST

The past has always held pride of place in psychoanalytic theories. Although theorists have disagreed about which experiences in early life are the really crucial ones for forming character and symptoms, and also about at exactly how early a period the formative forces make their impact, few people now doubt that experiences in childhood and infancy are of fundamental importance in understanding a person's current life and play some part in shaping how he

1

will meet his future. But the illumination to be gained from the past reconstructed as an explainer of behaviour is no longer so widely thought to be as magical a therapeutic instrument as it was imagined to be in the early days of psychoanalysis. (It of course continues to be hugely important for educational policy, preventive child psychiatry and the new field of infant psychiatry.) In fact, from as early as 1905, Freud had begun to learn that intellectual insight was not enough, that understanding in the here-and-now of the transference relationship with the analyst, with its attendant emotionality, was the crucial area where change could take place (Freud 1905a). Later he also drew attention to the process of working-through, emphasizing that insight, however momentous, did not involve an instantaneous miraculous revelatory moment, but a much more gradual and piecemeal process of slowly developing understanding (1914).

These sobering reflections about the sheer amount of time it takes to change one's nature have also been accompanied by changes in the theory of how the therapeutic action of psychoanalysis takes place and the manner in which the so-called insight is gained. There is now, for example, much greater attention paid to the interpersonal relationship between the patient and his analyst, that is, to the patient's changing transference and to the analyst's changing counter-transference – the feelings and reactions evoked in him by the patient. It is not only the patient who has had to slow down and attend to more minute happenings in the here-and-now; so, too, does the analyst or the psychoanalytical therapist. The attention to and study of these responses in the therapist have been stimulated in Britain by theoretical developments following from the work of object-relations theorists such as Klein and Fairbairn but also from other thinkers in Europe and America as well (Klein 1937; Fairbairn 1952; Sullivan 1953; Bion 1962; Spillius 1988; Stolorow, Brandchaft and Atwood 1987; Greenberg and Mitchell, 1983).

Klein's work suggested that it was not enough to look for missing aspects of the patient in his repressed and buried unconscious: these missing parts or feelings could sometimes lie much further afield, in someone else's feelings. This phenomenon, called 'projective identification', includes situations where, for example, some people you meet always make you feel intelligent and attractive, while others always make you feel that your slip is showing. Human beings, often quite unknowingly, can evoke very specific and often powerful feelings in other people, and we may do this repetitively in certain systematic ways in order to rid ourselves of unwanted or simply unacknowledged parts of our own personality, or because we genuinely believe a particular feeling or thought or talent could never be ours. A child may indeed have an elder brother who is more intelligent or more academic than she is, but if this fact of her family history has led her to believe that everyone is more intelligent and that she is stupid, she may not only see others as more intelligent (Freud's notion of projection – Freud 1911a), she may be doing something much more active and continuously impoverishing to her own personality than simply having a perception: she may really be allowing or even inviting others to do the thinking for her in situations where she could do it for herself (projective identification as described by Melanie Klein) (Klein 1946).

Her therapist may need to explore in herself, then, how it is that this patient always makes her feel so protective and intelligent and wise. To discuss these observations with the patient and show her how these processes keep repeating themselves moment by moment in the sessions seems to be far more effective than simply resorting to elaborate detective-like reconstructions about the past causes of the patient's beliefs about herself. Links with the past, of course, are important, but they are no substitute for the study of the living interactions and of the often dangerous erosions of precious parts of the personality which may take place in these interactions (Joseph 1975).

In some ways, this attention to the present makes the work for the psychoanalytical therapist much harder and more demanding, but it also makes it much more interesting and infinitely more lively. The popular image of the zipper-mouthed, detached and frosty analyst-scientist really no longer applies. The comparison, instead, should perhaps be with a trained and skilled but constantly improvising musician who, like the patient, has to live and learn from felt experience and – not surprisingly – also from practice.

A second factor which has led to more emphasis on work in the present is the development in the theory of how psychoanalysis works. Early theories had to do with catharsis and with the liberating effect of uncovering and unmasking repressed material. Such methods, of course, do often bring relief, but two modern European analysts, Wilfred Bion and Ignacio Matte Blanco, have laid much more stress on the interpretive, hermeneutic function in producing change. (See also the Americans Stolorow, Brandchaft and Atwood 1987.) Matte Blanco has written of an 'unfolding' or 'translating'

3

function, where the patient is helped to see new or deeper meanings in ideas which may in fact be quite conscious (Rayner 1981). Bion, observing in himself the type of projective identification processes I mentioned earlier – that is, feelings evoked by the patient – began to notice that sometimes his schizophrenic patients were using these processes neither as a defence nor because the unacknowledged part of the personality was simply unrecognized as theirs, but rather because, in some situations, the patient seemed really to *need* Bion to carry feelings the patient himself could not bear. Bion suggested that some projective identifications expressed a need to communicate something to someone on a very profound level; he began to see this as related to a fundamental process in normal development, and compared the analyst's 'containment' and 'transformation' of the patient's feelings and thoughts to the primitive but powerful pre-verbal communications that take place between mothers and tiny infants. The mother's capacity for reverie, he wrote, could contain the infant's crises and excitements and transform them into bearable experiences. He suggested that this was a normal maternal function, and many analysts have begun to consider this quality of understanding as central to their work with all patients, not only the psychiatrically ill (Bion 1962, 1965).

This notion of containment has much in common with Winnicott's concept of 'holding', and has been of immeasurable importance for the clinical work of child psychotherapists (Winnicott 1960). For children, the pathogenic past may be beyond our reach, not because it is over and done with, but precisely because it is not, that is, because it is continuing to do its damage in the present in the child's outside life. We may be able to do a little to change these outside factors, but most often we cannot do enough. What we can try to do, however, is provide an opportunity for something new to happen within the child. The reliability and regularity provided by the psychoanalytic setting – the child is seen in the same room at the same time – and the firm structure of psychoanalytic technique provide an opportunity for structure and order to begin to develop in the child's mind. The results of this opportunity for 'containment' are particularly striking with very ill, borderline psychotic, sexually abused children or with deprived children. Many people working with children know well how useless in taming the horror are facile explanations of whatever it is that has led to the child's breakdown. Yet brave receptive listening, and a firm and not too masochistic attitude to the child's possibly quite horrible projections – that is,

4

to the child's desperate need to do to us what he feels was done to him – do seem to help.

SEXUALITY, REPRESSION AND THE THEORY OF PERSONALITY

As Freud learned more about the stubborn resistance of his patients, not just to unpleasant insight, but to the very health and happiness they claimed to seek, he began to take more seriously the destructive forces in human nature, and the shadowy, often deadly power of unconscious morality. The domain of the 'id' was widened beyond its early somewhat narrow sexual terrain, and the conscience, instead of being seen as not much more than a repressing lid on the cooking pot, began to acquire a human, sometimes even an encouraging voice. Freud's and Melanie Klein's studies of mourning (Freud 1917; Klein 1940) led to an interest in the growth of love, concern and creativity. Sexuality had to take its place in the pantheon alongside the 'higher side' of man's nature that critics like Carl Jung had originally accused Freud of neglecting (Storr 1986: 184). Anna Freud's work with children and adults who managed to survive emotionally such disasters as the concentration camps led to much more interest in the ego, and more respect for the achievements which sanity, even neurotic sanity, may involve. Thanks to Anna Freud, and others such as Hartmann and Sandler, the so-called 'defences' have come to be seen – in a developmental perspective – as achievements rather than mainly as impediments (A. Freud 1936; Hartmann 1964; Sandler with A. Freud 1985).

Klein, too, linked particular groups of defences with particular phases (not stages) of personality development, in particular, with different types of anxiety. Her far-reaching distinction between anxiety related to fear and anxiety related to guilt and concern, together with her investigations of the different defences against, and responses to, fear and guilt, has led to the building up of a quite complex and subtle picture of personality and character development. These considerations have enabled analysts and therapists to be more sensitive to the vast variety of manifestations of states of mind which might appear, on superficial examination, to be similar: self-confidence based on arrogance is seen to have very different origins and consequences from that based on pride, for example; bravery arising from the denial of fear has very different

5

implications from bravery arising from the overcoming of fear; one type of depression may lead downhill to illness, another may lead to recovery and mental growth. The Kleinian interest in distinguishing between different types of learning, and motives for learning, together with Bion's investigations into how some of his schizophrenic patients with thought disorder developed a capacity to think their thoughts, have led to a deeper understanding of some of the conditions and preconditions for thinking (Spillius 1988a: 153ff).

Bion's ideas about what enables a thought to become thinkable, in terms of its prior containability in the patient's analyst or in the baby's mother, has led to much creative preoccupation among a whole generation of analysts with the technical implications of these ideas. There is now more stress on the need for the analyst to feel his way through to whatever is the patient's experience of the moment, and on the need to allow time for such experience to be explored carefully; it enables the patient to give greater form and meaning to his thoughts and feelings. In the Kleinian group, but also in others, there is something of a shift away from earlier techniques which involved interpretations of a more explanatory kind, and which focused on exchanging one content for another, such as: 'you feel this because you are afraid to feel that', or 'you think you feel this, but what you really feel is that', or 'you think I dislike you, but this is really a projection of your dislike of me'. This change to a more cautious, somehow more respectful approach to the patient's unconscious is exemplified in Joseph's emphasis on the importance of the analyst's tolerance of *not* understanding and in the practice among analysts and therapists of developing awareness of their own feelings toward the patient and of how these may change from moment to moment in a session. The analyst, according to Bion, has to help to make the thought thinkable before he attempts to pass it on to the patient. Predigested or, worse, undigested chunks of psychoanalytic explanation would not pass this test (Bion 1962; Rosenfeld 1987; Joseph 1983; Casement 1985).

PRACTICAL APPLICATIONS

These developments in psychoanalytic theory and technique (and I have mentioned only a few among many independent lines of growth) have been of enormous benefit to the work of child psychotherapists. The changes have extended the range of patients

who can be treated, although of course it is really the patients themselves, and their awkward refusal to fit the theories, that has led to
the slow, but mostly continuous stretching and breaking of moulds.
The better understanding of processes of splitting and fragmentation has enabled psychotherapists to include in their caseload the
patients who are the subject of this book: the psychotic, borderline
psychotic and also the seemingly amoral and conscienceless children
and adolescents who were previously thought to be unreachable
by psychoanalytic methods. Just as the neurotic may repress or
project the more unpleasant side of his nature, the psychopathic
or delinquent patient who appears cold and unfeeling may well
be projecting a quite gentle self, as well as his conscience, into
someone else.

There have been further developments, many in the area of
preventive psychiatry. The teaching of Donald Winnicott, the great
paediatrician and child analyst, has inspired child therapists, already
trained in infant observation, to begin working in baby clinics and
obstetric and paediatric units in general hospitals to help mothers
of distressed infants with feeding or sleeping problems (Daws
1989). Some are being asked to help mothers with babies who
seem too withdrawn for their own good. Some are consulting to
day care centres for babies and under fives, some to residential
children's homes and some to units for premature babies. Others
are working with the emotional suffering of physically handicapped
or terminally ill children and of the parents and nurses who care for
them (Sinason 1986; Judd 1989). Although this work is not in every
case always straightforward psychoanalytic therapy, it involves the
use of many of its skills, especially sensitivity to and familiarity
with primitive, nearly unbearably painful states of mind. The
popular myth of the cool, complacent, unfeeling psychoanalyst or
psychoanalytical therapist doling out recipes from his or her sexual
cookbook to comfortably-off, suggestible middle-class neurotics is
a far cry from the truth. Practitioners of intensive analytic work pay
dearly in emotional terms when they undertake to treat patients as
damaged as those I have mentioned. Many of us, when we began
this work, had a dream of releasing the inhibitions of depressed or
repressed people, the neurotics who were thought by Freud to need
to remember the past in order to be freed from it. We thought of it as
dramatic, exciting work. In practice, much of the time our task is to
help our child patients to learn such things as restraint, self-control
and thoughtfulness; not to remember the past in order to be freed

from it, but to forget it in order to be freed from it. The problem for the therapist is to keep a balance between getting close enough emotionally to the patient to stay in contact – which, with very mad children, will tend to involve grave worry and concern, outrage and despair – and staying just far enough away to be able to think. I know of no one who gets the balance right every time.

EXPLAINING CHANGE, NOVELTY AND THE MENTALNESS OF MIND

Psychoanalytic theory is nowadays much better equipped to account for change, development, novelty and mental growth in ways impossible before. In the early, more mechanistic system where instincts (usually sexual) sought gratification or discharge, but never stimulation or mental enlargement, the basic unit of personality was a packet of self-centred energy (an instinct or drive). 'Objects' – that is, other people or aspects of other people – were simply a means to gratification or release (Greenberg and Mitchell 1983). Babies, for example, were said to love their mothers because they were associated with the provision of nourishment and care, and so on. But for British object-relations theorists the basic unit of personality is a relational one, and the basic building block of human character is the baby's first relationship with its mother – with her eyes, voice, smell, touch, in addition to but not because of her feeding functions. According to the old theory, the need to 'let it all go, have a good cry' would be seen as a need for catharsis and discharge; the difficulty would be seen as an 'inhibition', a sort of lid or obstruction. (I am caricaturing a little, but not entirely.) In object-relations theory, on the other hand, the recognition of a person's difficulty in unloading unbearable tensions would be accompanied by the question 'What kind of object (imagined person or aspect of a person) is refusing permission for these tears or is not available for them, or can't bear them?' A person's motives are by definition, even at their most mindless and bestial, always seen as directed towards and influenced by the phantasy of a someone – however unconscious, unacknowledged and forgotten that someone may be. This emphasis on the phantasied qualities of the object is particularly important in Kleinian thinking. Klein stressed the way in which the 'internal object' (a phantasied or imagined figure or aspect of a figure) colours and shapes relationships with real figures – 'objects' – in the real world. An adolescent girl may dream of evil crones in the night and fear the ill will of female teachers throughout the day in ways which may bear only some relation to the actual behaviour of the teachers concerned, or, for that matter, of actual maternal figures from the past. The interaction between the child's own feelings, projections and introjections and the real qualities of real figures is seen as a highly complex process, one which leads to the gradual building up of internal objects which have a durable, determining and structuring role in development and in the creation of personality. A one-person psychology has been replaced by a two-person psychology of a highly imaginative and mental kind.

This relational model is more in accord with post-Einsteinian relativity theory in which there is no such thing as a context-free event and even a force as fundamental as gravity is seen as a relation between two bodies. Freud, in contrast, was a pre-Einsteinian thinker; despite all the wisdom and subtlety displayed in his clinical writings and in many of his philosophical musings, his scientific summings up were almost always in terms of Newtonian mechanistic science. The trouble with machines, however, is that they move but they do not grow. The newer models are also more in accord with recent research carried out by developmental psychologists, who find that the new baby is pre-structured to be as keenly interested in things like the expressiveness of his mother's face and voice, and in what one worker has described as the pre-music and pre-speech dialogues he has with her, as he is in her purely need-satisfying functions (Trevarthen 1974). The latest research is demonstrating the devastating effect on the personality and intelligence of babies born to mothers suffering from depression, who may meet the ordinary physical needs of the baby but cannot engage in the reciprocity which seems so important for developing hope and mental growth (Murray 1991). Klein was certain that infants sought love and understanding in addition to nourishment, and Bion pointed out that right from the beginning of life there seemed to be a desire for knowledge which was to some extent independent of emotional and bodily needs. He suggested that the mind needed the nourishment of the experience of *getting to know someone* as much as the body needs food, and terrible stuntings and bluntings resulted if the mind were starved of it. One researcher has ingeniously tackled this complex question of whether intellectual curiosity really is only a roundabout search for food. Peter Wolff showed that periods of something very like intellectual curiosity – when the new baby has a bright, shiny,

9

'what-is-it?' look in its eye, and studies novel, intricate stimuli with great concentration – take place *after* feeds, not before. These states of physiologically measurable alertness seem to be, as it were, freed to operate when the child is physically content and not, as the early psychoanalysts and many contemporary behavioural psychologists would have us believe, when the child is restlessly driven by a search for food or comfort (Wolff 1965).

In a way, psychoanalysis and its theories are now more respectful of its own early clinical observations concerning the existence – the naturalness – of hatred, suffering, love and even unselfish concern. The new need no longer be defined solely in terms of the old and the relationship of the higher with the lower is nothing like so simple as was first thought: pop versions of the Freudian concept of sublimation tend to view activities such as artistic endeavour, or friendship, in reductionistic terms, as exhibitionism and covert sexuality manifesting themselves in disguised and socially acceptable forms. Of course, many such simple substitutions do occur in life, but so do other genuine and profound developments to 'higher' levels. Klein insisted that reparation – the action of restoring a person (or cause or standard or ideal) damaged by one's own ill-treatment or neglect – was not a defence or 'reaction-formation' against guilt, but a creative outcome: that is, an overcoming of guilt and mental pain, a going forward and development (Klein 1940: 265). There is, I believe, a huge meta-theoretical leap in this Kleinian theory of reparation (see Chapter 11), which takes psychoanalytic theory right out of the old see-saw, push-me-pull-you model and, in its place, utilizes notions of growth. The forces for change are seen not as mechanisms but processes. Such a relational model implies the type of interactive process between self and object which enables genuinely new elements to emerge: the self may, for example, project something into an object who transforms the projection and returns it in a modified form; the self may reintroject this, with further modifications so that what is then re-projected is different again. Instead of a cycle, there may be an upward spiral. In cases of pathology, instead of a dead end, there may be deterioration.

The general problem of how to account for change has preoccupied philosophers since the beginning of philosophy. In his book *Gödel, Escher, Bach*, Douglas Hofstadter described the 'strange loops' and spirals that occur, not just in Godel's mathematical theorems, Escher's hallucinatory pictures and, supremely, Bach's

Musical Offering, but in areas as diverse as the genetic DNA system (where strands act upon enzymes and enzymes then act actively back upon strands to produce new information) and the strange, loopy fact that a mind can be conscious of itself (Hofstadter 1981). He said that all these things reminded him, in ways he could not express, of the beautiful many-voiced fugue of the human mind (see Chapter 11 for a fuller discussion of this). Hofstadter does not write about psychoanalysis, but it is cheering to think that psychoanalytic theory has reached a level of beauty and complexity deserving of a place on Hofstadter's list.

SUMMARY

I have tried to outline a few of the developments in psychoanalytic technique, theory and meta-theory which are important for the work of the contemporary child psychotherapist. These include: less emphasis on interpretations which invoke the past as an explainer of behaviour and more attention to the patient's need and functioning in the here-and-now; the supplementing, in the theory of the therapeutic action of psychoanalysis, of the lifting of repressive barriers with a process which involves, by means of analytic containment, the extending of the boundaries of the self to include the regaining of lost, split-off and projected parts of the self; the supplementing of the theory of sexuality with a greater attention to, and respect for, the 'higher' side of man's nature; and finally, the development of a meta-theory which is more relational, less reductionistic and mechanistic, and more able to accommodate novelty, growth, change and the mentalness of mind.

1

THE LONG FALL

In Milan Kundera's *The Book of Laughter and Forgetting*, an exiled widow, Tamina, tries desperately to recover some lost notebooks from her homeland, Czechoslovakia, in the hope of restoring her shrinking memory of her life with her husband. She is aware that there are many unpleasant things in the notebooks,

> But [says Kundera] that is not what counts. She has no desire to turn the past into poetry, she wants to give the past back its lost body. Because, if the shaky structure of her memories collapses like a badly pitched tent, all Tamina will have left is the present, that invisible point, that nothing moving slowly towards death.
>
> (Kundera, 1981: 86)

Tamina fails. She ends up on an island full of sensual children who have no memory and no past. This is how Kundera describes her last moments on the island before her escape and virtual suicide:

> Tamina is hiding behind the thick trunk of a palm tree. She does not want them to see her, but cannot tear her eyes from them. They are behaving with the provocative flirtatiousness of the adult world, rolling their hips as if imitating inter-course. The lewdness of the motions super-imposed on the children's bodies destroys the dichotomy between obscenity and innocence, purity and corruption. Sensuality loses all its meaning, innocence loses all its meaning, words fall apart, and Tamina feels nauseous, as though her stomach has been hollowed out.
>
> And as the idiocy of the guitars keeps booming, the children keep dancing, flirtatiously undulating their little bellies. It is

little things of no weight at all that are making Tamina nauseous. In fact, that hollow feeling in her stomach comes from the unbearable absence of weight. And just as one extreme may at any moment turn into its opposite, so this perfect buoyancy has become a terrifying *burden of buoyancy* and Tamina knows she cannot bear it another instant. She turns and runs.

(Kundera 1981: 188)

A frantic woman whom I once saw in a psychiatric hospital used to grab every passing nurse or visitor by the arm and tell them that something terrible had happened to her. She would make the visitor look at the clock on the wall, and then explain that she could see perfectly well that the clock said a quarter past four, but it didn't *mean* anything to her. She had the symptom known as 'derealization' and she, like Tamina, soon took her own life.

Both these women were desperate about the loss of meaning and reality, but they were desperate because they could remember a time when life had value, thoughts had weight and density, and memory lent meaning to the present. They had a measuring rod and perhaps this gave them their will to escape, however terrible the means they chose. Sometimes, where there is no such memory and no hope, there is something which goes beyond despair to a kind of doomed acceptance. Some of the psychotic children I shall be describing do appear to have forgotten, if indeed they ever knew, that there might be any other way of being. They do not, in these states, turn and run – not even into suicide. They tend not to scream or cry. They seem to have gone beyond hope, memory and even fear. Nadezhda Mandelstam suggests that it is right to scream under torture, because screaming is a concentrated expression of the last vestige of human dignity. She says it is a man's way of leaving a trace, of telling people how he lived and died (Mandelstam 1970: 42). Yet, for children in these very withdrawn states, it is as though there is nothing left on which to leave a trace, no imagined listener. At their worst moments, they seem to give up. For the psychotherapist who may have seen previous signs of life in her patient, it is terrible to be a witness to this. But it is even more terrible if she joins with her patient in becoming accustomed to this state of affairs. As Tamina found, it can be seductively peaceful and lulling to allow one's soul to slip away.

I want to describe a young man now in his early thirties who has

13

been with me in psychoanalytic psychotherapy of varying degrees of intensiveness since he was a child. Sadly, he did not have intensive therapy until he was 13. He had been diagnosed at the age of 4 as suffering from infantile autism. When I began seeing him at the age of 7, following upon the departure of his previous therapist, I found him exceptionally difficult to reach, partly because of what were to be for many years inadequate treatment conditions, but also because his withdrawal was so deep and chronic. The diagnosis has been confirmed on several occasions by professionals of differing schools of thought, but I should say that he was very different from and, in a way, much iller than the type of autistic child who presents as more actively withdrawn, and who has some structure in his personality. Robbie's personality seemed almost entirely formless. He has taught me, almost by virtue of the very sluggishness of his improvement, a great deal about the nature of states of dissolution and collapse, but also about the conditions in himself and me under which some regeneration has been possible.

REFERRAL

Robbie was referred to a consultant at the age of 4 with a note from his family doctor that he was backward in speech and behaviour, and at times very withdrawn. He was psychologically tested then and on several occasions since and has on most occasions been estimated to be of at least average intelligence. Five times weekly treatment was recommended but could not be arranged, and Robbie started at the clinic twice weekly with his first therapist when he was 4½. His mother was seen by a caseworker, and they met most of the time in a foursome.

Robbie spoke little, used to wander into ponds, run into the road and would try desperately to stick fallen leaves back on to trees. He never used the word 'I' and once in nursery school said that a jigsaw was a 'broken mummy'. I used to see him on the stairs of the clinic and he was an appealing, delicate-looking child with a lost, floppy rag-doll look about him. He did not have the muscular agility and grace that many autistic children have. After one year of treatment with his first therapist, he finally referred to himself as 'I'. This was after a dramatic episode with his mother. She had become very fed up with the way he constantly confused her with his grandmother, who had helped raise him. She had shouted at him, 'I'm your mother, and you've got to face it!' Like so many other apparent developments in the early years of treatment, this new capacity soon disappeared again.

HISTORY

Robbie's parents, together with his mother's parents, came here from abroad a year before he was born. He is the middle child, with a brother two years older and a sister eight years younger. He was born three and a half weeks post-mature, and his mother suffered considerable haemorrhaging. She herself was deeply depressed at the time of his birth, and was left alone a good deal throughout a long labour. She said that, by the time the baby was born, she simply wanted to die.

He was breast-fed for three weeks, but for the first three months could not hold his food. He cried after almost every feed. He drank from a cup early, was saying words by eleven months and stood at one year.

The event which seems to have precipitated his illness, or rather its obvious features, took place when he was eighteen months old. His mother became extremely preoccupied and upset while nursing her dying father, and sent Robbie to stay with friends in the country for three days. He did not know the family, and became terrified of some dogs there. Then the grandfather died and, eight days later, his mother was rushed to hospital with pneumonia and in a state of shock. Robbie was sent back to his dogs again. It seems that he became more and more withdrawn after this episode, and seemed, literally, to be frightened of everything. By the time he came to me at the age of 7 he was attending a school for maladjusted children, in a class consisting mostly of psychotic children.

TREATMENT

The first session

Freud agreed with Adler about the special importance of the very first communications made by patients (Freud, 1909: 160). Some clinicians have gone further and suggested that everything we need to know about the patient is contained in the first session, if only we had the wit and understanding to see it. That is true, I am sure, but it is nevertheless difficult to be a microscope and a telescope at one and the same time. We must attend with great care to the detail which presents itself, but also to that which does not, or which is only remotely and faintly visible. Much that was in Robbie's first session gave me reason to feel hopeful. In some respects he was much less withdrawn than other autistic children I had seen. He did respond to my interpretations about his feelings, but I did not understand then on what fragile and slippery foundations his seeming responsiveness was based, nor with what devastating rapidity every gain could be lost. Yet, however weak his moves outward were, he did come out of his isolation to make two quite different types of contact with me. One of these seems, to this day, to promote some change and growth and life in him. The other is death to development.

Robbie was an attractive child, with an uncoordinated, floppy, boneless look about him. He came into the playroom in a very lost and bewildered state, muttering 'gone' and looking frightened. However, after a few minutes in which he began to relax and perhaps to feel my remarks indicated I had understood some of his worries about what had happened to his previous therapist, he picked up a little arched brick, saying 'bridge'. I suggested that perhaps the bridge was like a link between his previous therapist and me, and perhaps he felt I might not be such a dangerous stranger after all. I did not interpret to him, but I felt sure, that the bridge material also involved a moment of real living contact with me. In the first part of the session, although he said a few single words, they were muttered to no one in particular, whereas by the time he spoke of the bridge, he had begun to look at me and speak to me with a sober look. This sobriety, unfortunately, was soon lost. He found a roll of string which he began to wind around himself and attach to my hand with growing delight and pleasure until finally he became entangled in it. He then said 'stuck' with obvious pleasure and no trace of claustrophobic panic. I interpreted his hope that I would stay stuck to him and not leave him as his previous therapist had had to do.

A little later he resumed the string game, then let go his end of the string, while insisting I keep mine, and began to roll some plasticine. This was difficult for him, and he said, 'Mrs Alvarez make it soft'. Indeed, this request, in various disguises, has been repeated endlessly by Robbie over the years, and has involved many technical problems for me in just how soft to make 'it'. I took it at the time as his request for a malleable, soft mother-person in me who would fit in and around whatever demands he should make on her. This request unfortunately has had its correlate in the demand, and need, that nothing whatever should be too hard.

The string game had somewhat touching connotations for me at the time, in terms of Robbie's wish for contact. I did not understand until much later that it was not a touching *symbol* for contact – unlike the bridge, it did not open up a living, firm, movable relationship; it was far more limited and dead end. Tamina's terrible sensual island lay waiting for us. In fact, it was the sole form of contact he desired much of the time, – something concrete, physical, sensual and very soft. When it was lacking, as we shall see, he simply fell apart. The real living bridge was much too tenuous to sustain him.

The fall

Robbie's difficulties in retaining links with other human beings of an imaginative and mental kind left him enormously affected by separations and changes. He had already had a change of therapist, and his hopes of becoming stuck to someone in the entangling total way I have described were dreadfully disappointed by the births of, first, his mother's baby, five months later, and then mine, in the second year of treatment. I was, in any case, seeing him on only a once a week basis, which was of course not enough but was all the clinic, I or his parents could manage at that stage. He returned after the birth of his baby sister in a very desperate, wild, frantic state, giggling helplessly in a hollow manner, falling about and expressing many suicidal fantasies which continued for some months.

Yet the hardest thing both to bear and to face was the emptiness in him. It was also, for me, the hardest thing to understand. Except on the chronic wards of psychiatric hospitals, I had never seen such emptiness in anyone's eyes, certainly in no child's. I had a kind of faith in the salvageability and ultimate reachability of the mentally ill; also, I had the help of the theories of Melanie Klein, which declared that we were social beings from birth, and that even our interest in the non-human world and universe had its foundation in the human one, in the earliest intimate and intense relationship between the newest baby and its mother. Klein and her co-workers who were managing to psychoanalyse psychotic patients found that even the most bizarre fantasies and nonsensical and neologistic speech could be decoded and found to have a human and interpersonal meaning. This meaning was by no means always positive. It was learned that destructiveness could be turned against the mind itself to produce terrible rifts and explosions and debris in

17

mental life. But it nevertheless meant that meaning could be found in non-meaning. Yet in Robbie it was not the weird behaviour or garbled speech such as I had seen in other psychotic children that were the real problem, even though he had his share of those, too. Rather it was the sense at times of there being simply nothing there at all.

I think a lot of the time I rather beat about the bush on this issue. When I reread my notes, I sense a quality of pained disbelief as I tried to record what I saw. I had to keep saying what wasn't there, circling around, perhaps afraid to see the truth. Here is a brief example from the period shortly after the birth of his baby sister when he had been in therapy for six months:

> Seemed wild – reminded me of a hebephrenic schizophrenic – giggling desperately – tried to throw the string out of the window – tried to undress – tried to run out – seemed determined to get me to follow – but there was something terribly despairing in the weak laughter – very little even nasty pleasure in it.

A month later I noted that occasionally a little colour would come into his face towards the ends of sessions, that he was less wild and more verbal, but there was also at times something more dead about him. Here is a session in detail:

When I came into the waiting room his only reaction to seeing me was to turn around with an expressionless face and ask Mrs D (the lady who brought him from his school for treatment) for sweets. She said 'afterwards' and he then came towards me with an empty look about him. I held his hand on the way down. He didn't look at me. Something very empty about him and the way he walks. He went to his drawer at once and took out some blue plasticine, walked over to a desk near me, looked at me briefly and with a lifeless gaze, muttered, half under his breath, 'wants to roll it', and gave it to me to roll. I began rolling the plasticine, and as I did so, he gazed out the window with a look which I would call dreamy if that word didn't have pleasant connotations. He had gone far away – but the place he had gone to wasn't pleasant. I gave the plasticine back to him after it was about six inches long – he measured it again and again, in the same dead voice, said 'wants to roll it'. This play (if that is the word) with the plasticine continued for some minutes. Sometimes he indicated he wished me to roll it, sometimes he rolled it. I made various pseudo-psychoanalytical interpretations about his wanting to make a long penis for himself, but I think now these were both useless and wrong. Useless, because they elicited no response from him and because they evaded the issue of what it really felt like to be with him, and wrong because he was wanting so very little at that moment. Wanting was what in large part was missing from his sessions at that period. Yet his lack of wanting, I think, did not signify that he had a sense of arrogant or omnipotent completion about him. He did not behave as some autistic children do, as though he were in, and had found, paradise. He wanted something in the way of an automatic repetitive activity and he wanted something to be longer, but he didn't seem to want it very much, and anyway, it was years before I discovered what it was. Perhaps he had indeed wanted the sweet from Mrs D, but when he didn't get it his whole body and mind seemed empty.

I think, as I have suggested, that I rather backed away from the powerful impact his emptiness and hopelessness had on me. I searched for meanings or signs of life where these were minimal. However, a little later in the session I seem to have got a bit nearer to it, and I think it helped him:

The plasticine play went on for some while, and again he looked out of the window with a dead gaze. Then he ran to the door, with his hands on it, and turned around with a sly look. There was something cold and nasty in his expression. I said I thought he was threatening to run out (he had done this before) to make me follow him, and to tear me away from myself and my links with the husband he imagined I had and who kept me away from him so much. Also, he wanted me to be frightened for him and worried about him. This I am sure was true. He did want this, and also I did worry, because he had no self-protective sense, and could start running all over the clinic or out of it in a totally directionless way. When I said that he wanted me to be frightened and worried about him, at first the sly and empty look was there but gradually his face relaxed a little. It didn't exactly soften, but it looked merry rather than sly – still naughty. He came forward, looking at me, and flopped on the couch. He stared into my eyes with his chin cupped in his hands, at first a bit dreamily, but then the cold, dead, empty look appeared and he stared into my eyes in this way for a long time. I said, 'I think you feel you are looking inside me and with your eyes you've got right inside me, but you don't like what you see. It isn't nice – you seem to feel you see something awful.'

That last interpretation was a bit nearer, but was rather timid. What he saw was nothing. A little later he picked up some wax off the top of a jar of paste, and called it 'ice'. Then I interpreted that he was experiencing me as a sort of cold, dead, icy mother-person who had no warmth in her for him. That, I think, was right, but I was late, and anyway I was hitching a lift from the content of his remarks – he himself used the word 'ice'. But in truth ice had been in the atmosphere for weeks. We were in a morgue together. There were no living thrusting penises, and probably no delicious comforting sweet-breast-mothers either.

During this period, he began to draw pictures of trees – leafless, barren, stiff, forbidding yet drooping things – which I felt conveyed the feeling that I was bearing no fruit for him and was really offering him no link. It also conveyed something about the nature of his imaginative inner world. Remember he had had a symptom at age 4 of trying to stick leaves back on to trees. Something in Robbie had not held together in himself or in his inner world. Was it that the sap didn't flow from the mother-root to nourish and hold the leaf, or was it that his own hatred and jealousy and despair had killed off the warming enlivening influence of love in him? Perhaps both. What I do know is that this Tree of Death bore no relation to Robbie's real mother or father. They were warm, lively, sensitive and extremely caring people when I knew them and their other children were normal. Maybe his mother's depression when he started life played a part – a tiny baby may not be able to tell the difference between an unresponsive mother who is depressed and one who is indifferent in a colder and more callous way. And perhaps there was something frail in him or in his brain from the start which made him so vulnerable. Some other children have survived the type of separation he had at 18 months without being destroyed. Whatever the cause, his inner world was extraordinarily impoverished. He seemed to have virtually nothing, not even the most pathological of the mental mechanisms of defence, to fall back on in times of stress.

In the summer and autumn when he was 8, during the period leading up to the birth of my child and a few months after the birth of his sister, I felt as though I might have lost him for good emotionally. I had told him I would have to stop seeing him for some months. I had considered, together with colleagues at the clinic, a change of therapist, but in the end I decided to stick with him, in spite of the long break. This was in part because no one experienced was available to take him on – very few people were treating autistic children by the psychoanalytic method at that time – but it was also because he had already had one change of therapist. I still wonder whether or not this was the right decision. Precious years were certainly lost. He was 13 before he had five times weekly treatment. On the other hand, another therapist might have left the clinic. Other patients whom I handed over did sometimes eventually lose their treatment. I also felt Robbie was *my* patient, and my responsibility, and in the end I think this was important. But, at the time, he clearly felt abandoned by me. He would simply crumple or stare blankly into space. In later years, when he could get sufficiently outside and away from such feelings to find words for them, he could describe the sensation of having been 'down a dark well', and of having 'fallen down, down into the evening, like the rain – but it takes so long to fall'. It is difficult to convey the dreadful feeling I often had of how far he had fallen or drifted. My attempts to show him that I understood how abandoned he felt, which might have helped a more mildly or even a more deliberately withdrawn patient, were useless. I was too far away. In Malcolm Lowry's *Under the Volcano*, the estranged wife of an alcoholic Consul returns to try to save him from himself. When she finds him beyond reach, she cries, 'Don't you love me any more?' He thinks to himself, 'Doesn't she realise – of course I love her – but her voice is like the voice of someone sobbing in a distant room.' I suspect that Robbie felt much the same. As for me, I was like someone dragging the bottom of a river: hoping for signs of life and tugging on a dreadfully inert weight.

There were, however, tiny variations on this Doomsday theme. Some situations were much harder for him to bear than others. He sometimes came to – a little – in the middle of a session, and he made occasional weak attempts himself to link up with and reach out to something outside. Beginnings and endings of sessions involved particular agonies for him. He could not enter or leave the playroom without touching the walls all the way along the corridor leading to it. Sometimes he simply brushed the wall, at other times he touched his nose and then the wall, as though trying to link the two. In later years, when he could talk with me about such things, he agreed that he was saying to the wall something like 'Hello – are you still there?' At that point he thought it was funny, but not in those early years. In fact, I would prefer now to say he wasn't asking the wall if it was still there – I think it and I and all substantial reality had dis- appeared in the week between sessions – I think he was asking it

21

something like 'Are you there? Is there anything or anybody there at all?' But in those early days, these minimal attempts at linking, these little brushes with reality, usually failed. On one occasion, near the end of a session, he drew a picture of a caterpillar emerging from its skin, and, when the session ended, he simply fell down three or four times as we made our way upstairs to the waiting room. Neither the wall nor I was adequate to hold him up. He had almost no internal supports, so external supports were desperately essential.

Many disturbed children have difficulties about separations. For all human beings a parting is like a little death. But Robbie did not experience a parting as a loss of something or someone. Nor did he experience himself as being left somewhere he did not wish to be. Rather he felt left nowhere. He hadn't lost someone or something in the parting; he had lost everything, including himself. In later years, he called it 'Wiped out – no more Robbie'. And I was wiped out, too. This nowhere state meant that the world – a possible imaginative world with human figures in it, the one that the non-psychotic part of us inhabits, and that sustains us through lonely periods – disappeared. He once described his world as a 'net with a hole in it'. It was an insubstantial universe and he was perpetually falling through it. How was I ever to become dense enough, contracted and concentrated enough, real enough, to catch him?

In his outside life, certain things were very real indeed: his terrors. He was terrified of dogs barking, the thud of a taxi's engine, the sound of its windshield wipers, men working on building sites, almost any loud noise. He often felt that bright lights hurt his eyes, and once, when a lorry thundered past, he covered his whole head, not just his ears, saying, 'It hurts my brain'. He seemed to lack a mental membrane to put between some central self and experience, particularly visual and auditory experience. It came too close, so he withdrew or else fell to a great distance, and then rescue was too far away.

He did keep one or two lines open. His main avenue of sensory investigation was his nose. He rarely looked at me or listened to me during this period, but he smelled literally everything. If I could have spoken the language of smells, I think I could have reached him earlier. Later, when he could talk more and knew the names of colours, yellow meant the smell of a lemon, which he loved; and later still, when he wanted to describe people's voices, he didn't describe them in terms of different sounds, he described them in colours. Someone had a yellow voice, one had a bright orange voice, and another had a dark green voice. Most normal people and all the poets use images from one sensory modality to describe experiences in another, but Robbie in the early years had no other choice. His nose and his sense of touch were almost his only sources of good experience. As much as he was able, he closed himself off to sights and sounds. Or perhaps they were closed off to him. I shall discuss later the problem of when this was volitional and defensive, and when it seemed that it was more helpless. I had to learn that he had many different types of withdrawal. But his interest in smells meant he was somewhere interested in something, and it also meant that he ate well. He stayed alive physically, although at this period I was in doubt about his mental survival.

I have said earlier that Robbie seemed to lack even the most pathological of mental defence mechanisms. Naturally this is a question of degree since no one can be altogether without defences. But what was most noticeable about Robbie's intermittent, flickering capacity for self-defence or self-protectiveness was its weakness.

He also lacked even the most pathological method that many other autistic children employ for protecting themselves from too powerful experiences. Frances Tustin has called this encapsulation, and many workers have described the impression such children give of being in a shell. Tustin distinguished between the 'crustaceans', who are able to interpose a bit of developed behaviour between themselves and the unwanted reality, and the 'amoeba'-type, who lack even that ability (Tustin 1972). Many years ago in Canada, I took an autistic child to the zoo, imagining that even he, with his preoccupation with lights, would show some childlike interest in lions, tigers and monkeys. But there was an electric fan above the cages which created, as it whirled, a complicated play of light and shadow on the ceiling. He fixed his eye on it, and that was simply all he saw, and all he allowed himself to see. Another child I knew from the same hospital spent all day listening to a particular static noise on his little transistor radio. Both these children managed almost a kind of self-hypnosis. Tustin calls these rigidly adhered-to love objects, which can be used so effectively to shut out the living world, 'autistic objects' (Tustin 1981).

But Robbie was really more like a defenceless amoeba. Sometimes, I am sure, he switched off voluntarily, and in fact the volitional element increased as the years went by and he began to develop something akin to a will. My difficulty was that much of the time during this early bad period, he did not seem to have gone anywhere; he wasn't hiding, he was lost. If there exists a mental equivalent of the deep coma that the brain can undergo, I think I saw glimpses of it. When the amoeba got hurt, something happened to it which was like a death. I had only seen it before on the back wards of mental hospitals. Kundera's Tamina was able to feel such hollowness, such nothingness, as a persecution and 'a burden of buoyancy'. But there has to be some part of the personality strengthened by awareness of a world elsewhere in order to feel the burden and in order to hate the burden. Naturally this was not the whole story: there were fleeting moments of hope, as in the first session; there were moments of cold sly hatred, as in the session described on p.19, and moments of dreamy merging. But for much more of the time than I can possibly get across without describing weeks, months and years of silent empty sessions, there was simply vacancy.

What do most of us do when we feel persecuted? We go into exile, real exile perhaps, or imagined exile, if we are imaginative or autistic. Or we stay and protest. But Robbie almost never protested. He lacked this other vital mechanism of defence. He seemed to have practically no capacity for methods of projection and projective identification of bad feelings or parts of the self in the sense first described by Melanie Klein. He couldn't go into exile and distance himself from fear or pain, but neither could he stay and fight. The mechanism of projective identification is very complicated, and it would take a whole chapter to describe the many different types that have been studied by psychoanalysts. But one type explains what the developing infant can do after he has had a bad experience: he can evacuate it.

Mothers do a great deal to protect tiny babies from distress, but much is known about the enormous degree to which, from the beginning, babies too have, and quickly improve upon, their own capacities for self-protection. One of these is like a milder version of the encapsulated little boy with the static. They withdraw their attention and apply it, when they can, to something more palatable. They may look away from too bright a light to a softer one. They may attend only to their mother's voice in a room full of talkative strangers. But what happens when the unavoidable happens and the frightening or painful stimulation gets through? The baby startles, then screams or cries. Adults do the same after a shock, or they talk emotionally to their friends. There are of course degrees of

24

pathology in these projections and evacuations. If we knife someone because they passed us too aggressively on a motorway, then we are probably a paranoid schizophrenic or a psychopath. If we shout at our spouse or partner because we've just stubbed our toe on a chair, then we are just having a tiny passing paranoid breakdown. If we say 'Ow' when the toe hurts, that is an everyday and apparently rather essential projective mechanism.

The Kleinian view would be that the projection went into an imagined human figure of various degrees of receptivity, friendship or enmity. But Robbie never screamed or cried or exploded. Occasionally he whimpered. I do not know what strength may have been in his cries when he was a baby, but I doubt there was much. Nothing inside him seemed capable of catching bad experiences, holding them and throwing them back out again, and perhaps he felt that no one was waiting to receive them. I mean, of course, bad experiences, mental or physical. He did hold onto bodily products all too frantically when his help was needed with the mental ones. He suffered from constipation and sometimes winter-long bouts of catarrh. He could not bear to blow his nose. The more it filled up and blocked up, the more he felt he had to sniff it back. He really seemed to feel he dare not let go or he would lose all of himself, and this was indeed a real danger: his one method of ridding himself of distressful feelings was to run back and forth half dragging his feet behind him, shaking his hands out in the direction of the floor. He would emerge from this, not relieved but simply empty and lifeless, perhaps less despairing but even more dead.

Bion wrote that some psychotic patients project into a mental space so vast that all the bits of the experience and of themselves thus projected are dispersed at great distances from each other (Bion 1962). Bion himself did amazing work with very ill adult schizophrenics, and did manage to link up bits of patients' material which sometimes appeared four years apart in time. He pointed out that the vast mental space may translate itself into huge time periods. I could believe that something like that was happening to Robbie at such moments. Too much went out of him and it went too far. The net was still too loose. It was years before he could use focused methods of projective identification onto or into an identifiable and receptive object or manage what he called 'making a mark'. In the meantime, he finally succeeded in re-establishing the entangling link he had made with me in the first session.

2

VEGETABLE LIFE AND AWAKENINGS

My vegetable Love should grow
Vaster than Empires, and more slow.

Andrew Marvell

Bion, whose work with schizophrenic adults I have already mentioned, made an interesting distinction between two types of link which human beings may make with an outside living reality. The first is the articulated link: it permits, through its flexibility, aliveness to be sensed and experienced. The second, the rigid link, restricts experience and thinking to manageable but mechanical chunks. Bion often compared the baby's approach to the mother's breast with the patient's emotional response to his analyst, and both of these with the mind's attitude to its own thoughts. He seems to have chosen the concept of articulation deliberately because of its double meaning of freedom of movement and flexibility of verbal expression. He found the rigid link very common in the thought processes of his psychotic patients (Bion 1957). Although I would prefer to call Robbie's thought processes, such as they were, flaccid rather than rigid, they shared with those of Bion's patients the absolute negation of action, movement, novelty and change. The effect on me and others who tried to make real contact with Robbie was to produce terrible feelings of despair and impotence.

There was, as I said, a brief moment of real contact and life accompanying the bridge material in the first session – but the feeling of hope changed straightaway into the cloying, entangling string contact – which is the story of his life, for he was an amazingly floppy, boneless child – and, in those early years, moments of happiness changed only the quality, never the strength of his response. It was a long time before he discovered he had bones, muscles or joints in his body, or power, will or freedom of choice available in his mind. Objects fell from his limp hands, as his very limbs seemed to hang from his trunk, and as words and thoughts seemed to drain out of his helpless lips and empty mind.

Late in the year, when Robbie was 8, he began to make a new drawing. We were due to stop for ten months, as I was soon to have a child of my own, and my advanced pregnancy must have been obvious to him on some level. The theme of this drawing and its variations preoccupied him for many more years. He called it 'the hook-of-a-door'. It was a drawing of a door which looked as though it might be a sort of wrought iron gate. It appeared to involve something of a development or, to be precise, perhaps a recapturing of the hopeful moments from the first session. Compared to the empty barren trees, it was more elaborate, intricate, graceful and controlled. It was framed, yet with its curves and arabesques it was much more lively than the trees had ever been. Also, this drawing seemed to coincide with his sessions being somewhat richer, and himself more talkative, and also with his making a new claim on me. He insisted that instead of his simply drawing his 'hook-of-a-door', he should be allowed to copy my version of it. Because I wanted to know what particular version he wanted in a session, I would therefore ask him to draw it first, and then would copy his. But he simply pretended that this first half of the encounter had not taken place; he insisted that he had copied mine.

This seemed to be a way of ensuring that I was permanently stuck and tied to him in the sessions. What I did not understand then was how successfully my playing in with this request colluded with his disbelief in his own existence. Yet he had found a way out of his dark well of nothingness. He had found something to hold on to, to hook on to, latch on to, rather like a Russian vine winds itself round whatever pole or cord or other plant it can find to support it in its search for sunshine. Yet his hook-hold did not help him to go on and up. He had little idea of a fuller, more extended, more living relationship, or a deeper one. He simply looked blank if I asked what lay behind his gate and clearly he did not consider that there might be anything inside me or *to* me. This method of holding himself and us together in fact positively interfered with my reaching him in a more alive way. I was kept simply too busy to think, while he, on his side, was totally preoccupied in getting a smooth unbroken line in his drawing, particularly where the curve changed direction. In the drawing, finally, there were leaves, but they remained unattached to the plant-like winding branches. He still could not conceive of, or perhaps bear, an articulated, differentiated link with a human being. He had to be curled up, merged, unnoticing. On the deepest level, perhaps

27

in his phantasy, his infantile tongue and mouth had found some kind of breast to curl around but, if so, they couldn't let go, and they still had very little idea of who owned the mouth and who owned the breast. They also had no idea that what babies usually do with breasts in their mouths is suck on them. A sucking movement involves pulling and slackening, pulling and slackening. Babies' mouths work very hard: there is huge activity, but hidden in the holding and pulling and drawing is the letting go – the fundamental rhythm of life, of all biology – in and out, forward and backward, work and rest. Robbie would have none of this, or else could not bear any of this. The breaks in smoothness were shattering for him and he insisted on making his own very smooth passage out and up. It was, however, unutterably slow. We were caught together in some pleasing but eternal still life.

Yet this situation was a little less concrete than the string play. Furthermore, he found something to hold on to during the long break. He dealt with this problem in the following way. He had, around the time of the 'hook-of-a-door' drawing, begun to bring long, unused bus tickets to the sessions – the longer the better. The last session before the break, he left the ticket in his drawer as usual. To my astonishment, when the ten-month break was up and he returned in September at the age of 9, he came into the room, saying, 'Where's the ticket?' And he found it.

At the time I was astounded at the ability of such an ill, lost and apparently mindless child to hold on to this long ticket of memory. It stopped him from forgetting me and must have helped him to feel, not exactly that I had remembered him – because it was a long time before he could understand such a notion as that of a person containing someone else in their mind – but that in my drawer, concretely, I did at least still keep his ticket.

In the next three years he alternated between falling back into states of disillusionment and apathy and recoveries of the copy-cat, hooking, entangling type. Yet within this rigid, slow framework some progress was made. His parents switched him from his maladjusted school to a school for psychotic children, where he could have somewhat more individual attention and he began slowly to learn to read. When he was 10 I had to reduce his sessions from once weekly to once monthly. He reacted with great depression to this situation, and even showed remorse and concern. He assumed it was because I was exhausted by him, and became considerably more helpful to his mother at home. He did not collapse into the sort of helpless floppiness I had seen before.

AWAKENINGS

The first

In December of the year Robbie was 11, we stopped for another three months' break while my second child was born. Robbie returned from this break in the most animated and sane condition I had ever seen him. His grammar was improved, the phrases and occasional sentences were longer, and he began to make certain claims, no longer only for tickets and soft plasticine and copyings, but for my perfectly sustained attention. If I stopped talking, even for a minute, he demanded, 'Mrs Alvarez, talk'. This doesn't mean he was listening – for the most part he wasn't – it was more something to link up to, hook on to and perhaps, to an extent, feel wrapped around by. A new and auditory line of communication was opening up, even if all he was hearing was something like a lullaby or a comforting background hum. But it did mean that I had a slightly better opportunity of having interpretations occasionally heard.

It is interesting to note the changes in his hook-of-a-door drawing. The leaves were finally attached, firmly and confidently, and there was much more differentiation of one part and one section from another. He had begun to learn, I think, on some fundamental level that, although his mother and I had left him to have our babies, we had both returned to him. There was a place for him too, and he could even lay claims upon it.

Robbie's parents had been pressing me for some time to see him on a more regular basis, but I was still unable to manage it. They arranged speech therapy with a very gifted woman who reported that his problem was not simply speech, but comprehension, causality and spatial disorientation. He had no idea of a time scale, of a before or after. The simple everyday crude notions of causality by which we make sense of events were impossible for him. The cup broke because I dropped it, or my knee hurts because I fell, or I am soaking wet because it's raining: all such links invariably got turned around or muddled up. I shall return later to his problem with time. In addition, he was still relatively undifferentiated as a self living in a spatial universe. Now he was a little less likely to fall or drift into his faraway states; what he did

29

instead was get too close to an object, too entangled with it, and so unable to get a proper fix or focus on what lay around him. Yet the drawing and his demands on me show there were developments, and his speech therapy began to help him enormously.

His last session before the summer break when he was 13 was a very moving one for me. I had been speaking to him about his difficulty in believing I could remember him over the holiday, and his difficulties in using his by now 13-year-old self to help him to think about me. When I knew he was in great distress, which he was sure to be about breaks, I had always to speak with considerable emphasis and intensity. I was never sure if he was listening, or even hearing me, or if anything was sinking in. It always felt odd talking to him about ideas like his mind, or time, since he did not seem to have such concepts. What I do know is that, because of all these things, I spoke to him with a great sense of urgency.

While I was talking, he had been shaking his hands and dispersing all his distress and anger in the ineffectual and draining way I have described before. Suddenly he stopped, came over and examined my face with great tenderness, then the area of my breast, and then said, slowly, 'Hello', almost as though he'd just recognized an old friend he hadn't seen for ten years. I wrote at the time that it was as though he had suddenly surfaced, but it was not for some months, until he talked about his 'dark well' that I understood that it felt exactly like that for him, too. There is no doubt that his entangling hooking measures were an expression of a kind of hope. He had come part way up his well; or rather his hook-hold had stopped him from falling further. But this 'Hello' was completely different. We were no longer gentle plants entwining round each other nor were we two identical mirror images of each other. I think he really saw me, for the first time since the bridge in the initial session, as another human being separate from himself, yet this time deeply familiar.

I felt that something extremely important had happened to Robbie, but the timing was dreadful. He'd said hello when we were about to say goodbye for two months (I was still seeing him only once a month). In later years, this has become a little ploy of his, a way of trying to prolong contact and put off the evil day, but at this period it was no such thing. I think the coming separation had helped to waken him; so had the long uphill slog of years of work. I also had the uncanny feeling that there was something in my *voice* that day that made the difference. But it was all so late – late in the session, late in the term and, in spite of the help he was receiving at home from his devoted and by now more hopeful parents, there was a long two-month break ahead.

A week after our last meeting, Robbie began a kind of breakdown at home. He was ill in bed with a cold and he suddenly sobbed and begged his mother not to go out to do some shopping. She told me (we kept in telephone contact during this break) that she had planned to be gone for only twenty minutes, but she decided not to go because she felt that something different was happening to Robbie, and she should take it seriously. She and her husband literally sat at his bedside for a week while he sobbed and screamed. In the beginning he was terrified that the dogs he had feared for so many years were coming to kill him. Gradually, as the week progressed, he began to talk to his parents about the dreadful period when, at $1^1/2$, he was sent away to the dogs, and his belief that they *had* in fact killed him. He seemed to be describing something like the beginning of his autistic breakdown, but also in a way announcing its end. He was afraid, he was broken-hearted, but he was screaming, he was alive, and he wanted the two most important people in his life to listen to his dreadful tale.

When he returned in September, he began occasionally to replace the door drawings with pictures of conkers, with spiky outsides and one or two cosy chestnuts nestled within. He sometimes brought real conkers that he had found on the street, and seemed utterly fascinated by the fact that such lovely smooth objects could be found inside such a prickly exterior. At the same time he became interested in other children's drawers in the playroom and in trying to undo my smock, but very frightened by my requests that he should leave such things alone. At these times I seem to have become something like a spiky cross father keeping him out of a desirable but forbidden mother-place. The phantasy was very primitive, and still very physical and concrete, but at least it was three-dimensional. He could feel real curiosity, instead of hopeless apathy or bland sticky contentment. Something finally lay behind the closed doors. His picture of the life beyond was, however, a very idealized one. In his drawing, there were two chestnuts inside the shell. But the boundary of the one perfectly followed and accommodated itself to the boundary of the other. There were no bumps, no sharp edges, no crowding, no collisions. All sharpness was outside. Years later, when I was seeing him at my home, he went to the lavatory, which

31

is across a tiny yard, just outside the playroom. Then, for the first time, he plucked up courage to look up at the sitting room window, which he had spoken about but never dared look into. He had an immediate hallucination of a green spiky monster looking down at him. It seemed that even then, when the figures in his imaginative world were beginning to take on a more-or-less human shape, it was still too dangerous to conceive of himself as ever having sharp edges or to allow himself to have a sharp penetrating eye, or biting teeth, or driving intrusive feelings of his own.

Robbie's usual way of penetrating into desirable inside places was instead very gentle and soft. One of his ways of doing this was to lie on the couch with his cheek on the pillow and his eyes gazing into mine, as though he felt this put him right inside me. When this state was not achieved, however, a veritable avalanche of feeling poured from him, which by now his parents were unable to contain. His fears, his distress and anguish over any separation, from them or me, his sexual mischievousness with women friends of theirs were overflowing even his parents' tolerant boundaries, and could certainly not be contained in once-a-month treatment. I arranged to start seeing him five times a week.

A second awakening

The change to five times weekly treatment provided a much stronger and firmer holding situation. Robbie's mother reported that, for the first time in his life, he was sleeping through the night, and not needing to be under about ten blankets. He seemed to interpret this remarkable alteration in my behaviour in two ways. First, he saw it in a way bearing many resemblances to the old copy-cat 'make it soft' mother of the past, that is, as a gushy, guilty rescue operation on my part. Second, however, he did seem to see it as a genuine lifeline thrown out to him.

I would like to illustrate the two situations by material from two sessions, one in January and one in February, after the Christmas break, the first break under the new arrangement.

Getting unstuck – his move

In Robbie's very first session at my house, he had dramatized his mother's or sister's voice saying to him, 'Darling Robbie, please forgive me, I'm so sorry I hurt you, let me bandage your knee.' She sounded all over him, while he lay back, the deserving but passive recipient of these frantic guilt-ridden attentions. In a later session close to Christmas, this cloying object grew even closer, became even more stuck to him in the form of a story about spaghetti stuck to a man's nose. The man could not get it off, as Robbie could neither defecate easily, nor blow his nose, nor expel his outraged feelings about the coming break. The greater his distress, the more he sniffed it up. He seemed unable to let go.

He returned from the Christmas break embittered, but finally able to push some of this feeling into me. He began the session by switching the light in the playroom on and off with a fast stroboscopic motion, so that it did literally hurt one's brain. He agreed with me heartily when I said that he wished me to suffer as he had from the way I switched him on and off at Christmas, and each day. Then he plunged us into darkness and sat on the couch with his coat wrapped around him, saying 'Y – I' in a cruel old man's voice, which he agreed was meant to frighten me. It was, he said, his grandfather's voice. I spoke to him about his reluctance to come out in the light and be himself. He was hiding inside grandfather's voice, as under cover of darkness, but it was really he, Robbie, who was furious with me, and was afraid to let us be a you and I. He then separated the two sounds a little more. 'Y – I.' He was silent. I asked what he was thinking a few times and he eventually said 'Prancelot' – 'Spaghetti'. I tried to show him how he tried to create a spaghetti mother in me – stuck together with him in the darkness; how I had to keep asking questions, making guesses, pulling replies from him as though blowing his nose for him, thinking about him every minute, always stuck to him.

He responded with great feeling to this, and said 'Throw spaghetti away – get it all off – gooey toffee everywhere – get it all off', gesturing vigorously all the while. He became very lively but, as so often in these moments of coming to life, he gave the impression of not knowing what to do with this unfocused, diffuse surge of feeling that was bubbling up. It was partly aggressive, partly loving, partly sexual. He came over to me, as though to hit me, then half patted my hair, then he tried to undo my smock. I stopped him, and he tried to open the door to the garden, and I prevented that. Then he stopped in his tracks, slumped a little, stared into space and said in a desolate voice 'Kisstone', and then, 'Not much mita in the water'.

This session seems to me to demonstrate two important developments: first, Robbie's ability to expel into me in a focused, aimed way his suffering over the torturing switching on and off experience; second, his ability, for almost the first time, to shed the apparently good, soft, but terribly cloying, suffocating object he tried to produce in me and inside himself. The session shows, too, the price he feels he pays each time he gives this object up. He comes to life, his feelings and sensuality mount towards a more separate alive object, but any move the object makes to limit his advances is taken as total rejection and he is paralysed again. A year later he could demonstrate how, if any aspect of him was rejected, he felt totally 'wiped out – no more Robbie'.

On the other hand, his confidence was rising, his constipation and catarrh began to improve, and his realization was growing that a separate alive object could still reach out to him in an unsticky way.

The long stocking – a lifeline – my move

In a session in February he revealed, I think, some belief in the possibility that there might be help at hand if he gave up his autistic methods of withdrawal. He told of a game he had played with his sister where a boy and girl had been kept imprisoned down a dark well. A long long long stocking, or a long long long penis, was thrown down, and each of them came flying up in the air, talking and shouting, landing on the other side of the street. So also did Robbie's loved ones, parents and old teachers, some reproaching him, but all talking and terribly alive. As he described this, his voice rose and fell and rose even higher in almost musical rhythms and waves. Normally, he spoke in a flat, small voice; his words were mostly like little wisps of smoke or puffs of wind – you could easily feel they hadn't really been uttered by anyone, and he himself forgot them within seconds.

It is probably a fact that Robbie's growing adolescent sexuality was helping enormously to rouse him out of the particular dead kind of withdrawal he was so habituated to down in his well. I think, however, he must also have interpreted the new five times a week arrangement as a genuine lifeline.

There is a third element in the long stocking material which has helped me enormously in subsequent years to understand the feeling Robbie so often gave me, that my reach did in fact have to be very long. I felt at times and, I am certain, showed dreadful urgency and despair about what would happen if I could not reach him and help. I often had literally to move my head into his line of vision to remind him I was there. He seemed so dead, or, at best, so in danger of psychic death, and yet so utterly incapable of taking any steps whatever to bring himself to life. It does seem probable that my urgency was absolutely essential to him at a certain point, as he could not feel it for himself. I have come to learn something about the considerable degree to which, unfortunately, he exploits this situation.

Robbie's lack of grasp

Earlier I have described how Robbie seemed to need to keep me talking and interested in him all the time. No breathing spaces were allowed; my silences seemed to mean to him that I had drifted off and left him to drift. This perpetual flow of speech from me was not, much of the time, used by him for purposes of understanding. The copy-cat spaghetti mother stuck eternally to him stimulated no feeling or curiosity. He seemed not to understand that he could follow my words. Nor did he appear to try, except when he was very desperate. Now that he had more or less what he wanted from me, he gave the impression of settling down for a life-long sleep on my couch.

I began to wonder where the ordinary, forward-moving, life-giving, volitional impulses were in him: why, for example, he never grew bored, and why he so seldom grasped the 'stocking' when it was there. Why did I have all the urgency, all the sense of time, impatience, concern about his lack of development and at times unutterable boredom? It is well documented by psychoanalytic authors that autistic children do have a genuine need for others to act as an extension of the self and to perform ego functions for them. This avoidance of separateness is not thought to be simply for purposes of omnipotent control (Meltzer 1975; Tustin 1972). This, I believe, was true of Robbie but it was also true that he exploited this situation of genuine need and genuine deficit.

He resisted effort of any kind partly because he was afraid, but also, I think, out of inertia due to a lifetime of immobility. His hands had hardly any knuckles; instead they were splayed out and boneless, as though they had never grasped at or clutched anything. He had, after all, been autistic for a very long time. His autism had become not only a reaction from the earlier horrors, but a positive life-style. He withdrew or, as he called it, 'drifted off',

35

not just when he was in distress but to avoid situations of really quite minor discomfort. He called this the 'lazy Robbie'. It was simply easier, for example, for him to let go of a thought or feeling that he had had two seconds before, and let it disappear for ever, than to go back and pick it up. He lacked powers of recollection and memory and methods of integrating himself, but he was also peculiarly reluctant to acquire them.

A sense of time

After much work on this 'lazy' aspect of himself, Robbie did begin to experience some impatience of his own, then a growing preoccupation with time. At first, his concept of time had been virtually non-existent. As we came to examine it, it began to take on very much the shape of the old, flat, closed-door situation of the 'hook-of-the-door' days. As he began to dramatize this problem in sessions, it was clear that sessions had beginnings and endings but no middle. Both beginnings and endings squeezed him out brutally. The beginning produced a perpetual feeling that 'it's a bit too early', that I could never be ready for him; the ending was so dreadful that it invaded all the way back to the beginning. The agitation he experienced even many years later when I would glance at my watch was indescribable. In his sleepy days, time did not seem to pass at all. Now its fleeting quality was as tormenting to him as his 'strobe' light had been to me. Time was not something he could fill, nor could it fill him with anything of any interest or value. He could not seem to get hold of a period of time that he could experience as sufficiently long. His own attention was so fleeting and he drifted so frequently that he was in fact present only for a few seconds at a time. His experience of a substantial, reliable, permanent object was by definition very limited. Gradually, he did begin to talk about his hatred and dread of time, and this seemed to pave the way for him to take more active steps towards ensuring that he get the maximum amount of pleasure and security from the sessions and also from his life outside. He became able to plan a little.

Movement – forward and back

Around the time of the summer break when Robbie was 15, I gave up much of my previously 'soft' adaptation to certain of Robbie's obsessional rituals which slowed us down on our way to the playroom. Although irritated by this, he seemed struck by one remark I made: I said that although I wouldn't let him mess around at the top of the stairs, he should come to the session room and 'we could talk about it together down there'. He made me repeat this suggestion for weeks afterwards, especially the 'we'. Early in the autumn, it suddenly occurred to him one day, as I persisted in my refusals, to ask me to join in a pretend game. In the game, we pretended that I had not denied him these rituals, but had permitted them all, and even made all the old interpretations relevant to them. He had played imaginative games before, but only rarely was I in them, and they were never organized like this. These games ramified and grew and were elaborated on until they soon included almost our whole history together since he started coming to the house. They described his journeys, his arrivals, his departures, his drawings, even his pretend games within pretend games. Part of this history was acted out in our play, and part of it was embodied in enormously long lists he made of subjects which had been talked about in his sessions.

A second type of game arose from a dramatization of his parents' telling him that he should not try to play sexual games with his sister and that he 'mustn't touch' her sexually. It seemed also to connect with the birth of a realization that the 'we' I was constantly offering him to replace the old YI stuck-together couple was not a promise of sexual intercourse. He dealt with this fleeting awareness of growth, frustration, change, separateness and sexual differences by making his sister change into all sorts of boys of his own choosing. He even began to lay plans for one or two weeks ahead, concerning which day of the week these astonishing changes (which were to astonish his parents, but never him) should take place.

These games did, I think, involve genuine efforts to deal with matters which were of great moment to him: time, change, growth, separation from his objects, external and internal, but also separation from his own past self. They gave him enormous pleasure and I am certain did help, as all imaginative play does, to enlarge his internal world. He often reminded me of someone who had been paralysed all his life and was flexing an almost atrophied muscle he had not known he possessed. He loved adding to his long lists, and checked the next day that I had remembered the whole list, together with its latest addition. He was delighted when I remembered, and always pretended not to notice if I left an item out. (I did not understand then how important it was to show him that he had indeed noticed my failings, and the chinks in the ideal world he persisted in creating.) However, his joy in this mental muscle flexing or mental playfulness was real enough. It was as though he had not previously realized that he could use his imagination and do things with his mind. These long lists, unlike the long stocking, were his creation.

The games represented, I think, a considerable development in the direction of Robbie's relinquishing external, sticking techniques in favour of imaginative reconstruction; or rather, they began this way. Each game began with some meaning and function; it usually dealt with some anxiety past or current. After several days of repetition, he looked much less worried as we played the game, and could even sometimes smile at the him who had been afraid a short while ago. But at the point where another child would have moved on to a new game, the process entered a third phase of glacializing, deadening, ritualistic and dreadfully boring rigidity. It would have remained in this immutable form for ever if I had not begun refusing to play my part. He had got stuck, not simply to me but to his old self and his old way of doing something. (He has found over the years ever more subtle methods of avoiding thinking. He will do anything, for example, to get me to make an old interpretation rather than a new one.) I have had to learn to resist the pressure to be the soft conforming object that is felt to be an extension of himself and that plays in with this comfortable but sleepy inertia. While I was dutifully proving what a good remembering mother-person I was by reciting my lists or my lines, I was prevented from thinking, and from understanding whatever he was really feeling on a particular day; and he was prevented from developing.

The difficulty was that while he appreciated this on one level, and friendly figures in his imaginative play began to reassure him that it was safe to move forward, change and meet new situations, that it was 'OK to make mistakes', to 'stick up for himself', to 'come out of the deep freeze and learn to walk', he was still faced with another menacing figure, in human form now, but extremely vicious, which warned him that to take any step forward towards grown-upness – to observe, listen, talk, protest – carried enormous risk. He would be 'left to be dead for ever and ever with no eyes, no ears, no mouth and no penis'.

Gradually, as Robbie became more aware of his own need and wish to develop, to 'catch up' as he put it, the brutal figure no longer planted itself so often in his path; instead it goaded him on from behind, telling him he 'must talk to people', 'stop staring' and 'get in line'. This object seemed to dog every step he took, but its grip was loosening slightly. Out of the 'net with a hole in it', where Robbie's persecutors were inhuman stray noises and lights and sensations, there began to crystallize a frightening, sometimes terrorizing object whose human form was nevertheless beginning to take on manageable proportions. It had, however menacing, a location and a shape.

A complication – mischievous autism

It is interesting to note how one unfortunate consequence of his more fearless attitude was that he was now able *actively* to use his autistic habit of withdrawal to avoid any situation he disliked. In the early years of my work with him, it was often impossible for anyone to get him back from his withdrawn states. Then came a time when both his parents and I found that, with difficulty, we could manage it. Then, as his awareness of time increased, and there was some ego development, he began to be able to pull himself back from these states, and even prevent their taking place. Later, however, it became increasingly obvious that he could go into these states almost at will for defensive purposes. He did this to avoid any situation he disliked or any unpleasant fact of life: recognition of his illness, of what it had cost him, his inability as yet to earn a living, his 'baby brain', his jealousy of my other patients and my family, and his awareness that the 'make it soft' mother figure could be related to a husband and other objects, a hard fact of life for him to swallow at his age and level of sexual arousal. He simply announced threateningly when he disliked the course a session was taking, 'Mrs Alvarez, I'm going to drift off', or 'Mrs Alvarez, I'm going to become Toby', a very ill autistic child whom Robbie remembered from a past school. What had been originally, and still was at times, a real dissolution and collapse was now put at the service of a more active and mischievous part of his personality. Yet he was also more actively helpful with the work of treatment, so it was extremely difficult to predict the course of the next few years.

Possibilities

Robbie was by now 17 and his hatred of novelty and the unknown produced incalculable interferences with opportunities for mental growth. Yet he showed me clearly the possibility of, and difficulties in, coming to life. On one occasion he dramatized a situation where someone was releasing him from a deep freeze where he had been 'left to be dead for ever and ever with no eyes, no ears, no mouth and no penis'. He showed me a person struggling forward in thick ice, beginning to use his legs and gradually moving and walking more freely as he got further out. This gave me tremendous hope: it seemed that he really knew and felt that he was coming to life and could value it rather than fear it.

But two problems persisted and constantly dashed my hopes. The first was the tragic fact that his senses were simply very unpractised (at times I wondered if they weren't atrophied) at functioning in a normal manner. True, they were finally switched on. But he preferred to use his eyes for something more akin to touching and merging than for looking *at* something or someone. He needed to learn to use his ears for listening to words and whole sentences, whereas instead he tended to get hooked on to the sound, shape and, I suspected at times still, the taste and colour of a word. Of course all babies listen to and most produce the music of speech long before they attend to individual words and grammar, but Robbie stuck to only a very few tunes. The meaning of words seemed irrelevant to him.

The second problem was that he seemed to have no concept of, or interest in, *trying* to change. The idea of mental effort itself was foreign to him. It had taken years for him to learn even that he could think his own thoughts. Furthermore, he had a powerful and abiding day-dream. He dreamed constantly of living in a country cottage where everyone did absolutely everything together all day long. The inhabitants, unlike the chestnuts, moved, but only in perfect unison. It was a sort of half-way house between autism and life – a hot-house which permitted some contact with other people, and some intellectual development, but under rigid and jealously defined conditions. Thus he could travel about London, use public telephones and restaurants, adapt if his absent-mindedness led to his taking the wrong train, and he could even take part in some athletic activities. Yet his educational and social life were far behind his 17 years and there was no way he had sufficient initiative to hold down a job. Still, he was beginning to dislike this situation and to be mindful of the impatience and annoyance his madness, vagueness and endless procrastinations produced in normal people. He had, finally, the beginnings – but only the barest beginnings – of some real motivation for being sane. He insisted that he wanted to 'catch up' but neither he nor I had any idea of how far he had to go. Nor did I realize then how powerful was his vegetative entwining grip on life. It appeared to be soft, gentle and harmless but it was truly deadly. It was a long while before I understood this, and even longer before I began to get some idea of how to put such understanding to use in Robbie's sessions.

3

BECOMING VERTEBRATE

Jacques Barzun, in his *Stroll with William James*, observed that only William James, staring at an octopus in an English aquarium, would have remarked on such 'flexible intensity of life in a form so inaccessible to our sympathy' (1987). One of Jacques Cousteau's amazing underwater films ends with a sequence showing a giant squid boxed in a huge crate on the deck of the yacht. The lid of the crate has been left off and slowly and horribly the creature slithers first its tentacles and then its slimy bulk up and over the edge of the crate and down the side, across the deck, then over the side of the yacht. Cameras must have been waiting in the sea below, because what one then witnesses is a miracle. The hideous, awkward, obscene slitherer is transformed into a ballerina of the deep. The tentacles undulate and stream behind the head like willows in the wind. All is flow and grace as the creature rediscovers its element. Many psychotic children give one the feeling that terra firma has too many obstacles, is too static, rough and rectangular. There is much written now of the need newborn babies have for being eased over the transitions from one medium to another, e.g. during the major change of medium from liquid to gas called birth, during the situation of being plunged into water – called having a bath – of being taken out of the bath, put on to the breast, off it, dressed, undressed.

Everyone who has worked at any depth with these very ill children knows how difficult they find all transitions and how important it is at certain stages of their treatment to smooth them over and ease them where possible. By this I do not mean that trained psychotherapists never take holidays from their psychotic patients or never confront them with painful truths. Changes are not denied. What I mean is that coming breaks or changes, e.g. a change of time or change of room, or, worse, a change of therapist, are prepared for and talked about before and after the event, so that the painful shocks can be absorbed, digested, borne, and therefore learned from, rather than denied. The difficulty with Robbie was that he had himself eventually found an all too effective but mind-destroying way of smoothing his own passage; he called it, in his first session, 'making it soft'. This, unfortunately, had become as serious a part of his illness, this passive hooking on to sameness and avoidance of novelty or difficulty, as whatever original panic and anguish might have called it forth. I had to find a way of being sensitive to the panic and pain where it remained – this I think I was fairly well trained to do – but also to find a way of loosening his cloying grip. This was much harder, especially as his methods grew more sophisticated as the years went by, and I think I played in with it and was fooled by it for far too long. I believe that I, with my misguided pseudo-psychoanalytic 'understanding', provided for much longer that I should have, an all-too-watery medium in which he thrived but failed to develop.

Frances Tustin coined a word for the toys and objects autistic children often carry around with them. She called them 'autistic objects' and distinguished them clearly from Winnicott's notion of the 'transitional object', the teddy or soft blanket the normal 1- or 2- or 3-year old takes to bed at night (Tustin 1972; Winnicott 1958). Winnicott's transitional object was half a true symbol, i.e. half a symbolic reminder of the mother, and half a way of forgetting her importance. It was therefore something half-way to being a true symbol.

There is some important psychoanalytical theory relevant here; it connects with a seminal paper by Hanna Segal on the difference between normal and psychotic thought processes (Segal 1957). Schizophrenics have often been described, even in the most organically orientated psychiatric or behaviourist writings, as typically concrete thinkers. Hanna Segal suggested that a capacity for symbol formation is characteristic of normal thought and language, that a true symbol is experienced as related to and representing the object, but also as fundamentally different from the object it represents. The irreplaceability and fundamental essence of the original is respected. A symbolic equation, on the other hand, equates the symbol with the object and denies their differences. Segal cited the example of a psychotic man who could no longer play the violin because he felt as though he were literally masturbating in public. This is similar to Freud's instance of the baby sucking his thumb and for a time believing it is the breast, as an example of hallucinatory wish-fulfilment (Freud 1900: 566). Winnicott's transitional object is half-way between the symbol and the symbolic equation. The child's soft cuddly teddy or silky blanket reminds him of, stands for, his mother's warmth and protectiveness and so helps him to go to sleep, as though she were still with him. In the transitional object stage, the child half knows the teddy bear is really only a substitute for the mother, and half denies this, telling himself that teddy is all it needs. When these transitional objects slide over into becoming all-important, just as good as – or better than – the real human mother, enabling the child to ignore permanently and chronically this mother and the need for a living human being, they become symbolic equations, or autistic objects. As Tustin points out, they then become used to avoid human contact, to keep the living, human, less controllable objects out of the child's mind (Tustin 1981).

In Robbie's childhood there were many objects, such as the bus tickets he brought to sessions, and obsessive rituals, such as touching the wall, which absolutely fitted Tustin's description. Tustin stressed that autistic objects are not used in terms of the function for which they were intended. She showed that they seem to have no phantasy associated with them and are used in an extremely canalized and perseverative fashion. She wrote, 'They are static and do not have the open-ended qualities which would lead to the development of new networks of association' (Tustin 1981: 96). That is a brilliant description of the pathology and dynamics of the child, but in order to convey what it feels like for parents, teachers and therapists on the receiving end of such perseverative blindness and deafness to human values, we also need Kundera. When I imagine myself witnessing Robbie's endless repetitive rituals, drained of all their previous meaning and with no end whatever in sight, with his horrific tolerance for timelessness, I think I felt like Kundera's Tamina – nauseous, desperate, my stomach hollowed out. 'It is little things of no weight at all that are making Tamina nauseous. In fact, that hollow feeling in her stomach comes from the unbearable absence of weight' (Kundera 1981: 188). That is it precisely – the unbearable absence of weight, the unbearable absence of meaning or significance in what he was doing. As Tustin says, not even phantasy remains – just debris. What, I often thought, had psychoanalysis, with its endless search for meaning, to do with all this?

44

BACKBONE IN ME

By the time Robbie was 20, although he had given up a lot of his more glaringly obvious psychotic rituals and was much more verbal, the insidious, passive, sensual lingering and malingering over the past had invaded his language. He no longer touched walls to ease his passage down a hall from one place to another; he simply stood stock still mentally, touching, caressing over and over again the same old thoughts. He had been for many years unable to speak in any coherent or narrative manner; thoughts or images simply passed through his head slowly, like fishes, often with little connection between them. As he became more coherent, I gradually came to realize that his lifelong habit of clinging to what we had together labelled 'old stuff' had invaded his speech, and of course the way in which he listened to the speech of others. He had become very proud of the fact that he was able to travel about London and even make trips to other parts of England by public transport. A recurrent problem at the beginning was not so much that of getting on the right train – he was usually nervous and therefore alert at that point – but remembering to get *off* at the right stop. He would sit down in the train, drift off to his own private psychotic preoccupations and wake up to find himself several stops beyond his destination. He came to a session one day in a very agitated but unusually awake and alert state, saying that he had been meant to meet his mother at Camden Town Station but had gone on to Tufnell Park. It sounded as though she must have eventually followed him there, because he gave a vivid description of her angry response and the expression on her face. He explained that her response when he met her properly was quite different, and he described the friendly expression, different lipstick, different clothes. This was during a period when he was struggling hard to make discriminations and distinctions, so it was important for us to distinguish between the kind of mother who had to chase him and shout at him to make contact, and the one who, he felt, smiled when he made some effort to meet her. For some sessions afterwards Robbie and I together took the names of these two stations as useful metaphors for his changing states of alertness and dissolving driftedness and the accompanying and changing views of his internal (i.e. imagined) mother and of me.

Gradually, however, it became clear that he had begun to stick to this previously lively metaphor in the same cloying, rigid way as he had with so many physical objects and rituals in the past. He began to use it not to go forward, but to stay where he was and to ensure that I did so too. We simply could not get off the train. Bion has described the psychotic's clear, articulated speech as one-dimensional, lacking in resonance and inclined to make the listener say 'So what?' because it has no capacity to evoke a train of thought (Bion 1962: 16). Where my patient often fooled me was that he inevitably picked ideas which had once been three-dimensional but in fact had no fresh meaning whatever attached to them now. He seemed to feel that letting go of the old familiar stuff would leave him with no means of achieving a new and different link again. Renewal was a concept almost entirely missing from his imagination. Concerning his old wall-touching ritual, he had explained to me, years after, when he was able to verbalize it, that he touched the wall to 'see if it was still there'. When he went to see Buckingham Palace and I asked him about it, the only thing he could say was 'There is a flag on the top to say whether she is there or not'. Yet the thereness of his objects rarely stimulated his interest or curiosity; it merely reassured him. I began to become more and more vigilant about the question of whether he was making a real communication or a false one, and whenever I was sure the material was dead, I refused to collude by using the metaphor any longer. I tried to indicate quickly when I thought he was starting to settle too comfortably into a verbal rut, because there was a dreadful downward spiral; if I left him too long, or interpreted too mildly, the material took on various fetishistic and perverted qualities and he became very excited.

It was my impression that over that year (he was 20 by then) he did not experience this firmness or backbone of mine as pushing him away, but rather as attempts to draw him close, to hold out for another less gluey kind of contact. Often he was irritated and bewildered by my refusals, but he did seem to become gradually more able to distinguish between the two kinds of communication. It was hard work and I was forever falling or catching myself about to fall into some comfortable and comforting familiar word trap. Over subsequent years, I became even more vigilant but also, alas, more awed by the unbelievable power of the psychotic process. It was like making one's way across tussocks in marshy ground: if I could keep my head and balance and stick to fresh language every time, i.e. avoid Robbie's psychotic addictive words and phrases, we might make a tiny move ahead. If I made a slip, or simply let him go ahead a bit too long without making my bid, we were sinking in the marsh. The word, with whatever comforting and then exciting sensual, textural, crazy associations it had for him, took over and it was by then much stronger than I. With a neurotic or less ill patient, a mistake or a delay in interpreting can be corrected or made up, the patient can be brought back by the next interpretation, one would not be in danger of sinking into the marsh, one would simply say the word and then analyse the response. But with Robbie, once these words were allowed to take over, it was like quicksand; he fell into his swampy psychosis and I lost him.

BACKBONE IN HIMSELF

In one session early in July when Robbie was 21, he came on time in a relatively integrated state. After a little while he turned around on the couch and looked at me. I asked him what he had seen and he said, 'You – looking – straight and stiff'. But he said this gently, admiringly and not afraid, nor did he seem at all excited. A few days later, he told me 'I've been to the Natural History Museum and I have bones and muscle and they are how I move'. He told me all this on his own initiative and I took it that he was beginning to be aware that he had bones to hold himself up and muscles to move him; in the same way, he had held the ideas up and together in his mind and had told me all this about the museum and moved towards me in the conversation, without waiting for me to do all the pushing and pulling and questioning. It was as though he were discovering the bones and muscles of his mind. Some years before, his shoes had become important to him and he said, 'They hold me up'. At the time this had seemed a valuable development, but it was a long way from a feeling that he had any central core of his own which held him up. Because he was so floppy, I always had difficulty in believing that he had any backbone at all, so it was strange and hopeful to hear him show an interest in his bones.

Later that week, he said he wanted an operation to get rid of his bones. He had been angry about some men on an overcrowded train who hadn't left him room to get on, and made him late. He wanted the bones removed so that he wouldn't hurt, and Vic, the foreman at work, couldn't hurt him when he hit him. (Robbie had a simple job by now, and sometimes his apathy and dreaminess was terribly irritating to workmates, so perhaps Vic had indeed hit him.) He wanted to be all soft in his tummy and arms and legs.

A few days later, he wanted to go straightaway to his book full of drawings connected with the Camden Town and Tufnell Park material. By then this was all dead old stuff, and I interpreted accordingly. He returned to the couch, but then said: 'I want to draw just one more drawing.' However, he stayed on the couch when I interpreted and said: 'I want to hit Julie (his sister) – women make mistakes – men think – women don't sort the dirty clothes – they leave them in their drawers.' I said perhaps he felt it was a girl or a womanish part of him that didn't sort out the old, stale, dirty thoughts connected with that book, the thoughts that never get washed and renewed. (I now think he might well have felt it was time I got rid of his old book.) He said, with great feeling, 'I don't want to be a man – I want to be a little boy – I want to grow down – begin again. I want to drown myself – die – be a little boy.' I said I thought he was a bit muddled, because if he drowned himself he wouldn't be able to begin again; all he would do is die. Then I asked him why he wanted to be a little boy again and, instead of giving the kind of placating rote answer I had learned to expect to this type of question, he began a kind of avalanche of painful and sorrowful regrets for his missing childhood. He said passionately, 'I want to play with bricks and build a house. I want to collect chestnuts and conkers, and have a doll.' I started to say something, but he interrupted me, saying, 'I want to put furniture in the house – a TV set – a camera – take a picture – set up the camera scream' (he pronounced it with an 'm').

I pointed out that it was true he never had played with bricks or dolls as a child, and had never done so with me either, but that he could do so here and now. Words and thoughts could be collected like chestnuts and put together to make a conversation, like bricks make a house. (I had been trying to show him for some years that he was unaware of his own capacity to collect, store and order his thoughts, but what I now thought was more important was not that he *could* do so, but that he *was* doing so today. Often he lay like someone at the bottom of a fish tank watching his thoughts float past, never realizing he could claim them as his own and do things with them or to them. But today was different, and I felt it was important to show him that.) I also said that we had opened up the chest of drawers of his mind and feelings and it wasn't empty and it wasn't filled with the stale, old, dirty stuff either, it was filled with something important and fresh. He said – still very involved and alert – 'I want a teddy that I can cuddle'. But this led off into talk about a quite different kind of teddy, along with some familiar masturbatory ritualistic talk. When I pointed this out, however, he came back to his more awake state and talked about his longing for the first kind of teddy. I interpreted that he wanted to find a way of keeping me with him always, and cuddling me, and he said – still with great emotion – 'I want to go to the adventure playground and climb things. Climb them to the top. I want to kick a ball.' I said, 'But you can and are kicking the words over to me and climbing over me with your feelings and ideas.' I should have shown him how free he seemed to feel to interrupt me today, but I failed to. I did say, however, that he was discovering he had bones and muscles inside him which made all this possible and made him feel strong, able to move and to take action with his feelings and thoughts and words. He began hitting his chest, and said, 'I want to hit that bone – at the centre – I want to break in – I want to see what I'm like inside myself.'

There are many interesting things in this session. Everything, for example, seemed to have an inside: the drawers, the house, his body; indeed, each thought seemed to contain further thoughts both within and beyond it. There was also the wish to build and put things together. But the element I want to draw attention to is the movement. It is difficult to convey without describing hundreds of dead sessions just how foreign movement was to this vegetable-like creature. This session, however, was full of imagined movement – building, collecting, filling, taking pictures, cuddling, climbing, kicking, breaking in and, most of all, wanting. The language, for him, was extremely vigorous, full of verbs, full of verbal bone and muscle. There seemed, first, to be a picture of an object that he could do things to and with and, second, a picture of himself as a doer. I suspect that an important prelude to this development was the day on which he saw me as 'stiff and straight', and that this heralded the beginnings of an important introjective and identification process. He was beginning to have some backbone and substance of his own.

4

GROWTH OF A MIND
The function of reclamation

Oliver Sacks' book, *Awakenings*, tells the story of the reactions of deeply Parkinsonian, post-encephalitic patients who had been sunk into deep states of 'sleep' or stasis since the sleeping-sickness epidemic of 1916. In 1969, half a century later, they were given the drug L-Dopa. Sacks describes the profound and disturbing return to health of his patients, and expresses his own amazement that 'the potential for health and self can survive, after so much of the life and structure of the person has been lost, and after so long and exclusive an immersion in sickness'. He adds in a footnote:

> The comparison of such awakenings to so-called 'lucid intervals' will at once occur to many readers. At such times – despite the presence of massive functional or structural disturbance to the brain – the patient is suddenly and completely restored to himself. One observes this, again and again, at the height of toxic, febrile, or other deliria: sometimes the person may be recalled to himself by the calling of his name; then for a moment or a few minutes, he is himself, before he is carried off by delirium again. In patients with advanced senile dementias or pre-senile dementias (e.g. Alzheimer's disease) where there is abundant evidence of all types regarding the massive loss of brain structure and function, one may also - very suddenly and movingly – see vivid, momentary recalls of the original, lost person.
>
> (Sacks 1973: 203)

A central feature of the psychoanalytic theory of Melanie Klein is that it is an object-relations theory, not, in its later formulations at any rate, an instinct or drive theory. It is a two-person, not a one-person theory. A psychotherapist working within an object-relations framework would consider it vital to note not only that Robbie came to life at moments, but to whom or to what kind of figure or landscape or object in his imagined or real world he awoke, and by what figure or landscape or object a particular awakening was facilitated. It seemed important to ask three questions: first, how had the tiny, undeveloped, unexercised, but none the less alive part of his mind managed to elude the mire of his mad indolence; that is, what conditions in him had enabled it to happen? Second, what variations in me might have facilitated this? And, third, what was the relationship between us that may have been instrumental in getting the vital juices flowing again? I speculated often about events and changes in his outside life that I was certain played a part in improvements, but the only thing I could observe directly was the ongoing events taking place in the consulting room, between the two of us – that is, in what psychoanalysis would term his trans-ference attitudes to me and my counter-transference attitudes to him.

The most moving recovery from madness in literature is the scene where King Lear, senile and wandering on the downs, is rescued by Cordelia. For some moments, the raving and broken King believes that she must be a spirit, or else, if real, she will surely mock him for thinking she is his daughter. He claims she does him wrong to take him out of the grave. She persists, begging him to look at her. Her forgiveness, her tender consideration of his dignity and pride (he reminds himself later that her voice was ever soft and low), some sort of redemption, all these seem to play a part in saving Lear from madness. But this is luxurious speculation for my purposes. King Lear had a sane mind to which to return. Robbie's situation was more dire and the Cordelias of his inner life evanescent, fleeting, long-gone and long-forgotten. For much of the time in the early years, he hardly knew anyone was in the room with him. How could I, a 'net with a hole in it', ever become sufficiently knitted, woven, dense and substantial to catch and hold his attention and his hope? How could I ever hope to mobilize his own life-giving energies? On the rare occasions when he or I did manage to stir the ashes and evoke a flicker of life, how were we to catch the moment and reproduce it?

I have already implied, in Chapter 3, a partial answer to my three questions. I think that my eventual firmness - or, if you prefer, hardness – in refusing to be too pliant a colluder with his entwining methods was probably an important element in his developing some mental backbone, some mettle of his own. The very collisions with reality which destroyed him at an early stage of his illness seemed to have had an invigorating and bracing effect later. In fact, images of fresh air colour all my thinking about that period because, in the middle and late years of his adolescence, once he had come to give off more masculine smells but not yet to care about personal cleanliness or appearance, it was sometimes nearly intolerable to sit in a room with him. He smelled like an old vagrant. The stench, however, from his unused, unrefreshed, decaying mind was even worse. He had latched on to a repetitive, highly sensual, mindlessly titillating type of language; he would, if left to his own devices, go on for years repeating the same phrases or stories. My mistake in the early years had been to think that because he was repeating them, they still had as yet ununderstood meanings which required my serious attention. Gradually, I faced the fact that the emptiness and unbelievable staleness of these stories was filling me with impotent rage, disgust, despair and, worst of all, unutterable boredom. In fact, what meaning there was lay in the sensual qualities of the words themselves, not the stories. Robbie was excited and tickled, not by the content of the stories, but by particular words which he loved to roll around on his tongue. He was fascinated, as I have mentioned, by the colour and texture of people's voices. Someone had a dark green velvety voice, another had a bright orange voice. And these were no mere metaphorical experiences: sounds were felt, quite literally, to touch him, caress him, tickle him, or, strangely, to provide visual thrills.

But I did not understand this then. I simply began to know that the stories were utterly dead. Often I could envisage him ending up on a back ward for chronic psychiatric patients – despite everyone's efforts – and, worse, being quite content to be there. Notions of psychoanalytic neutrality and even of human compassion seemed, at times, to imply a state of positively lunatic collusion on my part. Civilized human beings choose to bury their dung heaps and their dead, and they provide asylum for people who prefer their hallucinations and delusions to 'reality'. Was I, by listening so carefully to his gigglings and mutterings, really taking part in some sort of necrophiliac perversion?

But I am getting ahead of myself. I want to return to the question of what kind of relationship, in the early and most broken-down periods of Robbie's illness, may have helped to bring him to life.

THE PSYCHOANALYTIC ATTITUDE: NEUTRALITY, CONTAINMENT AND RECLAMATION

The psychoanalytic attitude of neutrality has a long, distinguished and well-tried history. Freud pointed out that experience taught that the analyst's taking over of repressive, guiding or even encouraging functions could interfere with the process of self-knowledge and self-realization in the patient (Freud 1912). Analysts have subsequently warned against the dangers, not only of literal seductions of patients, but also of more subtle but equally powerful seductive attitudes on the part of the analyst who, because of the patient's dependence and because of the powerful nature of transference feelings, is in a highly privileged but therefore extremely responsible position. Reassurance, or encouragement, or what has been called 'corrective emotional experiences' have been considered by many analysts to interfere with the patient's bringing his true inner imaginative world, however cruel and devastating, into the transference relationship where it can be subjected to real, rather than superficial, change.

Bion provided a somewhat different model of the analytic function. His concept of containment stresses somewhat more what the attitude should be than what it should not. It seems at first sight to be quite close to Freud's concept of neutrality, but in fact it arises from a different theoretical underpinning, an object-relations one. Neutrality seems somehow to imply a rather static state of affairs, whereas containment is a much more dynamic notion, referring to the holding of and the managing of a balanced play of forces, and also to the methods by which such balanced holding is achieved. It refers to the thoughtful emotionality and emotional thoughtfulness, that is, to the work done inside the analyst upon these forces. Bion compared this to a state of maternal reverie in which the mother feels the impact and upset projected into her by her distressed baby, but contains it, and returns it to him in a modified form. Later, Bion gave a name to the modifying process which went on inside the mother or analyst as a sequel to the impact of the initial containment: he called it a transformation and likened this to the activity of the artist. He said: 'An interpretation is a transformation . . . An experience, felt and described in one way, is described in another' (Bion 1965: 4).

Bion's notions of containment and transformation seem to me to bear a much closer correspondence to what actually goes on between therapist and patient in the consulting room than does Freud's rather static image of the neutral mirror. Mirrors are not changed by what they reflect, therapists are. But because of the obvious importance of the therapist's being open to feeling the impact of the patient's projections, I think the receptive elements in Bion's model were sometimes over-stressed (in my own thinking, at any rate; for a fuller discussion of the problem of neutrality and containment see Alvarez 1985). Thus, what sometimes seemed to be the rather passive implications of the function of containment, with its notions of thoughtful reverie, seemed to leave something to be desired, as I sat week after week, month after month, searching for the emanations and projections from Robbie that failed to materialize. I began to feel a need and urgency to be more active and more mobile than with other patients for whom the containment model had proved helpful, and, at the time, this worried me. I felt, as sometimes other despairing therapists working with vegetable-like psychotic children have felt, that perhaps analytic therapy is really not the right treatment for such children. Robbie didn't even want merging oneness with me at this early stage of his illness; he simply didn't know or care that I was there at all. He wanted, in fact, almost nothing.

This situation seemed to require an extension of the models of the analytic function with which I was familiar. I did not feel Robbie was projecting into me his need to be found, nor did I feel that he was even waiting to be found. I believe he had given up. I began to feel that I, as the mother or father in the transference, had to chase after him, not because he was hiding, but because he was deeply lost. It seemed to me that my function was to reclaim him as a member of the human family because he no longer knew how to make his own claims. I could not, and still cannot, forget how he stressed again and again that the *length* of the rope was so important. And this exactly corresponded to my feeling that I had, indeed, to traverse great distances – distances created, I think, both by the degree of his withdrawal and also by its chronicity: he was a terribly long way off, and he had been there a long time. Ideas of neutrality, of adaptation, and even of reverie were inert and inadequate solutions to his plight. Robbie's own image of the long long long stocking which rescued him and all his loved ones from the dark well seems to imply that rescue was felt to come from somewhere a long way off, that its capacity to awaken, enliven, stimulate and, I think, stir hope was central, and that even the most Cordelia-like compassionate receptiveness would have been inadequate. It was not enough for me to go on, like the Consul's wife, sobbing in a distant room. The enormous psychological distance through which he could fall had to be spanned, not only to call him into human contact, but even more urgently to recall him to himself.

There is no doubt that the mother's receptiveness to the baby's unfolding attachment, or the therapist's to the patient's transference, is a fundamental maternal and analytic function. But there are other maternal functions, and perhaps other therapeutic functions as well. What I cannot forget about the day Robbie told about the rescue of the boy and girl who had been imprisoned down the dark well is that, as he described the way they flew up and over to the other side of the street, his voice changed radically. He began to talk in rising, almost musical cadences, with a tremendous urgency and flow. His ideas had direction and purpose. They, like all the rescued people talking and shouting in the story, had somewhere to go – to a place which he called 'the other side of the street'. This fountain of life in him had clearly sexual and birth or rebirth significances (the long stocking was also a long penis, he said), but the rising note seemed also to have a lot to do with notions from everyday speech such as the heart lifting, spirits rising, hopes soaring. Yet one point continued to puzzle and disturb me: Robbie had stressed that the rope had been thrown down, and also that it was very, very long. It seemed to be an image of a lifeline. He seemed to be describing not only an awakening, but an experience of being *awakened*. It seemed to me that in his illest, most withdrawn state, he surfaced and came to when I got through, when I made some fundamental move to reach him where he was in his lost stuporous state. I chose at the time the word 'reclamation' to describe the situation. Waste land does not ask to be reclaimed, yet its hidden potentiality for growth may flourish none the less when it is reclaimed. (Eleanora Fe D'Ostiana, in describing her work with a deeply withdrawn and previously unreachable psychotic boy, describes viewing him as down a dark well, completely alone. She made herself imagine vividly what it was like to be in a place of such emptiness and loneliness, and as she did so the child came to life and sang a song about flowers and spring. She seems to be describing something related to, but different from reclamation: a type of profound empathy (Fe d'Ostiani 1980).)

A classic view, put by James Strachey in 1934, was that the analyst, by means of his neutral attitude, acted as an auxiliary superego – that is, as a non-judgemental and non-seductive figure who could eventually be seen to be different from more extreme inner parental imagoes and voices. By lending this new neutral viewpoint to the patient, and by resisting the patient's effort to identify him with these parents, the analyst could help the patient to get outside his fears and guilts and illusions and be freed from them (Strachey 1934). But psychoanalytic experience and theory has had to go beyond this notion of the analyst as auxiliary superego. It is now understood that people project not only aspects of their parents on to the person of the analyst or therapist, but also basic and precious parts of themselves, even ego functions such as their common sense or their intelligence. Bion has written of an even more drastic situation with severely ill schizophrenics, where the whole of the personality may be evacuated, even the will to live (1962: 97). For Robbie, the word 'lost' seems more appropriate than 'evacuated', as it accords more with my experience of patients like him who have given up, who seem to have abandoned hope rather than projected it, and for whom one may have to carry not only their will to live, but even the very knowledge that they do exist.

Rosenfeld, who analysed several psychotic patients, suggested that Strachey's model needs extending, and that at times the analyst functions as an auxiliary self for the patient, performing certain functions he cannot perform for himself. Rosenfeld stressed the ego functions, the perceiving, introjecting, verbalizing functions that the patient cannot manage (Rosenfeld 1972). But what was lacking in Robbie was something even more basic: his very sense of existing, and therefore any awareness of how near he might be to psychic death. He later often spoke of the time when he had been sent away to the country as the time when he had died and, truly, something did seem to have died, or nearly died in him. For patients whose depersonalization is deeply chronic, who are as burnt-out and as long-forgotten by themselves as Robbie, the therapist's feeling of dire urgency about their situation may need to be taken absolutely seriously as being utterly appropriate. At such a point, the therapist may be temporarily functioning as almost the whole of the patient's self – that is, not only the rational thinking, sorting ego, and not just the infantile dependent self either, but as something possibly prior to both: the very sense of being alive.

Urgency, horror and desperation may therefore be appropriate responses to some stages of mental illness, mental dissolution and psychic near-death. The therapist may have to feel this urgency without losing her balance and her capacity to think, in order to help the patient to know the seriousness of his plight. It may be that in cases of chronic mental illness or chronic depression or chronic apathy, *even in children*, the chronicity itself has to be addressed, long before luxurious questions such as the child's original motives for becoming depressed or apathetic or mad can be dealt with. Autism may, indeed, start off as a defensive flight from shock and mental pain. There is plenty of evidence in Robbie's history, with his rather joyless birth and the two traumatic separations in the second year of his life, to suggest that these factors played at least a precipitating part in his illness and withdrawal. But years of withdrawal bring further consequences in their train. Malnutrition, or a state of starvation, is a condition vastly different from hunger. Mental starvation may, indeed, be very different from mental need. It is no good telling someone with advanced lung cancer to stop smoking. Prevention is of a different order from cure and interpretations directed to the why of withdrawal may ignore the perilous facts of the degree of withdrawal. They ignore, too, the huge problem of defining, grasping, and then of traversing the enormous unmapped mental spaces through which the patient has retreated.

So far I have touched briefly on some of the theories of how the curative process of psychoanalysis has been thought to work. Early psychoanalytic notions of psychoanalysis as an uncovering, unmasking activity seemed fairly irrelevant to Robbie's condition. Notions of growth, learning, inadequacy, even of defect seem to offer a better description of the therapeutic problems with such a patient, and I shall return to the psychoanalytic theories of learning in the next chapter.

RECLAMATION AND PROJECTIVE IDENTIFICATION

Yet a further theoretical question remains: do the powerful feelings of alarm aroused in the mind of the therapist arise as a result of being sent there by the patient? At the very least, are they evoked by the projective identification processes described by Klein and Bion? Bion stressed that one type of projective identification, normal to infancy, involved a very primitive, perhaps the most primitive, form of communication (Bion 1962: 36). Is the withdrawn patient's arousal of alarm in us a communication of alarm, or even an evacuation of his unacceptable feelings of alarm, or neither? Much depends on how one defines a communication. Gregory Bateson makes a clear distinction between two types of communication, signs and signals. He has speculated that an important stage in the evolution of communication is reached when the organism ceases to respond 'automatically' to the mood-signs of another and becomes able to recognize the sign as a signal: that is, to recognize that the other individual's and its own signals are only signals, which can be trusted, distrusted, falsified, denied, amplified, corrected and so forth. He describes his own astonishment when he went to study meta-communicative signs (that is, signals) at the Fleishbacker Zoo in San Francisco and saw two young monkeys *playing*. They were play-fighting, and he explains that this phenomenon could occur only if the participant organisms were capable of some degree of meta-communication, i.e. of exchanging signals which could carry the message 'this is play'. Mood-signs, on the other hand, are thought to be like sexual odours – automatic, involuntary, but outwardly perceptible events which are 'part of the physiological process which we have called a mood' (Bateson 1955: 120). It seems probable that Bion's projective identification as a primitive form of non-verbal communication may be referring to something which falls somewhere between a mood-sign and a signal. I would suggest that some of the symptomatology seen in the most psychotic of patients may be operating at an even lower level, namely at the level of a mood-sign. Some of the alarm one feels about a deeply withdrawn patient may be partly a response to a powerful projection of despair that the patient is unable to feel for himself. But the alarm may also be a response to something even iller in the patient, something which has given up, and become incapable of sending out any communications at all. The patient has broken down; he has, in part, ceased to send out signals, but nevertheless something like mood-signs remain. The therapist's response to this aspect of the situation may be, in a manner of speaking, called up within himself by an active act of the imagination. It is taken for granted that people who are acutely ill with physical conditions receive emergency treatment and intensive care. But first, the condition has to be identified as grave. I suspect that the emotional perception required to identify the need for the intensive emergency treatment appropriate to severe psychological illness in children is some of the time akin to the receptive senses of vision and hearing in humans; at others, where there is insufficient light

58

from communication processes, it is perhaps more like echolocation, the sending out of ultrasound pulses by bats in order to 'see' in the dark. It perhaps draws closer to a projective process than an introjective one. Sometimes the shadowy shape of the child within can be located by such methods: at others, the reclamatory moves may have to precede any evidence that there really is a mind in there to reclaim.

5

RECLAMATION AND LIVE COMPANY

Normal counterparts in the caretaker–infant relationship

Haydn surprises us with the unexpected; Mozart surprises us with the expected.

Alfred Brendel

I now wish to inquire whether there are any normal and ordinary maternal functions which might correspond to the responses of the therapist described in the last chapter. Do the 'reclaiming' activities connected with alarm, urgency, intensive care, echolocation, empathy, directed to desperate situations in desperately ill patients, have anything to do with more normal 'claiming' activities engaged in by ordinary mothers of ordinary babies? I shall first examine some fairly straightforward examples of what seem to me to be everyday reclamations, and then go on to discuss activities which seem to involve something closer to 'claimings'.

Bion's concept of maternal containment goes like this: he describes how the mother, through her reverie, carries out a type of mental digestion which, due to her more mature mental digestive processes, enables her to experience in a bearable form the baby's distress or rage or fear (1962). She is thus able, without panicky over-involvement, but also without too great detachment, to soothe and calm him. Bion discusses this as a normal and everyday maternal function. It is important to consider, however, something else: what ordinary mothers do when their ordinary babies are mildly depressed – that is, not when they are expressing or showing their distress but when they are failing to show it because they have temporarily lost interest or hope and have become somewhat withdrawn. Mothers, I mean, function also as alerters, arousers and enliveners of their babies.

The studies by child development researchers of the reciprocal

60

interactions between mother and child seem to suggest that inter-actional contact is rhythmic and cyclic, that the ups are as important and as mutually sought as the downs, and that alerting and arousing functions are as significant as soothing ones (although these are muted and highly sensitively engaged in with a very young or particularly delicate baby). The research points to notions such as intensity curves, to a sort of wave function, to contouring, to rhythm, to periods of intensity followed by quiet, to intense mutuality followed by retreat, peaceful withdrawal and isolation. Apparently the normal mother permits and respects some degree of withdrawal on her baby's part, but she also plays, however gently, *an active part* in drawing him back into interaction with her. Too much distress evokes something which bears a resemblance to reverie and containment (Bion 1962), too much withdrawal evokes sensitive drawing into contact (Brazelton *et al.* 1974; Trevarthen 1984; Stern 1985).

I had not read the child development research when I first began to wonder about the notion of reclamation, but two observations of normal infants made me feel that Robbie's long long stocking had some perfectly normal connotations. In one observation, a little girl baby named Lucy had been prematurely weaned and had become, in comparison to her usual sunny self, somewhat depressed and withdrawn. During the observation, the mother got down on her knees facing the baby, was tirelessly concerned and sympathetic, and gave far more of her face and voice on that day than on previous occasions when her breast had been available. This type of 'cheering up' needs to be distinguished from the kind of manic reassurance and denial of depression which could encourage the development of a 'false self' in a child, who, for example, then has to cheer himself up in order to cheer his mother up. It seemed to me, however, that the mother in that instance may have been demonstrating something different to her child: namely, her sympathetic understanding that although something was lost – the breast – not everything was lost, and that, where there had seemed to be emptiness, there was still fullness and ripeness after all. Sheila Miller has suggested an example of an ordinary everyday occurrence in a child's life: a toddler was playing with his teddy on his own near his mother in a happy and animated fashion, but gradually his play became a bit automatic and lifeless. The mother came over to the child, played with the teddy for a little while, whereupon the child and his play came back to life. These examples of input

61

from the mother seeming to pull the baby out of depression lead one to think of other ordinary situations where input, or, to use another highly inadequate term borrowed from psychology, stimulation, does not lift a depressed child to an ordinary level, but takes a child *already at an ordinary level* to a level of delight, surprise, wonder, pleasure. The words 'input' and 'stimulation' are inadequate; they are based on a behaviouristic machine-model of personality which ignores the object-relations implications of the research on intersubjectivity and interaction. But they are, for my purposes at the moment, useful counterweights to 'containment'. 'Cheering up' is an object-relations term; 'stimulation' is not. 'Delighting', 'entertaining', 'playing with' are all object-relations terms. So is 'singing to'. Some of the thinking in psychoanalytic theory, especially that derived from Freud's early reliance on a somewhat reductionist model, implied that interventions on the mother's part are only to gratify, to adapt, to fit to the baby's needs. There seems, in such a model, no concept of *adding to* his enrichment.

The following are two other maternal interventions, both observed by me, which were experienced by the babies as a stimulus to curiosity, interest and attention, rather than as intrusive interferences. These arise from observations of normal infants, observations carried out according to the method devised by Esther Bick at the Tavistock Clinic (Bick 1966; Miller *et al.* 1989). In the first example, a 3-day-old baby girl named Cathy had just completed an apparently satisfactory feed at the breast, but was still awake. The mother held the baby in front of her face and began talking to her in a gentle but animated manner. One could see quite clearly the baby turning her head this way and that to get an even better fix and focus on the source of this amazing noise. She seemed to be trying to grasp or puzzle the thing out. She did not look troubled by this novelty (research suggests the mother's voice is recognized by the neonate from its learning of the identifying prosodic features in utero (Trevarthen 1986)); but she did look highly interested, possibly even fascinated. Another mother observed to me around the same time that her very young baby seemed fascinated by this experience *after* a feed, but found it too stimulating before a feed. In the second example, Martin, a 5-month-old baby boy, had been fed mostly on a demand schedule and was accustomed to waking in the morning, crying or gurgling for a little while until his mother heard him and came into his room to lift him up and feed him. He was accustomed, that is, to drawing his mother to him with his voice – a good example of maternal 'adaptation' and not inconsistent with hydrostatic theories of the mother as a need satisfier, tension reducer, etc. However, on one occasion, the mother heard the child stirring *before* he was fully awake and waited by his cotside till he awoke. When he opened his eyes he saw her face, and slowly revealed absolute and astonished delight. These examples may seem simplistic, but they may serve to remind us that there is more to mothering than the passive and mechanistic concepts of adaptation and fit, or receptiveness, would allow. Surely novelty, surprise, enjoyment and delight, in manageable quantities, play as vital a part in the infant's development as their more peaceful counterparts – structure, routine, familiarity, lullaby. The mother of Lucy, the baby who had been recently weaned and seemed depressed, was engaged, I am suggesting, in a fairly everyday type of 'reclaiming' activity; the mothers of Cathy and Martin were providing interest and surprise by engaging in what might be called a 'claiming' activity. They were *seeking* their babies' attention not because the baby was depressed, and not because they were even showing a particular need; the mothers made the first move, and their babies seem to have taken pleasure in this opportunity for communication.

THE PSYCHOANALYTIC THEORIES OF LEARNING: THE PLEASURE PRINCIPLE RECONSIDERED

What struck me at the time in Cathy and Martin was the element of pleasure in their alertness – or, rather, the element of alertedness in their pleasure. Many psychoanalytic theories imply that it is the negative experiences in life that are the great teachers, the great stimulators, that pleasure soothes and feeds illusion and unpleasure awakes and alerts us to the great outside world of 'reality'. The most concise expression of this idea occurs in Freud's 1911 paper 'Formulations of the two principles of mental functioning'. Although the identification of what the essential stimulators to thought are has been greatly refined since the days of Freud's stress on the frustrations of sexual longings, the teacher is still somehow often seen as rather negative: disillusionment with Winnicott, frustration and separateness with Bion. (Balint's stress on the importance of primary love and on the need for a not-too-contoured early object is an exception.) The reality which needs digesting, however much it is felt to be balanced with love and happier feelings, is a painful one (Freud 1911b; Winnicott 1971; Klein 1940; Segal 1957; Bion 1962; Balint 1968: 167). (See Chapter 13 for a fuller discussion of this issue.)

An interesting paper by O'Shaughnessy stressed one aspect of the frustrating quality of the object: its absence. She pointed out that the first object of attachment, the feeding breast, is, when present, prima facie a good object because, whatever its difficulties, it sustains life. She pointed out that the feeding infant has a relationship to the breast, not an association – a relationship which spans presence and absence. The experience of the absent and therefore frustrating object is a spur to development. She added that this is not a coincidence, because there is a logical connection between thought and absence. 'You can be asked to think of something that is absent, a painting in a gallery (say) but you cannot be asked to think of a painting you are already looking at. You can think about – in the sense of reflect upon – anything, things present as well as absent, but before you can 'think about' you must develop the prior capacity to "think of"' (O' Shaughnessy 1964). She went on to suggest that the capacity to 'think of' is essentially linked to things absent; developmentally speaking, to the absent breast. In her later writing, she stresses the element of separateness, rather than separation and absence, and this does seem to be a much subtler way of looking at things (O'Shaughnessy 1989). I shall try to show in later chapters that, whereas certain patients need to be helped to learn about separateness and the differences between themselves and their object in order to become aware of its aliveness, others may need to learn about its availability, familiarity and similarity. Arrivals and returns can be just as stimulating and thought-provoking as departures, especially if the patient is more accustomed to departures than returns. What provokes thought must surely be the *noticeability* of the object. Absence would be noticeable where the object is usually present, but presence would be the operative factor where the object is more usually absent.

ARRIVALS AND RETURNS

I suggest, therefore, that the notion of perspective may be a useful complement to the notion of absence and the notion of separateness. (See Chapter 6 for a fuller discussion of the notion of perspective.) Separateness allows for the distance between the self and the object necessary for thought to operate, but cannot account for situations, like Robbie's in the early years, where the object simply seems to be too far away, too separate, to be thinkable about. A concept of perspective allows for situations where the patient may need to be alerted to feelings of closeness, of shared experience, however fleeting. Perhaps, indeed, the breast–mouth model is too narrow for all the interactions which take place between mother and baby in the first weeks of life. It lends itself too easily to images of fit, adaptation, presence, absence. Yet a mother's speaking voice cannot be said to fit itself precisely to a baby's need for sound. There are, indeed, hundreds of different languages and dialects in which mothers speak to babies. The mother's speaking voice is, to my mind, a cause for positive wonder, if not amazement; so is her unexpected appearance under not too sudden or intrusive conditions. Babies like to look at light and colour and pattern and to listen to certain sounds, not only because these 'stimuli' focus and hold their attention in a soothing way, but because they were at first sufficiently strong to catch and attract their interest. Tustin writes of the infancy of some psychotic children:

> I have always been puzzled by the fact that some psychogenic psychotic children are reported as having been withdrawn from birth. Whilst writing this paper, it has occurred to me that these children may have chanced upon autistic objects very early in life and have thus been diverted from turning to the suckling mother. A depressed or underconfident mother would not be able to muster sufficient firmness and resilience to attract her infant away from the illusory delights of his sensation-objects to the real enjoyment of her breast.
>
> (Tustin 1980: 102)

And, one might add, such a mother might not be able to muster sufficient liveliness or rather aliveness *to attract her infant to the real enjoyment of her face and voice.*

By the time I came to know Robbie, whatever the reasons for his withdrawal, an invigorating maternal presence was by no means adequate to his situation. Yet the lifeline provided by his parents during that dramatic week of his breakdown, and then by me the following September, to some extent was helpful. There is no doubt that my most obvious reclamatory move – the increase to five times weekly treatment – played a considerable part in the awakening process. The difficulty was that he did not seem to know what to do with powerful feelings when they eventually flooded through him. The risk was always that they would drain away and dissolve into something so undifferentiated as to provide no sustaining, coherent link with his world. Later, however, as he became able to organize and order his feelings and sufficiently able to value contact with human beings, it was clear that firmness in his object, something provoking a kind of collision (something more like Freud's and Bion's notion of 'reality'), played a far more vital part in keeping him awake. I wish to stress strongly that the different situations applied at different levels of his illness. There is no doubt that firmness on my part was not adequate to arouse curiosity or interest or attention in Robbie in earlier times. His reaction then was that he felt he was 'kissing a stone'. There was no interesting 'stiffness and straightness' about me then, only a lovelessness and hardness, an object unmoved and unmoving.

THE PROBLEM WITH DRIVE THEORY AND THE NEED FOR BION'S 'K': SOME RESEARCH EVIDENCE

My work with Robbie has led me to speculate upon the narrowness of the old dualisms of pleasure–pain, illusion–disillusion, presence–absence. The usefulness of equating pleasure with symbiosis or illusion has been questioned by Klein; I have also questioned the view that it is the negative, frustrating experiences which are the main teachers and stimulators of thought. The child development researchers have tackled both these questions in experimental situations. A particularly fascinating and ingenious experiment, designed by Wolff, tackles both at once. It throws serious doubt on the early psychologies and psychoanalytic ideas that assumed that only the pressure of deprivation of the drives stimulated interest in the outside world. It seems to me to lend support to Bion's concept of 'K', the innate need to get to know the world. Wolff has defined with careful physiological measures states of 'alert inactivity' where the child has a 'bright shiny look in the eye'. The child makes conjugate eye movements and visual and auditory pursuit movements to appropriate objects. Another worker called it the 'What is it?' look (Eisenberg 1970). These states, Wolff suggests, are the equivalent of what another researcher, Kleitman, has called 'wakefulness from choice'. Before his studies, Kleitman had thought this came only some weeks after birth, after a long period where

66

the only wakefulness was wakefulness from necessity, i.e. under pressure of bodily discomfort. Wolff says that these states of alert inactivity, wakefulness from choice, come only *after* a feed or *after* a defecation, i.e. when bodily discomfort is at a minimum, and are demonstrably different from distressed states. He also says they do not last for more than half an hour a day in the early weeks, and this may be why they have not been studied in the research before (Wolff 1965; Kleitman 1963). The implication, as I see it, is that in these situations the baby is not *driven* to learn, he is freed to do so. I should make it clear that I am not suggesting that frustration cannot stimulate thought, I am simply presenting evidence that this is not the primary stimulator. Pleasure should not be thought inferior to pain in its capacity to disturb, alert and enliven.

RESEARCH EVIDENCE CONCERNING MATERNAL CLAIMING AND ALERTING FUNCTIONS

O'Shaughnessy has suggested that the infant's first object is a psychological object, i.e. not simply a breast, but something partaking of mental and psychological qualities (personal communication). The research findings concerning the qualities of the object world to which the baby is sensitive and alert have important implications for the argument that, even in earliest infancy, pleasure is by no means opposed to the reality principle, and may indeed play a major part in developing it.

Wolff's study suggests that satisfaction of bodily needs may be a precondition for, but *by no means a cause of*, the condition of alert inactivity to take place. Another set of brilliantly observed and described preconditions is to be found in a study by Brazelton and others on the origins of reciprocity (Brazelton *et al.* 1974). They describe, in touching and lucid detail (more of which is to be found in Appendix 1), how mothers themselves appear to provide the functions of organization and focusing necessary for the baby to begin to learn to pay attention to the mother. Brazelton suggests that when the mothers do this well the babies may learn about the self-organization necessary for cognitive acquisitions. Child psychotherapists and remedial teachers know that it is no good trying to pump knowledge or understanding into a child who has a short or scattered attention span. The work has to begin with the problem of the attention span and the child's difficulties in concentration. 'Organizing', in fact, seems rather too cognitive a word to do full justice to what Brazelton and his co-authors describe: I prefer to think of the mother as claiming her baby as her own, claiming his attention, calling him into relation with her and, in a way, calling him into psychological being.

It is in the particular area of the alerting and amplifying activities which Brazelton describes that I feel our psychoanalytic theories may need enlarging if they are to be relevant to the treatment of the illest of psychotic children. So many of his observations describe improvisation, alerting, amplification, deliberate alternations, movement, change, variations on a theme – activities which are, by definition, issuing only from a live object. These notions seem to be needed to breathe life into the image of the mother and to help us to see her as more than simply a feeder, caretaker and container, however important and vital these functions are. Brazelton, for example, describes how the mother often *exchanges* one activity for another, sometimes soothing when alerting has contributed to the child's becoming upset, sometimes alerting when his interest is flagging.

> Her speech is high pitched, she uses alerting consonants, simple rhythms, she speeds up when necessary, her eyes bright and dull in a measure appropriate to his state, all in order to intensify his attention and keep it focussed on her face and on their interaction .... When she pats or strokes him, she does so with a rhythm and an intensity designed to alert as well as soothe (e.g. there was a two-per-second rythm which most mothers used for soothing AND alerting, and a slower rhythm for simple soothing.)

Brazelton also points out that the part of the baby's body that the mother touches also serves the double purpose of soothing and alerting. 'For example, as he quiets to her stroking his legs and abdomen, she moves her hands up to his chest and finally to his cheek in order to arouse his attention and focus it on her.' He suggests that the mother seems to be teaching the infant how to suppress and channel his own behaviour into a communications system (Brazelton *et al.* 1974: 65).

What is striking about these descriptions is the degree to which the alerting activities are as central as the soothing activities to focusing the babies' attention. Indeed, the very alternation in the two, the play of one against the other, is apparently in itself focusing.

It is striking, too, how musical much of the imagery and language is. The babies seem to be being invited into contact with another human being not only through their own bodily or emotional needs, and not only through their own interest in such contact, but very much with the guidance, active assistance and obvious desire of their mothers. The word I chose originally to describe the function of Robbie's lifeline was reclamation, but perhaps one needs to consider the prior claiming, the drawing into contact, the active but sensitive calling forth and naming which must precede any reclaiming and which takes place at the very beginning of life as mothers get to know their new babies and claim them as their own. Brazelton's description of how mothers deal with the newest born of babies, the neonates, at their most unresponsive is even more telling.

> The mother takes on facial expressions, of great admiration, moving back and forth in front of him with great enthusiasm; or, again in response to an unmoving infant, she takes on an expression of great surprise, moving backwards in mock astonishment; or, in the most exaggerated manner, she greets the infant, and, furthermore, carries on an animated extended greeting interchange, bobbing and nodding enthusiastically exactly as though her greeting were currently being reciprocated.

Brazelton adds, 'It is interesting that surprise, greeting and admiration seem to share the common elements we have mentioned earlier; raised brows, widely exaggerated eyes, and in two cases even a faintly pursed mouth . . . . [The mothers] insist on joining in and enlarging on even the least possible interactive behaviours, through imitation' (p.68).

The work of Klaus and Kennell on parent–infant bonding is also relevant to what I am calling the phenomenon of naming or claiming (1982). Klaus and Kennell filmed mothers' and babies' behaviour in the delivery room for ten minutes during their first contact. As Macfarlane puts it:

> The results of these observations showed that each mother went through an 'orderly and predictable' pattern of behaviour when she first examined her newborn infant. Beginning hesitantly with her fingertips, she touched his hands and feet and then within four or five minutes began to caress his body

with the palms of her hands, showing increasing excitement
as she did so. This examination continued for several minutes,
and then diminished as the mother dozed off with the naked
baby at her side. During the ten minutes of filming there was
also a marked increase in the time that the mother positioned
herself and her baby so that they could look into one another's
eyes (if the baby had his eyes open). At the same time, she
showed intense interest in waking her infant in an attempt to
get him to open his eyes, and this was verbalized by nearly
three-quarters of the mothers: 'Open your eyes, oh come on
now, open your eyes,' or 'If you open your eyes I'll know
you're alive.' Several mothers also mentioned that, once their
infants looked at them, they felt much closer to them.

Macfarlane also filmed the first moments after birth, and in some of
the transcripts the mother verbalizes her detailed initial examination
of the child: 'Mrs. C. goes over the baby, touching here and there
with her fingers and remarking to her husband, "Look at his little
mouth. Look at his little face. His little nails. Oh. His little
squashed-up nose, like your nose. Look at his little head. Look
at his hair"'. Macfarlane comments, 'A sort of joyous, wondering
inventory and, at the same time, a serious check to make sure that
everything is there as it is meant to be.' Macfarlane, like Klaus and
Kennell, noted the 'mothers' intense interest in their babies' eyes
. . . . Mrs. C. does not actually greet the baby directly until he
opens his eyes, and then she says, 'Hello!' to him seven times in
less than one and a half minutes. Just prior to this she has asked
her baby to open his eyes' (Macfarlane 1977: 50–3). He can have
had little doubt of her thereness or of his own, after such a sustained
and determined invitation and such a joyous greeting.

RESEARCH ON THE INFANT'S
SOCIAL CAPACITIES

Babies themselves are now known to be 'hugely precocious socially
at birth' (Newson 1980: 49). Newson cites findings from the research
of Trevarthen and others which suggest that the human infant is
'biologically primed, or pre-tuned, to enable him to communicate
with other human beings. He has all the basic equipment he requires
to begin to engage in face-to-face interpersonal communication –
initially of a non-verbal kind – right from birth.' In fact, Trevarthen

70

has studied the dialogue and conversation-like exchanges as something he terms 'pre-speech' and, more recently, as the 'pre-music' of these dialogues. Apparently, motherese is high-pitched, initially in an adagio, later in an andante rhythm, and the dialogue has certain rhythms in common in every language (Trevarthen and Marwick 1986 and lecture at Tavistock Clinic, July 1991). Newson points out that when these conversation-like exchanges are examined in detail it immediately becomes clear that the baby himself is by no means a passive or non-participant observer. And he has been shown by Papousek and Papousek (1976) and others (Bower 1974) to have a set of visual structures highly sensitive to those aspects of stimulation that emanate from other people's faces and auditory equipment selectively attuned to the human voice. The infant pays far more attention to these human stimuli than to inanimate or static objects. In particular, Bentovim points out, it has been noted that the infant pays attention to the mother's eyes (Bentovim 1979). Robson (1967) has commented on 'the stimulus richness of the eyes, their remarkable array of interesting qualities, such as shininess, mobility, variability of size of pupil, width of fissure'. Schaffer says that it is increasingly difficult to avoid the conclusion that in some sense the infant is already prepared for social intercourse, and this should not surprise us (Schaffer 1977). Trevarthen asks, in the quote at the beginning of this book, how the infant mind might identify persons. His answer in 1978 suggested that intentional behaviour would be revealed by its self-generating vital rhythmic movement: subsequently he has stressed the infant's innate capacity for communicative and emotional interchange with another mind, and for developing cultural intelligence (Trevarthen and Logotheti, 1989).

Schaffer says: 'If an infant arrives in the world with a digestive system to cope with food and a breathing apparatus attuned to the air around him, why should he not also be prepared to deal with that other essential attribute of his environment, people?' Schaffer points out that the type of research that measures total amounts of behaviour collated over time is inadequate for the study of social interaction. It requires techniques of sequential analysis (baby does something, mother responds, baby responds to her response, she responds to his response, and so on). This type of research is appearing more and more in the literature (Schaffer 1977).

But what happens if the mother's naming and claiming activities are insensitively synchronized with the baby's moves outwards, or, because of her own depression, worry or withdrawal, much reduced? Brazelton's work has a good deal to say about the first instance; there is evidence that the babies do withdraw to some degree from contact. Murray and Trevarthen found with 8-week-olds that failure of communication due to lack of response or paradoxical response of the mother may lead to expressions of confusion, distress and crying, inert dejection, or withdrawal into self. Murray also employed voluntary immobilization of the mother's face to observe stereotyped expressions of unhappiness in infants of 7–12 weeks. 'The baby becomes unhappy, looks puzzled, stares at his fisted hand, avoids the mother's eyes but makes quick glances at them, and makes contorted grimaces' (Murray and Trevarthen 1985). Murray has subsequently demonstrated the powerful effect of real maternal depression on the cognitive development of infants (Murray 1991).

It should be clear from the evidence and the arguments for an interactional object-relations theory, that the 'cause' of cognitive deficit or emotional withdrawal, or both, in a baby can never be entirely in the mother. The child development research itself has been careful to show that social and cultural supports (a companion, preferably the husband present at the birth, support in the home afterwards, a good marriage, socioeconomic level) all affect whether there is a benign or vicious cycle of development. Decades of observations, at the Tavistock Clinic and the University of Turin for example, of infants seen in the home environment with their parents over a two-year period have shown how complex the question of causality is, how a depressed mother may be helped to come out of her depression by a lively responsive baby, and a depressed mother may become more depressed with an unresponsive unrewarding baby. And depressed mothers often recover in time to reverse dangerous vicious circles. We cannot neglect the new findings about the importance of the intrauterine environment (Piontelli 1987; Liley 1972) nor the presence of genetic factors in the baby's constitutional make-up. Help is often available from skilled health visitors and other types of worker – physiotherapists, child psychotherapists and sometimes helpful nannies, grandmothers and friends – if the situation is treated soon enough. Often, time is on the side of health, and the mother and baby get together in the end. Where not, psychotherapeutic treatment may have to step in where prevention has been lacking.

To return to the theoretical issues of the maternal function of naming-claiming-greeting and its link with Robbie's long lifeline: I suggest that those babies being handled all over, talked to, and gazed at are not only being called into awareness of the human world outside themselves, they are being called into awareness that they themselves exist. The research seems to link with 1) my feeling that my reach had to be long, 2) the need, in the early days, to put my head into his line of vision, and, often, to call his name, and with his own early request that I should make the roll of plasticine very *long*, possibly to combat his own brief and tiny attention span and his sense of the fragility and tenuousness of the world. Robbie's mother was severely depressed at his birth, but it seems likely that he was born an infant who was difficult to satisfy and difficult to rouse. It is often the case that a vigorous responsive baby will help to pull a depressed mother out of her depression. The lifeline can work both ways, but it seems that in states of severe withdrawal, it not only calls the person into contact with a human object, it also calls him into contact with himself. The striking thing about autistic children is that they have as little sense of self, of existence as they have of the other person.

STERN AND BION

Daniel Stern has studied the ways in which mothers 'tune in' to their babies' states of feeling. He shares with the British object relations school (Klein, Winnicott and others) and the American analyst and psychiatrist, Harry Stack Sullivan, the view that infants have a very active subjective life, filled with changing passions and confusions. He stresses that the baby is born with social capacities at an extremely high and subtle level. In many respects his views are close to Klein's belief in the existence of some rudimentary ego in the neonate and to Bion's theory of the innateness of the desire to make contact with psychic quality ('K') (Bion 1962). Stern cites a huge body of fairly recent and growing experimental research, the evidence from which challenges the basic tenets of associationist psychology, stimulus–response models, classical Freudian drive theory and even Piaget himself. Infants seem, according to this research, to be not only especially attuned to, but also *seekers of*, forms and abstractions which facilitate their interaction with living human beings; they recognize the smell of their own mothers' milk within a few days of birth; they are highly attuned not only to the human face but to the changes in expression on it; they know before they experience it that the thing they touch is the thing they see. Stern quotes developmentalists such as Bower and Meltzoff who posit that from the earliest days of life the infant forms and acts upon abstract representations of qualities of perception. These abstract representations that the infant experiences are not sights and sounds and touches and nameable objects, but rather shapes, intensities and temporal patterns – the more 'global' qualities of experience. Stern writes, 'The need and ability to form abstract representations of primary qualities of perception and act upon them starts at the beginning of mental life; it is not the culmination of a developmental landmark reached in the second year of life' (Stern 1985: 138).

A third point concerns not only the baby's capacity for abstraction, but its capacity to attend to, be attuned to, abstract patterns taking place in the time dimension. The associationists and many psychoanalytic theorists assumed that events which occurred close together in time were learned to belong together through a process of association. But Stern says, 'I am suggesting that the infant can experience the process of emerging organization as well as the result, and it is this experiencing of emerging organization that I call the emergent sense of self. It is the experience of a process as well as a product.' Stern's interest is in the emergence of self, but he might as easily have added the emergent sense of the object – for that, too, is surely as much an experience of a process as of a product, in the sense that the attending, caring, feeding, holding, talking, murmuring mother is a living object. In fact, much of the work he cites is about the processes in the object, but he concentrates in his summaries on the development of the sense of self. He could as easily have tackled both. In regard to the notion of process, I myself have always mourned the disappearance of Freud's idea of 'trains of thought' which he makes so much use of in his great work *The Interpretation of Dreams*. Still shots of living processes can, of course, be very revealing, but they are always partial. States of gratification and frustration are surely an important dimension of psychic life, as is the balance between love and hate, but it is the shape and form in which these experiences come, and their shaping and forming through time which seem to be lost when the dynamic elements in psychoanalytic theory are neglected in favour of more static models of the mind. The writings of Betty Joseph bring this aliveness back; they give a sense of a dynamic play of forces and of moment-by-moment changes in these fluid media. We never step in the same river twice and, as the philosopher remarked, we really never step in the same river once!

Much of the research quoted by Stern examines precisely these living processes. There is, for example, evidence of innate capacities for 'amodal perception', i.e. perception which is not dependent on or tied to a particular sensory modality; this evidence runs absolutely counter to all forms of stimulus–response, associationist psychology. The baby can recognize a rhythm as the same regardless of whether he hears it, sees it or feels it through a series of pats. He recognizes the contourings regardless of the sensory modality in which they appear. Life, apparently, is not experienced, even by the new-born, as a series of moments in time, like pin-pricks, which have to be gradually strung together through experience, but rather in much longer waves or contours or shapings of time.

Stern adds that the experiments which demonstrate that babies have a capacity for global inner representations imply that we should add a second set of qualities to the affective, feelingful way the infant experiences the world about him. The first are the traditional Darwinian (and psychoanalytic) 'categorical' affects: of anger, joy, sadness and so on. The set of qualities Stern goes on to postulate, he calls 'vitality affects'. ('Affects' is an old psychological and psychiatric term for what the layman would term an emotion or a feeling such as love, hate, anger, greed, pleasure, disgust, happiness, joy.) Vitality affects, Stern claims, refer to the *form* of experience and they arise *directly from encounters with people*. He suggests that these may be captured by dynamic kinetic terms such as 'surging', 'fading away', 'fleeting', 'explosive', 'crescendo', 'decrescendo', 'bursting', 'drawn out' and so on.

Stern uses his arguments and evidence to defend his notion of the sense of an emergent self against more static definitions of the sense of self, and certainly against the theories which think no sense of self is possible so early on in life. It gives equal support, of course, to what one could call 'the sense of an emergent object'. His ideas and evidence seem to be of great relevance to Bion's notion of alpha function, the function of the mind that makes thoughts thinkable. Stern's vitality activation contours are incredibly good candidates for providing the form in which happy, sad, angry experiences are cast, and must surely play a large part in making the particular experience experienceable, recognizable, digestible and capable of being thought about. The content of the experience, good or bad, is only one important dimension. The other seems to be the formal qualities and contourings in which it is cast, and these may be as alerting, as interesting, as arousing, as notable when they surround good experiences as when they surround bad. Thus it would be the *level* of activation and intensity, and the *shape* of the contour (too explosive, or too flat and dull), which determines whether the experience is mentally digestible and thinkable about, *as much as* its actual positive or negative content. Research on trauma has studied the effect of shock when the experiences are bad, but perhaps as much attention needs to be paid in psychoanalytic thought to the stimulus to learning provided by the mother's natural everyday provision of pleasant surprises. In fact, Bion himself seems to leave room at some points for alpha function to make any type of thought thinkable, not only bad ones, but the weight of his work on containment and transformation in the practical clinical sphere and the mother–baby situation tends to have to do with the containment of anxiety and frustration. Containment of hope, exuberance, delight and joy would seem to be just as important for development and thinking. (Stern's work suggests that timing of interpretation and pace in psychotherapy are not just decorative frills on the basic classical structure of analytic work, but essential to it. If we are writing a duet for two pianos rather than composing a still life, timing is as essential as tone, thematic values, harmony; see Malcolm 1986).

By demonstrating the baby's sensitivity to the form and quality of experience, observation and research have changed the conventional picture of the infant. He is no longer just a sensual, appetitive little animal seeking gratification and a passionately loving and destructive creature, finding and losing love and nurture. He is also, when the conditions allow, a little music student listening to the patterning of his auditory experience, a little art student studying the play and pattern of light and shade and its changes, a little dance student watching and feeling his mother's soothing movements or playful vitalizing activities, a little conversationalist taking part in pre-speech dialogues with his mother in the early weeks of life, a little scientist working to yoke his experiences together and understand them.

6

MAKING THE THOUGHT THINKABLE

Perspective on introjection and projection

In this chapter I shall try to integrate the findings of psychoanalysis with those of the researchers on infant perception in a way which I hope may be relevant to questions of psychotherapeutic technique with the psychotic child. The most important of those findings is one that has long been suggested by psychoanalysis, and is now confirmed by child development research: for his emotional and cognitive development, the baby needs to have experience of, and interaction with, a consistent human caretaker, an 'animate object', or, in Trevarthen's phrase, 'live company' (Spitz 1946; Trevarthen 1978). A major technical problem for the therapist is how to provide such experience to children who have difficulty in assimilating experience in general and also a particular difficulty in assimilating the experience of a living human object. This technical issue may require an extension of the psychoanalytic model which stresses the centrality of mechanisms of introjection and projection for learning.

Such an extension may, I suggest, be provided by notions which take account of the perspective from which experience is had or viewed: notions such as the object's availability, its accessibility, graspability, proximity and its perceptual followability. Bion's concept of containment suggests some of the conditions under which learning and introjection take place, but his concept, even at its most mental, tends to have metaphorical links with something concave, a lap-like mind, perhaps (see Grotstein 1981a). Sometimes, however, the container is soothing, sometimes it as seen as something much firmer. I have already suggested that the maternal object needs also to be seen as *pulling the child, drawing the child, attracting the child or interesting the child*. I now want to stress another element, one that involves a metaphor that is more visual, and different in the tactile sense – a metaphor quite other than that of a lap or encircling arms. This arises from what is now known about the baby's need to have objects such as the mother's face, or her breast, presented, particularly in the early days of life, at *just the right distance* for the face to be seeable and the breast to be feedable from in a satisfactory way. The conditions under which babies are able to reach and grasp objects in three-dimensional space may also be of relevance to the question of the conditions under which an *idea* may begin to become graspable. Perhaps the developmental processes and stages involved in the functioning of the baby's eyes, hands, and even in the actual anatomy of its sucking have received less attention in the psychoanalytic models than they deserve.

INTROJECTION AND PROJECTION

Melanie Klein held to the view that processes of introjection and projection operated from the beginning of life (Spillius 1988b: xiv). As Paula Heimann put it, 'Life is maintained through an organism's intake of foreign but useful matter and discharge of its own, but harmful matter. Intake and discharge are the most fundamental processes of any living organism' (Heimann 1952). She agreed with Klein that the mind was no exception to this rule, and that, although previous psychoanalysts had accepted that the superego was built up through introjection, it took Klein to point out that so also was the ego. Klein was suggesting that babies, from the start, were capable of learning from experience, absorbing experience, but that they also had some capacity to defend themselves against experience by discharge activities. The model and metaphor was of a digestive system, but it was not, however, a reductive model, and Klein insisted that the baby took in love and understanding at the breast, not simply milk and sensual satisfaction; many of the experiences described as being taken in or evacuated were seen as mental and emotional.

Bion took up Klein's analogy of the mind as a digestive system, but added that the mother did much of the mental digesting for the baby via her function as container and transformer. There has been considerable clinical psychoanalytic work subsequently on the various different ways of 'taking in', or failing to take in, mental and emotional experiences, e.g. too quickly so that they are only partially digested. Meltzer has described the 'in one ear and out the other' quality of the mothers of some autistic children, a kind of auditory and mental digestive problem (Meltzer 1975). Modern use of the transference and counter-transference makes the analyst less attuned to whether he has given the 'right' interpretation, and more to whether he has communicated his understanding to the patient in a way that is receivable (see Spillius 1988b). The analyst would also be monitoring whether in fact the patient did feel understood by it, how he heard it, whether he heard it, what he did with it. Its correctness would therefore be as much a question of its hearability as its truth in some more psychodynamic or general sort of way. Did the patient take it in, take it over, get rid of it immediately, or feel so hurt by it that he couldn't take it in at all? Or did he simply not understand it?

The alimentary model has offered a rich source of metaphor for the ways in which experience is assimilated, but it nevertheless need no longer be the only one. Indeed, when the problem has to do with the patient's difficulties in listening, the breast–mouth model may be inadequate. The manner in which experience is assimilated through the visual modality, and also through tactile modes other than oral ones, (e.g. the ways in which babies improve upon their capacity to reach and grasp objects in three-dimensional space) may also provide a fertile source for both theory and technique with psychotic children. The fact, for example, that an experience can be assimilated only when it is located in someone else *may have more to do with questions of perspective, than with questions of projection.* Such locating may actually involve the *beginnings of an introjective process rather than a projective one.* The way in which a patient may or may not be able to follow his therapist's train of thought, or pursue one of his own, may be as analogous to the problem of the visual tracking of the trajectory of moving objects as to his response to the flow of milk in his throat.

However, I would like to keep to the alimentary metaphor for a moment longer, for, even here, notions such as perspective, proximity, graspability, accessibility are important. Before, for example, the infant can even begin to suck from the breast he first has to get a good hold on it. The sucking reflex is elicited by stimulation (tactile/chemical) of the palate by the nipple. According to Woolridge, much pain for the mother and feeding difficulties for the baby can be avoided, not only by ensuring that as much of the areola is got into the baby's mouth as possible, but also by ensuring that the baby's tongue and lower jaw are properly positioned underneath (Woolridge 1986). Many new mothers do, in fact, describe the amazing moment when their and their new baby's mutual tentativeness is overcome by a helpful midwife who almost pushes the two together, and the baby suddenly seems to react as though he feels, 'Oh is that where it is!' and never looks back. So the element of position, proximity and perspective may play a part even in the most bodily of all introjective activities.

Apparently it also plays a part in the activity of mutual gazing between mother and infant. According to Papousek and Papousek (1976: 77), the mother of the infant in the first months of life 'regularly carries out many movements of which she may be largely unaware, which are interpretable as attempts to achieve mutual visual contact with her infant . . . . She keeps moving her head to stay centred in the infant's visual field, with her eyes in the same plane as his eyes. She also tries to maintain the optimal distance (20–25 cm in the first two or three weeks) as if respecting the infant's limited capacities for focusing and convergence.' The Papouseks' research shows how important the variable of proximity is and how it varies as the babies get older. Bower's work on the development of reaching and grasping, and on visual tracking and object constancy with moving objects, trajectory problems, also explores the notion of proximity, position and the baby's concept of three-dimensional space in very interesting ways (Bower 1974). It is well documented clinically how little concept of three-dimensionality autistic children seem to have (Meltzer 1975) and also what difficulty they have in thinking their thoughts, collecting them and following trains of thought. Their thought processes are often stultified and under rigid control. Severely obsessional patients may also may be unable to let a thought go and then follow it.

I have been led to these speculations on the importance of perspective by the observation that some very withdrawn patients may be alerted to a new experience for what seems to be the first time not when it is happening inside them, but, rather, when it is seen to be happening inside someone else. Whereas in the past I would have seen this as the result of a projective mechanism, I now think this may be a mistaken formulation. This is because the concept of projection, even the more subtle Kleinian one of projective identification, tended in the past to carry the implication that, although the experience is taking place outside the self, *it must have originated within the self*. That is, the experience projected must have come originally from the patient's self and been been subsequently disowned. However, Spillius and Joseph have drawn attention to the fact that the term projective identification is often used to cover situations where what is being projected is not a part of the patient's self, but an aspect or part of his internal object which needs exploring. So a part of his internal world is being projected outside, but not necessarily a part of his self (Spillius 1988a: 82; Joseph 1978: 112). Both Grotstein (1981b) and Sandler (1988) prefer the term externalization, and I do not know whether it is useful to extend the meaning of projective identification this far, except for situations where the patient is really forcing the analyst to play the part of the earlier object. Joseph describes the pressure put on the analyst to feel hopeless and/or offer false reassurance in exactly the way earlier figures in the patient's life or imagined life, may have done (Joseph 1982). But where the patient expects external objects simply to be like his internal object and then observes something *different and new or even renewed but unexpected,* and this something really catches his attention, I think the use of the notion of projection can lead to premature questions such as whether the patient should be having the experience himself, that is, re-introjecting the lost part, when what he most needs is, in Joseph's terms, to explore it and examine it from a perspective or location that makes it viewable and examinable. He may then, at a sufficiently safe distance and from a cognitively adequate perspective, be able to manage what Americans call 'getting his mind around it' and find the thought thinkable. (See Byng-Hall and Campbell (1981) on problems in distance-regulation in families.)

The findings on the importance of live interaction with a consistent human caretaker for the emotional and cognitive development of the human infant raise, as I have said, important technical problems for the therapist of the severely withdrawn or autistic child. For this seeking out of, and apparent responsiveness to, animate live company and interpersonal contact is exactly what cannot be taken for granted in the autistic child. Careful observation may indicate indirect evidence of such sensitivity to other persons, often, in fact, excessive sensitivity, but the child's reactions are often delayed, disguised, confused and therefore impossible to decode without much study and attention to the clues specific to each child. A further problem is that the child's protective manoeuvres may have become so practised and habitual that to a large degree he has indeed become genuinely insensitive, and therefore unable to use and assimilate much of the ordinary human contact and help that is on offer.

LIVE COMPANY: THE NEED FOR AN INTELLIGENT ANIMATE OBJECT

There is now a fairly long established acceptance, with some refinements (Rutter 1981), of the findings of Spitz and Bowlby that maternal deprivation at a very young age may have consequences for the emotional and (in more recent studies) intellectual well-being of the child. These studies examined the effect of maternal deprivation in the sense of maternal absence. Until recently, there has been little research to examine the effects of chronic maternal absent-mindedness or chronic maternal depression. As I mentioned before, Murray and Trevarthen have studied the effects of temporary immobilization of the mother's facial expression – a blank face – on her baby's temporary mood, and have noted autistic-like reactions (1985), and Murray has subsequently shown the devastating effects of post-natal maternal depression on babies' emotional and cognitive development (Murray 1991). None of these studies on the importance of intersubjectivity can shed light, of course, on the *aetiology* of Robbie's condition. True, his mother was severely depressed during his early weeks, but there were many other factors at work in his early situation, and there is always the possibility of unknown organic aetiology (see Chapter 15 for a fuller discussion of aetiological issues in autism). It is possible that, if Robbie had had an easier birth, and if the hospital had left his mother alone less during her long labour, and if the family had not been adjusting to a disturbing change of country, and if Robbie had had a less limp, more thrusting personality at birth, he might have managed to draw his mother out of her depression. Some lively babies do precisely that (Di Cagno *et al.* 1984). But whatever the causes, he seems to have had a shaky start, and may not have been in good condition to weather the two separations which seem to have had such a traumatic effect in the second year of his life.

Thus, although the child development findings cannot give retrospective support for any speculations about the aetiology of Robbie's condition, they may nevertheless have implications for his treatment, and the treatment of other severely withdrawn patients. To return for a moment to Trevarthen's statement: 'The inanimate object does not surge in self-generative impulses . . . this rhythmical vitality of movement is the first identification of live company.' It is well known that autistic children are very preoccupied with inanimate objects. They also tend to treat human beings as though they were inanimate objects. Robbie was for much of the time totally absorbed in his 'long ticket', with touching a piece of wall, with his endless repetitive stultifying phrases, but only occasionally and gradually with people's faces, or the living *meaning* of their words. I have described the fact that one of the most striking features of the moment when he first seemed to come so dramatically out of his dark well was the sudden musicality of his speech. It rose and fell in waves, and cadences, and *kept flowing*. Previously it ran downhill within seconds exactly like Trevarthen's inanimate objects. It is interesting that so much of the language of these authors who are studying intersubjectivity in the young baby is of a quasi-musical type. They write of rhythm, synchronicity, dialogue, surging, turn-taking, conversation-like exchanges, amplification. Trevarthen has studied what he calls pre-music (Trevarthen and Marwick 1986), and Stern titles one of his chapters in *The First Year of Life* , 'Missteps in the dance' (Stern 1977). This new level of conceptualization, which is so much more complex than the behaviourists' stimulus–response models, has been able to arise precisely because of the fact that what is being studied is *interpersonal* behaviour *in sequence and through time*. These patternings through time can only be measured through time and the complexity seems absolutely central to the notion of 'live company'. These researchers, like psychoanalysts, study not responses to stimuli (two moments in time, a two-event model), but something more like answers to answers to answers to questions.

If, at two months, the baby can distinguish and seek animate objects, what conditions might enable this development to take place? Trevarthen puts it thus: 'The normal pattern of response by an infant of 2 months to an attentive talking mother . . . may be divided into a phase of orientation, a sign of recognition, then an expressive phase, and a close or termination which may take the form of a withdrawal, or a return to orientation and recognition' (Trevarthen 1977: 249). But it is precisely the initial phase of orientation which cannot be taken for granted in autistic and other psychotic or very schizoid children. Infant observation studies (Di Cagno *et al.* 1984; Miller *et al.* 1989) suggest that some babies seem to seek contact and life far more actively than others, but in all neonates some capacity to make these distinctions exists from the start. It is known, for example, that the newly born baby does make eye contact with its mother or primary caretaker, however fleeting, and it does recognize the mother's voice and smell within days of birth (Macfarlane 1977). But it is also known that the mother's gaze remains on the baby for longer periods than the baby's on the mother's in the early days. He looks away but her gaze is still there when he returns his gaze (Fogel 1976). Brazelton's observations on the degree of help babies get from their mothers in learning how to maintain attention and concentration in a human dialogue also seem particularly relevant (Brazelton *et al.* 1974).

Although Brazelton observed that patting and stroking accompanied the mother's gaze, I am not suggesting that therapists should engage in patting and stroking activities with their autistic and psychotic patients (although some people have found it useful to hold a child's flapping hands at some moments to draw him away from autistic activities and into more contact). What I am interested in pointing out, however, is that these activities of the mothers which help the normal baby to focus on, not simply a patch of sunlight, or a smell, but a human face and voice are by no means simply gratifying or simply soothing. They are, however gently and sensitively administered, alerting and apparently *interesting*.

In the 1960s, however, I was concerned about the degree of mobility and activity called forth in me by Robbie's state when he was at his most lost and dissolved. Well-tried analytic technique indicates that when the therapist overreacts to excessive projections, this can prevent the patient from getting in touch with his own feelings of urgency for himself. Yet underreaction has perhaps been less well explored as a technical problem, with some exceptions (Tustin 1981; Coltart 1986; Carpy 1989; Symington 1986). I often found I had to call Robbie's name, move my head into his line of vision, and, when he seemed at his utterly lowest ebb, I felt extreme urgency and alarm and spoke to him in a manner that showed this. It was on one of these occasions in July, just before a long summer break, that he seemed to surface and greet me like a long-lost friend. It was also immediately after this that he had his breakdown, or rather break-out from his autism, which made everyone feel he was coming alive, and both needed and could use more intensive treatment. In October I started seeing him five times a week, and a few months later, just after my return from the Christmas break, he described his emergence from the well. I would suggest that the strength of feeling I felt and conveyed on that July day, however melodramatic, unbalanced, uncontained and uncontaining it may seem, did have something to do with a reach which was simply, for once, long enough, or loud enough, or alerting enough or human enough to get his attention.

Of course, as the years went on, and Robbie became more able to stay in contact for longer periods, people often shouted at him because he seemed to have drifted off in, by then, fairly unnecessary ways. This shouting was usually counterproductive, because it played in with his complacent passivity and tendency to project his ego and initiative and sense of time into others. So I am not recommending shouting or even dramatic lifeline rescue work as a regular technique. Modern Kleinian work in the transference and counter-transference, as exemplified in the work of Joseph, Rosenfeld and others, would teach one to learn from such a dramatic moment, in order to convert it into the everyday ongoing use of a more vigilant approach to the patient's loss of attention or of faith or hope, and indeed, to one's own (Rosenfeld 1987; see also Brenman Pick's paper, 'Working through in the counter-transference', 1985). I suspect my own attention in those early years was sometimes almost as slack or as sagging as Robbie's own, for it was so difficult to believe, much of the time, that there really was anyone there inside his skull. Coltart and also Symington have described the effect of similar dramatic moments on their patients. I would agree about the powerful effect at the particular moment on the patient, but would stress that the therapist's task is to translate such an experience into a more ongoing awareness *in herself* of how far a very withdrawn patient may have fallen or drifted, and of what may be his *constant and recurring* need to be awakened to the peril he is in, and to the human possibilities for him and for his experience when he manages to discover he has live company. Emergency resuscitation may not be necessary where adequate intensive care is available.

I suggested in Chapter 4 that there are situations where the whole of the patient's personality may be lost, *even the very knowledge that he is alive.* Some patients who have given up have genuinely lost hope, or abandoned hope, not projected it. Here, to paraphrase Strachey and Rosenfeld, one may have to function as an auxiliary id, or, in Kleinian terms, carry the feeling alive part of the self for the patient. And this may involve feeling an almost constant alarm and vigilance which is not only appropriate, but actually necessary to the treatment. Dr R has described a similar phenomenon in her work at the university hospital in Turin with a very withdrawn autistic boy, Alessandro. At first, she frequently felt defeated and depressed by the sheer extent of his withdrawal, but gradually she summoned more strength, both to survive his quite perniciously cruel rejections and also to fight *for* him, in the sense of getting through his own devastating despair. She began to describe her feeling that there was a thin thread of contact between them which she 'tried to grasp and make use of as soon as possible', because, she said, 'I feel, when I can't grasp it straightaway, A falls back into a far world in which he tries more and more actively to keep me far away. I have the sensation that I make a great effort in trying to contact him in some way.' This sensation Dr R described is identical to my own feeling that the pychotic state itself – with its deadening and dehumanizing of the self and of experience – exerts, once it has got under way, a pull and force of its own which the therapist may then be quite powerless against. Thus 'great effort' may be required to survive the attacks, but it may also be required to catch and keep the patient when he is in a fleetingly more accessible state. The sense of cliff-edge urgency may, at certain moments with certain patients, have to do with carrying something for the patient that he is as yet unable to carry for himself.

Bion and Rosenfeld, both of whom worked extensively with psychotic patients, have hugely increased our understanding of the enormous power of processes of projective identification in psychotic patients. It is important to remember, however, that the patients of Bion and Rosenfeld were adults, and that where these authors refer to the analyst carrying parts of the self that have been projected, the implication somehow is that it must have once belonged to the personality before projection. Work with very young psychotic children, however, often makes one suspect that this 'projected' part may never have belonged to the personality in the first place, at least not in any solid way. It may need to grow, and this sense of being alive and human may need to be recalled or, in the case of the illest children, called forth (Reid 1990). This need in the patient for input from the therapist in order to be recalled to himself must always be carefully distinguished from the part of his personality which, as it were, can't be bothered to fight for life; the line between apathy consequent on despair and the apathy consequent on hostile indifference or complacent passivity is not an easy one to draw.

An example of some work with a patient who was not flagrantly psychotic but nevertheless quite schizoid, withdrawn and out of touch with feeling, may illustrate the problem of keeping a balance between notions of a projective process which is excessive and one which is too weak and inadequate, perhaps because the experience has never yet been located anywhere. The thought may not so far have been thinkable.

A very withdrawn adolescent patient of mine, a girl named Harriet, was involved, after some years in treatment, in a serious car accident. Although she was in a coma and close to death at one point, her life was saved by an operation which removed temporarily a piece of her skull – part of her forehead – so that pressure inside the brain could be relieved. She returned to therapy with this disfiguring hole in her head, and often expressed considerable anxiety and impatience for the operation to take place which would replace the missing piece of bone. After some months, the date was finally fixed when her local hospital would do the surgery. This meant that the bone had to be sent from the hospital in another city where the original operation had taken place. She (and I) had assumed that such a precious piece of a person would be sent by something like an ambulance or by courier. Or perhaps the first surgeon, who was both eminent and caring and had, after all, saved Harriet's life, would bring it himself! Harriet came in one day and said quite casually, and in her flattest of flat voices, that she had just heard it was being sent by post. There were postal difficulties in the area at the time, which we both knew about, and I felt a moment of absolute horror at this news. Harriet was, as I have said, not psychotic, and although at times she was very cut off from feelings out of a genuine depersonalization and difficulty in finding them, at other moments she was extremely skilled at projecting them. I knew from long experience with her that if I overreacted at such a moment, if, for example, I had revealed my own anxiety for the fate of her bone, she would simply ask me coldly and contemptuously what I was making such a fuss about. I also knew that if I tried too neutrally to insist that *she* felt horror or anxiety about her bone, she would deny it, feel nothing, and my attempt to put her in touch with herself would also fail. Betty Joseph has stressed the importance of not pushing parts of the patient's self back at them prematurely or too crudely: she points out that the analyst may have to contain unassimilable parts for some while, and the patient may need to explore these in the analyst (Joseph 1978). I would add that, with the more withdrawn patients, in order for the process of containment, exploration and eventual re-introjection of the lost part to begin at all, the patient first has to register that there actually is an emotional state worth exploring. I think I managed on that occasion to get the balance right. I pointed out to Harriet that she was telling me this fact without any feeling at all, yet she had previously been very worried about the arrival of the bone. I tried to show her how she seemed to be posting into me, with truly terrible casualness, a very precious part of herself, namely her feeling of anxiety about her bone. I did, I may say, put this interpretation to her with some feeling: I believe that if I had spoken too strongly, she would have closed up even more and projected the whole of the experience into me; on the other hand, if I had spoken too neutrally, or too slackly, or without sufficient seriousness, she would simply have experienced me and the feeling as too far away. As it was, she did really seem to hear the interpretation because she suddenly said, in for her a very spontaneous and relieved way, that she had suddenly realized how very worried she was. She rang the specialist later and he told her that the bone was safe on his desk and that he was sending it special delivery, and in the end the operation was carried out successfully.

This, I think, is the other side of the coin of the neutrality principle. It is a serious mistake with a projecting patient to carry too much of the projection. But for a very depersonalized patient, even if the depersonalization is the result of previous massive projections, we must not carry too little. Some patients may not be able to be in touch with their own feelings until they have been in touch with *a* feeling. At that point it hardly matters who has the feeling first. In fact, Harriet began to say with surprise that it was odd that someone else often had to feel things for her first, before she could feel them for herself. At such moments I do not believe she was using other people as vehicles for ridding herself of unwanted parts of herself. I think, rather, that she was using them as places for the exploration of whether or not it was safe to have feelingful states of mind at all.

Matte-Blanco has suggested that there are two distinct processes in the course of therapy. One is the lifting of repression and the undoing of defences; the other is an 'unfolding or translating function'. According to Rayner, this is 'helping the patient to see new or deeper meanings in ideas that are not repressed but quite conscious'. Rayner has pointed out that the patient usually quietly enjoys this sort of process as enhancing (Rayner 1981: 410). Not all enhancements, of course, are pleasurable, but even unpleasant ones seem to be quite life-giving for cut-off patients. I believe Bion's concept of alpha function suggests that the thought may have to be thinkable long before the therapist should concern himself with luxurious questions about who is having it. This may imply, in order of priority, first naming it and containing it (implicit in child development findings and in Bion and Joseph), only afterwards locating it in the self or object (stressed by Klein), and only after that considering the even more luxurious question of why the patient is having it (Freud). I suspect I learned this lesson in reverse order in my work with Robbie.

PERSPECTIVE

The examples of Robbie, Alessandro and Harriet are all situations where psychotherapeutic technique involved bringing the patient nearer to an experience. In other situations, where the psychotic patient, or the borderline psychotic in a psychotic episode, is feeling overwhelmed by too much feeling, the problem is quite different. Here, the patient needs help in getting some distance from the experience. Where the idea is too far away, it may need amplifying, where it is too close for perspective, binocular vision and alpha function to operate, it may need containing and distancing. Such a patient is in no doubt of his being alive; his problem is that he feels overwhelmed by terror of death. Dr U was seeing a borderline 9-year-old autistic boy in regular four times weekly treatment. On one occasion she had to see him in a different room, as their usual room was occupied by a group of noisy children. Autistic children, with their rigid personalities, are especially disturbed by changes of time or venue, but unfortunately there was the added problem that the noises were taking place at the end of the same corridor as their temporary session room. Although they were at the far end of the corridor, the child began to panic. The therapist felt that he was in no condition to listen to interpretations about why he was upset, e.g. that he was jealous, or that he was disturbed by the change of room. She saw that his panic was rising uncontrollably, and she said firmly but calmly, 'Julian, the noise is *outside*'. She might have said, to a less ill neurotic child, or even to Julian under less overwhelming conditions (he was only borderline autistic and he had improved greatly with treatment), 'Julian, you seem to feel that noise is right inside your head.' Or: 'Julian, you don't seem able to keep that noise down at the end of the corridor where it belongs.' But it seemed that Julian had not got sufficient ego at that moment to draw the obvious conclusions. Psychotic children, and borderlines at their most psychotic moments, often have great difficulty in seeing the *implications* in things that are said to them. The thought may not be thinkable until it is recognized as being precisely that: a thought and only a thought, or a noise and only a noise. Robbie frequently broke down in terror at any loud noise, such as the sound of a Hoover or of a taxi's engine. He would cower, covering his head, saying 'the noise hurts my brain'. Tustin has suggested (1981) that autistic children lack filtering mechanisms for their sensory experiences. It would seem that, before we can indicate this lack to the child, we may, at his worst moments, have to provide some of the filtering for him or the child may be in too shattered a state to listen. I know at times when Robbie was stricken and desperate and on the edge of real violence from having been delayed on the underground and made late for a session (this was when he was much less withdrawn, but very obsessional and frantic about getting to his sessions on time) it was a waste of time talking about *why* he was so distraught and angry. He needed to be shown that I understood just *how* upset he was. The 'what' has to precede the 'why' when the patient cannot think.

This seems to be true regardless of whether the thing that has provoked the terror or despair is real, partly real or quite imaginary. For example, patients with terrifying or cruelly tyrannical and demanding hallucinations seem not to be helped by premature interpretations which try to suggest that these voices or figures are really either parts of themselves or aspects of the therapist as an object in the transference. It sometimes seems more helpful first simply to explore the power the voices hold, before worrying about shifting their location. Gradually, later, the power that the patient *accords* to the voices can be explored, and then, even more gradually, as a tiny bit of ego or self is reachable, the power that he seems to *invest* in the voices. This seems both to reduce their power and give the patient a little potency in his mind. He becomes able to think about the voices, instead of just submitting to having them. In the initial stage, it seems a mistake to ask a relatively egoless patient to think about re-introjecting lost parts of his ego when he has insufficient introjective equipment with which to do this. Perhaps the mind may need tube feeding until it learns how to digest previously unthought thoughts.

One anorexic girl suffered from auditory hallucinations of voices which forbade her to eat except at particular moments of the day, and only for one or two minutes at a time. If she defied the voices they threatened her with death, and she sometimes starved herself to danger point in order to placate them. Although she improved after some years of psychotherapy, it was interesting that the initial improvement was not that she acquired a much stronger ego and could defy the voices, although there were little glimmerings of these developments. The major new development was that she acquired a new set of voices which were 'amazed that the food tasted good instead of terrible'. These voices were 'strong and told her that she could eat and would eat'. What interested me about these new objects was not only their encouraging qualities, but also their amazement. In a way, they were somewhere half-way between a superego and an ego. They were, of course, still far from being recognized as being a part of herself that could acknowledge enjoying food and life, yet they seemed to represent an object which was interested in and aware of her experience of pleasure. It was an object which was quite respectful of and attuned to her self and probably arose as she began to introject a new kind of figure in the person of her therapist.

I do not believe one can help patients to re-introject lost parts of themselves in a surgical manner. We cannot stitch the lost part back on. More important, with some children who have been psychotic all their lives, the model of a severed limb is not accurate. Instead, something may need to grow for the first time. This is a slow delicate process and may be more akin to the way mothers, by attunement and shared mental states, provide alpha function for their babies, than to older psychoanalytic models of recovering lost splits and lost projections. The facilitation of such growth may depend on the distance at which the lost part is held by the therapist and the corresponding distance from which it is then able to be perceived by the patient.

7

THE PROBLEM OF THE NEW IDEA

Thought disorder and behaviour disturbance as forms of cognitive deficit

There has been much discussion in recent decades among American psychoanalysts concerning whether psychoanalysis, and its theory of cure or, more precise, of change, should be a theory of conflict, defence and resolution (classical psychoanalysis) or a theory of deficit and repair (Kohut and his followers). Classical analysts consider that a theory of deficit is too superficially environmentalist and denies the significance of the powerful givens, and of the powerful struggles between these different givens, which Freud suggested were at the heart of human neurosis and suffering. They imply that Kohut was too soft on human nature, and was offering only supportive psychotherapy instead of true psychoanalysis. Kohut, on the other hand, criticized classical psychoanalysis for its 'moralistic confrontative posture', and suggested that many so-called 'defences', such as grandiosity and narcissism, could be fulfilling a genuine developmental need in a very insecure person (1985).

Wallerstein is one classical author who has suggested that there is a false dichotomy here (1983). I would agree, but from an object-relations perspective: however seriously such a perspective takes the emotional givens – the potentials for love and hate – as well as the inevitability of conflict among these givens, it must by definition also acknowledge the possibility of deficit. In a two-person psychology, the 'object' is no longer simply the passive object of the early Freudian infant's drives nor is it simply the object of the early Kleinian infant's extreme passions. Klein later insisted on the importance of love and understanding (1937), and the Kleinian study of infants seen with their mothers, together with Winnicott's (1965) and Bion's (1962) stress on the importance of the maternal function of holding or containment, has led to increasing interest in the qualities of the maternal object itself and in its mental qualities. Bion suggested that the mother helped the baby to process his experience: she lent meaning to his experience by making his 'thoughts thinkable'. Infant observation and infant research suggest that, where either the baby or the mother, for whatever reason, is weak in the capacity for such processing, a negative feedback system may eventually produce a psychological deficit in the child which may bear relatively little relation to its original, possibly quite adequate, constitutional endowment (Murray 1991; Miller *et al*. 1989).

DEFICIT AS COGNITIVE

One way of looking at deficit in psychotic and deprived children is to see it as cognitive, as well as emotional. Yet the distinction itself may be false. Jerome Bruner points out that David Krech used to urge that people 'perfink' – perceive, feel and think at once (Bruner 1986). Spensley has questioned Rutter's (1983) acceptance of the view that the cognitive impairment in autism is organic and precedes the impairment in affect: Spensley observed that cognitive deficiency in an autistic girl seemed to be inextricably related to a profound collapsed state of psychotic depression (Spensley 1985). Urwin has criticized the cognitive researchers for seeing emotion as slowing down or speeding up cognition but not as entering into the structure of cognition itself (Urwin 1987). It is also true, however, that early psychodynamic thinking on autism may have been too ready to see defensive and resistive processes everywhere: the refusal to conceive of certain possibilities is quite different from the inability to conceive of them, not because the child was born without the necessary preconceptions, but because the preconceptions may not have met with the necessary realizations (Bion 1962). I would suggest that in certain instances repair of deficit may lead to the child's having a new experience, and this new experience may involve not only a new feeling or a new idea, but also the beginnings of a new way of thinking thoughts. Many psychotic children, especially those who have been psychotic for all or most of their lives, have practically no concept of narrative or of space or of time. They may also have inadequate or confused ideas about causality or intentionality. On the simplest level, they can rarely tell anyone that 'something happened': the child may be covered with bruises, but be unable to say that he just had a fall and that his leg hurts; he may be shaking with fear but be unable to say what frightened him. The ability to narrate seems to presuppose the most complicated advances in the inner emotional world of object relations. The quality of emotional experience is central to healthy development, but so too is the the way in which the infant comes to be able to reflect upon and process experience, to manage, in Bion's words, to think his thoughts. So although the distinction between emotional deficit and cognitive deficit may be a somewhat artificial one, cognitive considerations cannot be ignored.

This need not mean that the therapist has to become a substitute mother or teacher. There is a way of maintaining an analytical attitude while nevertheless addressing this important and, in the case of psychotic, deprived or abused children, very common clinical problem. It is possible – and necessary – to enable the patient to have a new experience or new idea without forgoing one's alertness to the ways in which a child may use his deficit defensively or destructively. A 'cannot' or a 'do not know how' may, indeed, disguise a 'will not' or, more subtly, a 'can't be bothered'; but it is also true that a 'won't' can easily mask a 'can't', or at least the patient's belief that he can't. Analysts and therapists have to be as sensitive to the latter situation as to the former.

Many authors, both psychoanalytic and psychiatric, have described the states of fragmentation and dissociation to be found in psychosis. Kleinian psychoanalysts have used the close analysis of such states to demonstrate that this seeming randomness may be the product of meaningful processes which involve mental activity and active, emotionally motivated, mentality: dynamic processes such as splitting, disintegration, pathological projective identification, dismantling, attacks on linking, all of them processes which are seen as designed actively, that is, defensively, destructively or protectively, to perpetuate some state of mind or avoid another (Rosenfeld 1965; Joseph 1987; Meltzer 1975; Bion 1959). Such ideas may seem to be light years away from deficit theory, since they imply defensive activities which interfere with possible integrations in a resistive way. Yet surely mental impoverishment which has become chronic in a young child who should be developing may, whatever the original motivations, result in deficit. Winnicott (1960), Klein (1946) and Bick (1968) all insisted that states of unintegration should not be confused with disintegration. I would add that anyone who has worked for long with the type of children I have mentioned does not always find evidence of previously acquired integrations.

It may be necessary to conceive of mental conditions where thoughts remain not dismantled but unmantled; not projected but as yet never introjected; not dissociated but as yet unassociated; not split defensively but as yet not integrated; and where thoughts remain unlinked not because the link has been attacked but because the link has never been forged in the first place. The complication in the live clinical situation is that such situations rarely appear in pure culture and the defensive motives and the defects are invariably mixed. But the distinction is nevertheless crucial for the practising clinician who treats psychotic children: thrusting premature integrations on an already confused child may only confuse him further.

STAGES IN THE DEVELOPMENT OF SPLITTING: A COGNITIVE PSYCHOLOGIST'S VIEW

Klein and Bion have taught that the process by which normal infants begin to put thoughts together is infused and suffused with emotion. Bruner, a cognitive psychologist who is less interested in emotional considerations, nevertheless has some fascinating things to say about the order in which certain cognitive comings together, which he calls co-ordination, occur in normal infant development, and about the sequencing of stages of necessary differentiation which seem to have to precede the eventual integrations. Bruner does not make use of psychoanalytic terms such as splitting, but he does insist that what he calls 'one-trackedness of behaviour' has to be firmly established, and only then, by a series of careful steps, does the baby move to two-trackedness. Bruner describes how babies learn to co-ordinate the two activities of sucking and looking in the early weeks of life, how, later, they learn to co-ordinate reaching and grasping, and how, eventually, they become able to maintain intentionality through a sequential series of acts.

He says that the relation between sucking and looking goes through three phases in its growth: 1) the *suppression* of one by the other. Mostly it is looking that suppresses sucking; that is, the neonate cannot suck and look at an interesting object both at the same time. He tends to shut his eyes while sucking. By 3 to 5 weeks he may leave his eyes open while sucking, but if he fixes on, or tracks something, sucking stops. 2) By 9–13 weeks there is a new development, a simple succession of sucking and looking, *organization by alternation*. The child now sucks in bursts and looks during pauses. 3) In the third phase, which Bruner calls *place holding*, the two acts go on, with one in reduced form that is sufficient for easy resumption, while the other goes into full operation. Bruner says that usually by 4 months the baby appears to be able to suck and look at once. Bruner explains, however, that although the baby seems to continue sucking while looking, the sucking is not of the suctioning type – the baby continues to mouth the breast but is not drawing in milk. 'By maintaining some feature of an ongoing act in operation while carrying out some other act in parentheses, one is reminded that the original act is to be resumed' (1968: 18–24). So the baby is 'tided over the distraction' until he can get back to nutritive sucking (p. 42). It is rather like putting a finger on the line on the page of a book, while holding a brief conversation.

Bruner likens this place-holding to the ability to 'think in parentheses'. Bruner, and also Bower, have carried out studies on the development of the co-ordination of reaching and grasping, which Bruner suggests is another interesting model for understanding how babies learn to maintain intentionality. Bower has shown that reaching develops from a stage of a unitary reach-grasp pattern that is visually initiated, to a stage where there are two separate, recombinable acts – reaching and grasping – that are visually initiated, but also, importantly, visually guided. After the age of 20 weeks, the infant can make 'in-flight corrections', that is, 'in older infants . . . the hand may start off on a miss path, but it is brought onto a hit path as soon as it enters the visual field. The hand is not withdrawn to begin again but rather alters its trajectory in flight. There is correction within the act, rather than correction between the acts' (Bower 1974: 175). Bruner suggests that the open hand during early reaching, like non-nutritive sucking in the earlier example, is a kind of place-holder, for it 'keeps the terminus of the act in evidence during the running off of the component parts'. At a later stage, he goes on, the rigidly opened hand is a 'tactic for maintaining, through exaggerated action, an intention whose fulfillment has been delayed' (p.43). This may be a very useful model indeed for the methods by which certain psychotic patients who are forever losing the thread – or worse, who never knew there was a thread – eventually do manage to learn to 'collect' their thoughts in order to be able to think them.

Bruner's and Bower's descriptions leave out vast numbers of emotional factors – in the baby, in the mother, in the context. It would be important to know, for example, whether the baby has turned to look at his mother's responsive face, her unresponsive face, someone else's face, or whether he has been distracted before he has managed to get a decent experience of sucking going at all, and so on. But Bruner's suggestion that suppression precedes alternation and only after alternation is established can place-holding be managed, and only with place-holding can true co-ordination take place tells us something important about some of the conditions under which human beings are able to concentrate on ever-widening areas of experience. It throws light on some of my own clinical impressions based on work with children with ego deficit and thought disorder or, rather, thinking defect. I am reminded of my own belated recognition of how important it was for Robbie to learn to forget over-exciting ideas and to be able to ignore over-stimulating sights. He was, for example, easily pulled into a psychotic state where he seemed almost to drown in ecstasy, simply by looking into someone's eyes. When he finally began to want another kind of contact of a more alert but sober kind, one of his first solutions to this problem was to close his eyes, just like Bruner's babies, when he felt it happening. Later, he described having to 'tear his eyes away'. Much later, he became able to change the way he met people's gaze. By then, he could keep his mental distance and feel that the object of his gaze was keeping hers.

In the middle years of Robbie's very long treatment, I think I often tried to produce what were premature integrations, in the sense that I interpreted that he was defending himself against powerful and overwhelming feelings of merging. Later, I came to understand that my very mention of this was enough to send him back into it and that, instead, it was necessary to acknowledge the fight he was putting up in order to have a normal conversation with me. If I referred too much to what the fight was against, he experienced this as my colluding with the powerful pull the madness had over him. At a later stage of treatment, when his wish for and his will to maintain sane contact were stronger, one could work differently with him, and interpret defences and conflicts. But earlier on, I believe I had to facilitate 'one-trackedness' and the suppression of powerful distractions, in order to allow one thought to be thinkable at a time, before he could afford to weigh the two alternatives of madness and sanity in the balance.

It is well documented that autistic children have difficulties with, and resistance to, notions of space, time and causality. I would agree with those analytic writers such as Tustin and Meltzer who relate these difficulties to the child's inadequate development in his inner world of a relation between his infantile self and, first, his maternal and then his paternal object. An adequate sense of space, time or causality involves the notion of at least two fixed points of reference, and these two seem to arise from those two great organizing principles, the 'perfinking' self in relation to the 'perfinking' parental object. But this sense of twoness (and, certainly, the subsequent oedipal sense of threeness) cannot be rushed. If the child cannot understand twoness, it may not be because he resists it. He may, for example, be unable to understand even quite simple interpretations of an explanatory type, for these involve holding two thoughts in the mind at once. 'Why' and 'because' interpretations involve an understanding of causality, yet the 'whatness' of experience may have to precede the 'why'. To understand an explanation as an explanation, you must first understand what it is an explanation of. If Robbie came to a session furiously upset because he was late, I wasted my time saying things like, 'You are upset and angry because you feel I should have made the trains run on time', because he was much too overwhelmed to think causally. First, I had to show him how *upset* he was, and then just *how* upset he was. Later, he could think in a more linear, causal and narrating way. He could begin to distinguish our two identities. As he himself became a less desperate and fragmented 'I', and 'I' became less muddled with 'you', 'this' became separated from 'that', and 'now' finally began to be separated from 'then'. He could begin to understand, 'this is happening now because that happened then'.

PROGRESS TOWARDS THE DEVELOPMENT OF INTENTIONALITY

Cindy was a little girl with autistic features in whom the problem of 'maintaining intentionality' was particularly marked. She had had a very difficult birth and her parents became worried about her development as early as 15 months, as she was so unusually slow and unresponsive. She came into treatment with Miss N at the Tavistock aged 4 with practically no speech. She had been born covered in faeces at a time when her parents were living in a foreign country and both had been in a very depressed state. She seems to have aroused, at the beginning of her life, mostly despair and distaste in them. As the parents began to recover from their depression and to come to life themselves, they began to feel concern and love for Cindy. No evidence has been found of brain damage.

Cindy, in many ways, seemed hardly to exist as a person. She seemed to be drifting through life, with few wants and demands, a constant lost look in her eye and a shapeless quality about her body and her movements. She appeared much younger than her 4 years. Objects and people did not seem to exert much attraction for her. She would stand apathetically just inside the door of the playroom with no apparent desire for anything. Miss N found it important to pay close attention to minuscule movements of Cindy's body or eyes. If she saw Cindy's gaze flick onto the cupboard, she would comment that Cindy seemed to be interested in going to see her toys. Sometimes she might take a few steps and then seem to lose her way and forget not only the toys but also herself. It perhaps needs to be said that this type of egoless passivity and helplessness seems to have had very different origins from a similar sort of behaviour in a child who is projecting his ego into the maternal object: such a child would be far more developed in his expectations that someone somewhere was capable of ego functioning, so long as it wasn't expected to be him. In Cindy, I suspect the ego function of maintaining intentionality had probably not been developed at all, a lack more to do with deficit than with defence. Perhaps she had never been fully awakened to the pull and power of an interpersonal relationship. It was almost as though she had, like certain fragile neonates, to be put together as a human being with a gradually growing sense of her own reality and her own existence, and that of her maternal object.

It is well known that some new babies need far more holding at birth, but it is perhaps less well documented that some need far more determined (although careful) drawing into contact than others. I have mentioned in Chapter 5 Brazelton's descriptions of the way the mother of the neonate amplifies and enlarges on every tiny movement or flickering gaze of the baby, and lends it meaning. She turns an interfering activity into one that serves their interaction. I think this is very similar to the work carried out by Miss N. Miss N gave, most of the time, a gentle running commentary on what Cindy was doing, or failing to do, or almost doing. Yet this was no mere containing or mirroring or receptive reflecting. If she was lending meaning, in Bion's terms, she was neverthless adding at times somewhat more than was expressed by Cindy. She often amplified, and thus gave more meaning to Cindy's wishes and to

Cindy herself, than Cindy thought was there. Sometimes, all Cindy would do was to open her mouth slightly, and Miss N would say, 'I think you want to say something'. It was not always clear that Cindy had indeed wanted to say anything. Brazelton says of the mothers with neonates, 'Perhaps the most interesting response to the challenge of facing an unresponsive infant is this. The mother takes on facial expressions, motions and postures indicative of emotion, as though the infant were behaving intentionally or as though she and he were communicating' (1974: 68). At times, there was the ghost of an intention, or more than a ghost; at other times perhaps Miss N really was, like Brazelton's mothers, reacting as if highly significant interaction had taken place when there had been no action at all. In any case, she was constantly bridging gaps between the child and her object, and helping them to be seen, by this child who seemed sunk in apathy, as bridgeable. When Cindy, at first aimlessly and absent-mindedly, pressed her thumb into some plasticine, her therapist commented that she was 'making a mark'. Much of the time there was only the hint of a gesture or movement to go on. But, gradually, she began to behave less like a little podgy lump and to take more shape as a person. The sluggish river of her mind began to move. She became more definite and developed the beginnings of a sense of purpose and a sense of agency.

Within a few months it seemed that the therapist's interest and attention had had the effect of increasing Cindy's interest in what she was doing. It began to be possible to comment on Cindy's own interest and her own liking for making a mark on her world. Gradually, her therapist's attention to her enjoyment and comments on it helped her to notice that she enjoyed enjoyment. It is this layer upon layer of self-observation which the normal attuned sensitive mother provides for her tiny baby in the first weeks and year of life without realizing she is doing it. She contains and calms upset and nurtures and provides care, as Winnicott and Bion have shown. But, as Stern and Trevarthen indicate, she also follows the baby's gaze, interests herself in his states of mind, in his interests, in his good and interesting mental states, too.

By the seventh month of Cindy's treatment, as she was becoming so much more sure of herself and of her own existence, it became possible occasionally to begin to make 'as if' and 'why' interpretations and links with transference experiences. When she made the doll fall, the therapist could say, 'Just like you feel I am dropping you at the end of the session' or whatever. By this stage Cindy was beginning to be able to hold two experiences and two ideas in her mind, so they could be compared.

In one remarkable session Cindy seemed to be making important discoveries about the notion of paradox. She was in the process of pretending that she was the big one in relation to the doll held by Miss N. She hesitated, however, looking from the doll to Miss N, clearly pondering the bewildering fact that, in reality, Miss N herself was a great deal bigger than she was. She also became increasingly irritated each time Miss N referred to her (Cindy's) outer garment as a 'coat' – she herself was using the word 'jacket'. Finally, with a combination of weary resignation and interested discovery in her voice, she concluded, 'You say coat, I say jacket!' Sue Reid has commented on the huge development involved when an autistic child becomes able to look at something from more than one perspective (personal communication). A dual perspective (like Bion's 'binocular vision') seems to arise from the infant's relationship with another living human being, but this particular development of 'two-trackedness' may also be compared to some work of Trevarthen. He has examined the development from 'primary intersubjectivity' (mutual gazing and interaction between the mother and baby) in the first months of life towards a development in the second half of the first year, which he calls 'secondary intersubjectivity': the baby's ability to engage in shared acts with inanimate objects, and to accept mother's directive regulation of his play and behaviour. Prior to this development, the baby prefers to examine and jiggle and bang toys without active manipulative interference by the mother. On the other hand, he appears to enjoy (and, presumably, need) the mother's responsive attention to his activities and her addition of synchronic and rhythmic comment. Trevarthen cites the example of Tracey at 7 months:

> When she shook a cage with a bell in it, her mother, looking at Tracey, synchronized her head with the movement and the sound. This caused Tracey to pause and 'think'. As soon as she moved again her mother moved her head in synchrony saying, 'Bang, bang, bang!' Tracey watched her mother closely and the effect became a game, leading to eager smiling and laughter.
>
> (Trevarthen and Hubley 1978: 195)

By 40 weeks (when, interestingly, Tracey was adept at two-handed play, and exchanged objects between her hands many times),

Tracey's mother became an acknowledged participant in actions. Tracey repeatedly looked up at her mother's face when receiving an object, pausing as if to acknowledge receipt. She also looked up to her mother at breaks in her play, giving the indication of willingness to share experiences as she had never done before.

(Trevarthen and Hubley 1978: 200)

Trevarthen appears not to have considered studying the baby's integration of his relationship to the mother's breast with his relation to her face and voice (is the breast an inanimate or an animate object?) or the multidimensional perspective gained when the father is present. Nevertheless, his emphasis on the step-by-step nature of these developments, and the conditions necessary for each step to follow the other, seems to underline Miss N's and my feeling that, although Cindy was indeed beginning to emerge from her early lost state, it was not useful at certain points to draw her attention too frequently to the therapist as a transference object. Her new interest in the plasticine, in making shapes on paper with crayons, in giving the dolls each his own bed was therefore usually not interpreted as being connected with her feelings about Miss N. It seemed to us that this would have interfered with her tentative attempts to have, and own, her own experience. It seemed enough to comment, 'you really like changing the shape of the plasticine' or 'that dolly has to go in exactly the right bed, doesn't she?' without adding 'just as you feel you have a special place with me'. The therapist remained alerted to this connection, but used her understanding that Cindy was indeed beginning to feel she had a place in her therapist's mind only at moments when it was more immediately evident in Cindy's mind – when, for example, Cindy was actually looking at her. But the jump from the doll to the person of the therapist felt too disruptive, intrusive and confusing at the point when Cindy was just learning to concentrate on a tiny piece of her new experience of, and impact on, dolls and plasticine.

Trevarthen points out that it was only after the stage when Tracey began to look up to seek her mother's gaze during pauses in her play that they began to play games where the mother was both giving and taking back, and where Tracey could allow her mother to instruct and direct her play. This careful developmental thinking helped us to be patient until Cindy had reached the point where her mind could contain what seemed to be a three-part relation: an image of herself, of the toy and of her therapist, and of the links between them. Then she seemed able to hear and use symbolic transference interpretations more easily, and the more usual level of psychoanalytic work could begin. (Balint's view (1968) on the importance of not providing patients functioning at the level of the basic fault with an object which is 'too sharply contoured' is of great interest here.)

By the eighth month, Cindy suddenly introduced her own 'thinking in parentheses'. By now her dolls had come to life and were often very busy. But on this day she instructed the therapist to look after one doll, while she did something else. She added, describing how the play was to unfold, 'I say, "I love you, Mummy".' Here she was not simply playing, she was anticipating, from one perspective, her playing in another, and also communicating her intention to play and her plans. Thus can begin the sense of a future within a future, the play within the play. It is a tremendously exciting moment when autistic children begin to discover the freedom to use their minds, to think in the subjunctive or conditional, to believe that one idea can contain another within it, that they can move away from their careful one-trackedness or one-pointedness and still have 'live company' while they move. Behind Cindy's new sense of purpose and intelligence lay, I think, a new sense of hope.

BEHAVIOUR DISTURBANCE AS A FORM OF COGNITIVE DEFICIT

If, as I have suggested, an object-relations perspective requires a study of a deficit in the self–object relation, then both terms need examining. Cindy had a weak capacity to approach her object, but she also saw her object as remote and faint. The work had to start from both ends, as it were. In the case of a second child, 4-year-old Rosie, the therapy also had to take as much account of the object's deficit as the self's. Rosie, who was at times a suicidally provocative child, did seem often genuinely lacking in a capacity to stop herself. She had been referred for hyperactivity and wild aggressive behaviour, and it was clear that she (or rather the relationship) was driving her mother to the edge of breakdown. Rosie seemed to believe that her mother believed that she was constantly wanting to provoke her. Her mother did, indeed, believe this and expect it, and Rosie expected her to expect it. Much of the time Rosie did not seem to have access in herself to any alternative belief that her mother might believe she had good or at least non-sinister motives for her behaviour. If she cried for her mother in the morning, her mother had no doubt that she was deliberately wanting to disturb her sleep. The child would start to sing somewhere at the other end of the house and the mother was convinced that the song was directed at her and meant to drive her mad with irritation.

The therapy with Mrs K began with frequent references in Rosie's play to objects being blocked, stuck, broken, and it seemed as if this child could not get off the treadmill of naughtiness which led to punishment from her mother, which led to more naughtiness and provocation in ever more vicious circles. Both were in despair, but neither could stop it happening. In the therapy, Rosie began to play a game where she was in a runaway car rolling downhill – an accurate symbol for the way she would do something mildly defiant or naughty, sense that she had produced irritation in the therapist, and then become more defiant, fearful and excited. This would lead to even more provocative behaviour and, eventually, to abandonment to despair. Her face would then change to a sort of crazy grinning mask and she would laugh hollowly, saying 'Who cares?', and call herself a 'binhead'. At such times, she seemed to have no idea that such runaway cars could be furnished with brakes.

If Mrs K could get in quickly enough with the interpretation 'You felt you'd made me cross, and you were afraid of me then', Rosie would sometimes calm down. It would be an instance of containment of a projection and transformation in such a way that the child (who has enough ego available at the moment to think and hear implications in what is said) has a chance to consider, 'Is she as angry as I think? Perhaps not.' But when Rosie was in a more disturbed state, the cycle of projection, re-introjection, re-projection into an ever angrier and more frightening figure led to worse and worse provocation, along the lines of 'Well, if you think I'm bad (and want me to be bad), then I must be bad, and so I might as well be really bad.' Here one often witnesses, in a matter of seconds, a child getting into identification with the image he feels his parental object has of him. He becomes what he feels he is. When these very rapid escalations took place, it was not always enough to say 'You feel you've made me angry', for Rosie heard this as a confirmation, if she heard anything at all. But she did sometimes hear, 'You seem to feel that I want you to go on getting wilder'. At times, however, it seemed even better, given the pressures of the moment, to try an interpretation which introduced the new idea of brakes. During a period when her mother was saying to Rosie and others that she really wished Rosie would go out and fall under a train (they lived near some railway tracks) Rosie took to teetering dangerously on the edge of a cupboard, sometimes provocatively in a mischievous way, but at other times more worryingly, as though she had really lost her sense of balance and the will and ability to stay upright. Mrs K and I thought that there was no doubt that her internal object was wishing her dead. Mrs K therefore began to point out that Rosie did not seem to be able to imagine that Mrs K really did want her to be safe, or really did want her to stop her wild behaviour (interpretation taking account of a deficit in the object), or that Rosie did not seem to be able to imagine that she could stop herself trying to irritate her therapist (interpretation directed to a deficit in the self). Rosie seemed to hear these interpretations in a different way and gradually began to emerge from her despair and suicidal cynicism. It was also, of course, very important to underline the moments of sanity and friendliness when they occurred in Rosie, because she hardly noticed them herself. Mrs K also often commented that Rosie seemed to expect her to want her to be naughty. These, although important, are in the tradition of a more usual containment and transformation of what is there, however fleetingly, in the material. It seems to me important, however, to acknowledge that in the 'brakes' interpretations the therapist is not containing a projected feeling or thought which 'somewhere' belongs to the child's self: she is containing, instead, a more or less as yet unthought thought. The alarm felt in the therapist's counter-transference does not arise from a projection of the child's. It is the lack of such a projection which is even more worrying (see Chapters 5 and 6). I would suggest that, although the child needs to explore fully the fact that she has a wildly provokable object or a very provocative part of herself, she cannot explore either while she is so overwhelmed. She can only explore from a relatively safe perspective, when she has some sense of the existence of another type of object and another more friendly type of object relation.

It needs to be said that such interpretations would clearly not have had such a calming effect on a child in whom sadism was more pronounced and who had become addicted to upsetting her maternal object. Rosie, however, was as yet by no means addicted to this form of object relation. She was only 4, and although she was in the grip of a provocative relation with a provokable object, when that grip could be loosened, from both sides as it were, she gave little sign of a genuine preference for a sado-masochistic relation. Nor did she seem to have any inbuilt resistance to the idea of brakes, and the idea that her therapist might not enjoy being cross with her was pleasant, but apparently quite new. A few years later, such features in her behaviour might have been far more embedded in her character and far more difficult to shift.

I have given in this chapter examples of difficulties in cognitive functioning of three patients. Such deficits need as careful attention in psychoanalytic work as do the emotional conflicts, splits and projections more central in less disturbed patients. In the case of both Robbie and Cindy, I have tried to describe a profound lack in the capacity to maintain intentionality and in thinking in parentheses in a two-tracked way. I have tried to link this with object-relations considerations. In Cindy, a much younger patient, I have also tried to demonstrate some of the technical considerations which I believe enabled her to achieve and maintain intentionality fairly rapidly in her first year of treatment. In the third case, Rosie, I have drawn attention to a more partial, but nevertheless severe type of cognitive deficit where the therapist may have to contain as yet unthought thoughts, unborn ideas which may have to be given flesh and life by the therapist. In the case of Cindy, the preconceptions of certain ideas were sometimes already there. The therapist took a gently active role in assisting their realization. According to Bion, when a preconception of a breast meets with a realization, a conception is born (1962: 91) That model is mostly adequate for what happened with Cindy. But what about Rosie, who genuinely seemed at times to be spinning wildly out of control? Or what if, for example, after a premature birth, a baby is too weak to open its mouth and go rooting for the breast? Its preconception of breastness may need awakening. Mothers in such instances help the baby to feed by giving the breast before the baby thought of asking for it. Some new realities press themselves upon us before we have preconceptions ready to meet them. If the conditions are not too pressured, a new concept may still be given time to be born.

8

A DEVELOPMENTAL VIEW OF 'DEFENCE'

Borderline patients

Bruner delineated the stages in the development of the capacity for co-ordination, or 'two-trackedness', which he suggested was the forerunner of the capacity to 'think in parentheses'. I have mentioned that when Robbie got beyond the stage of needing me to reach out to him in his far-off state, and could reach out himself, one of his problems was not knowing how to modulate and filter strong emotions. If he wanted to make contact with me by talking, he sometimes had to close his eyes, like Bruner's infants, so as not to lose himself in the process of gazing. By now he wanted to link up, but he still lacked most of the basic equipment to facilitate such linking. But closing his eyes was a start, both to defend himself against overwhelming excitement and also to preserve a more peaceful and solid form of contact. In the same way, stopping his ears against the noise of a Hoover was both a defence against terror and an attempt to find a place of safety. Gradually, he has become able to look and listen in more modulated and less drastically defended ways. This has involved developing functions which in a more mature, complex, structured personality may sometimes serve as 'defences', but in the case of Robbie and other psychotic or borderline psychotic, traumatized or abused children, may deserve a better name, one which stresses elements of a protective and developmental type. Notions of immaturity, of weak ego development, of deficit (Kohut), of equilibrium (Joseph) are helpful because they provide a sense of where the child is coming from and, even more important, where he has as yet not arrived (Bruner 1968; Kohut 1985; Joseph 1989).

THE BORDERLINE PSYCHOTIC CHILD

The case of the borderline psychotic child, where there may be some ego development, although of only a minimal or fragile sort, raises similar problems to those in the treatment of the psychotic child. The diagnosis is unfortunately not widely used among child psychiatrists who are not psychoanalytically trained. It does not exist at all in the ninth edition of the *International Classification of Diseases* (ICD-9). In the third *Diagnostic and Statistical Manual* (DSM-III) of the American Psychiatric Association, it is included as a sub-category of personality disorder, with its main features cited as: 'Impulsive, unpredictable, with unstable but intense interpersonal relationships. Identity uncertain, mood unstable, fearful of being alone, self-damaging' (Barker 1983: 145). I am using the term borderline psychotic in a much wider sense to include the other sub-categories of personality disorder such as compulsive, antisocial, paranoid, schizoid and avoidant, and so on. The psychiatric classifiers are, I suppose, uncomfortable with too wide a use of the word psychotic to describe children who are not flagrantly so, partly because the word still has pejorative associations in the lay (and organically minded psychiatric) mind. To the psychoanalytic psychotherapist, the notion of a psychotic part of the personality or the evidence of (hopefully brief) instances of psychotic thinking in everyone's life is perfectly comfortable, and so no more pejorative than the label personality disorder. Furthermore, when the quality and level of anxiety are understood (along with the content and form of some of the phantasies), the word psychotic attached to borderline seems perfectly appropriate. It also has important implications for theory and technique in relation to such children.

Most writers in the field tend to describe adult borderline patients as existing on a continuum between psychosis and neurosis. This vertical dimension, which describes both the degree of pathology and the level of ego functioning, is useful as a rough guide in unknown territory, but it should not be allowed to narrow one's focus, for most of the writers are in fact referring to an extremely broad range of illness. The categories – on the horizontal axis, as it were – tend to include everything from the psychopathic character disorders through the immature personality, the narcissistic disorders, severe neurotic conditions with psychotic features, excessively severe depression, to what used to be called latent schizophrenia but would now more likely be termed borderline schizophrenia (LeBoit and Capponi, 1979). The child psychotherapist might want to add many severely deprived, abused and traumatized children who sometimes have much in common with psychotic children, but in other respects are very different. They are different from borderline adults because psychotic illness in children, however temporary or however much only a threat from beyond the border, interferes with normal psychological development and therefore often produces developmental arrest and developmental deficit. Child psychoanalytic psychotherapists from the Autism Workshop at the Tavistock Clinic would also feel comfortable with the notion of borderline autistic conditions, although of course many organicists would not.

Therapists in the Anna Freud (then Hampstead) Clinic's borderline Workshop attempted to formulate the meaning of the concept 'borderline' in 1963. Kut Rosenfeld and Sprince concluded that the illness resides 'both in the quality and level of ego disturbance and in the precarious capacity for object relations' (1963). In a second paper (1965), on technical issues, they stated that they found that borderline children had an unusual reaction to interpretations: they experienced them as permissive, and interpretations of phantasy often caused phantasy and anxiety to escalate uncontrollably. Their conclusion was that it was necessary, therefore, to facilitate the very defence mechanisms which in a neurotic child one would attempt to undo: for example, repression and displacement. But there were differences among the members of the workshop as to how much ego support, reassurance and encouragement of the positive, as distinct from interpretation of the negative, should take place. Chethik and Fast, of the Borderline Workshop at the University of Michigan, do not agree with the notion of facilitating repression and displacement. They state that they no longer focus on getting rid of the phantasy but on helping the child grow out of it by delineating the underlying fears and anxieties. On the other hand, they do not recommend 'precipitating the child into an overwhelming state of non-pleasure' (Kut Rosenfeld and Sprince 1963, and 1965; Chethik and Fast 1970).

LeBoit, in a summary of the technical problems with borderline adults, concluded that 'the borderline patient in the past created a problem for psychoanalytic treatment, because he was deemed unable to form an object transference'. (He was thought to be unable to withstand the deprivation and 'abstinence' involved in classical analytic technique.) LeBoit continued, 'Currently the borderline individual is allowed to form the transference of which he is capable, usually a predominantly narcissistic transference, which develops into symbiosis.' LeBoit believes that during this early period of the treatment, the analyst may have to include modifications in classical analytic technique – that is, interventions other than interpretation, particularly those which indicate agreement of thought and feeling between analyst and patient, and those which reflect acceptance of the patient's unconscious wishes and understanding of his maturational needs (LeBoit and Capponi 1979: 57). Child psychotherapists are familiar with the kind of pressure child patients put on them when they come up in a friendly open manner and say 'My favourite colour is red. What is yours?' The therapist often feels compelled to offer a depriving type of interpretation – Grotstein has called it a weaning type of interpretation (Grotstein 1983) – in order to curb the child's omnipotence or intrusiveness, and in order to avoid gratifying the child's phantasies in a collusive or seductive way. However, I believe the argument over gratification versus deprivation is a false, a dangerously false, dichotomy. It is false because an interpretation may deprive the patient of real gratification of the information asked for, yet not be experienced as depriving at all. It may, in fact, be quite gratifying if it is an interpretation which is receptive to the child's wish to assure himself that the therapist and he have something in common, or like some of the same things, or belong to the same species. An interpretation can communicate understanding of this without being collusive or seductive. The dichotomy is dangerous because a too defensive interpretation may be experienced by a suspicious or already deprived child as cruelly rejecting of what may be his first overture of friendliness. I would suggest that the same question might have very different implications depending on the child: in one child, it may well be an attack on or a defence against separateness; in another child, it might be a first step in getting together with his object. In the first case, the child may be too close, too inside, and may need to be more separate; in the second, the child's object may be too remote, and he may need to feel it is approachable. This does not necessarily mean you have to tell the patient what your favourite colour is!

DEFENCES AND DEVELOPMENTAL
ACHIEVEMENTS OR OVERCOMINGS

Unfortunately, the useful elements in the notion of the theory of deficit are sometimes obscured by the technical modifications which many people seem to think must follow from Kohut's stress on deficit. One Kohut supporter, Ornstein, suggests it was probably a mistake over the years to think of deficit as a void that has to be filled, as Kohut implied (Ornstein 1983). Kohut believed it was important to develop what he called the normal narcissistic pole of the personality and he has been much criticized for gratifying the idealizing narcissistic transferences. It has been claimed that he was doing supportive psychotherapy rather than analysis, what some writers would call manipulating the transference rather than analysing it. That seems to me to be another too simplistic dichotomy, which could be clarified by considering some of the problems that may arise from the psychoanalytic concept of defence. In Kleinian thinking, for example, a paranoid-schizoid patient may be defending himself against the truths of the depressive position – that is, against his love or his guilt - but he may also be suffering from impaired development, so that he cannot yet proceed to the depressive position (see Chapter 10 for a fuller discussion). This brings up a vital practical question: what are the conditions under which development forward is possible at any stage? These considerations must shape whether the therapist interprets a patient's suspiciousness or detachment as a defence against a closer and better relationship, which it may be, or whether it is understood as a protection against what he perceives to be a genuinely attacking or intrusive or useless object. Joseph's term 'psychic equilibrium' provides us with a concept much subtler than that of defence. In 'On understanding and not understanding', she writes, 'The patient who believes he comes to be understood actually comes to use the analytical situation to maintain his current balance in a myriad of complex and unique ways' (Joseph 1983: 142).

In her novel, *Beyond the Glass*, Antonia White tells the autobiographical story of a young woman's collapse into madness and her subsequent recovery in an asylum. Clara has what seems to be a schizophrenic or possibly manic breakdown and is confined in a straitjacket and a padded cell. One day, after many months, the straitjacket is removed and she begins to emerge from her state of wild confusion. Remarkable things happen. Instead of going

111

through myriad changes of identity, she notices that she is always the same person called Clara. She has no memory of her previous life, but she does begin to know that she once had a previous life and her name was Clara in that life, too. Certain images from her daily life – the women's washroom, a creeper growing – begin to be fixed points of reference for her. As she puts it, 'A small space about her became solid and recognisable. In that space, objects and people were always the same, certain islands of time always the same.' Whereas before she felt she had fifty nurses, two emerge with some distinct and separate identities, and she writes, 'The red-haired one was Jones. *She must try and remember that*' (my italics). But the little islands of consistency continue to have no connection or thread of continuity between them. Thus, she says, 'It was extraordinarily difficult to remember things. Words like "before" and "after" no longer had any meaning. There was only "now".... Nevertheless she *continued to try desperately to piece things together, to find some connection between Clara here and Clara there*' (pp. 230–2, my italics). Eventually she does. She is moved to an open ward and then is allowed out to play croquet on the lawn. Somehow or other she remembers how to play croquet, and she realizes that none of the women will obey the rules and that they will play any old colour and any old way; she starts trying to tell them how to play properly. She cannot think why these women won't obey the rules, and it suddenly hits her that they are mad. After that, she recovers quickly (White 1979).

The notion of Clara developing defences is clearly not a useful way of looking at her attempts to emerge from psychosis. We should not, that is, confuse the building of the house with the building of the defensive fortifications which may eventually surround it. We build houses with walls to keep the weather out, but also to mark, frame and preserve that which may take place within. Surely it would not be useful to think of Clara's desperate efforts to piece things together, to concentrate on and remember the bits of clarity which are beginning to emerge from the mist, as obsessional defences against madness. Hoping against hope can be used defensively, but it can also be used for purposes of overcoming evil and despair. Robbie described a terrifying dream or hallucination he had had of hanging off the edge of a cliff, upside down, holding on to a piece of grass. Is the grass a defence against falling? Do we need lifelines only to escape death, or also in order to preserve life?

These issues may seem very clear-cut, but for the chronic

borderline case, who fluctuates back and forth between madness and sanity and where the amalgam of the psychotic part and the non-psychotic part may be very complex (see Grotstein 1979 and Steiner 1991), the issue is not quite so simple. It is important to know when obsessional mechanisms are being used defensively against an experience of a more living, free, less controllable object or feeling and when they signal perhaps the very first attempt, or at the very least a renewed attempt, to achieve some slight order in the universe. It is important also to distinguish between the moments when a manic experience of an ideal object or an ideal situation is used as a defence against a more sober reality and when it signals the first glimmer of emergence from lifelong clinical depression. Bion has taught therapists to distinguish between mechanisms designed to modify frustration and those designed to evade it. But is this a simple either/or situation or are there many developmental steps on the way between evasion and modification? There is, for example, the intermediate situation where a defensive evasion is necessary because the patient is not capable of managing the more mature modifications of his anxieties. His defences are all he has. What, then, are the conditions and even preconditions under which modification can begin to be possible?

The Analysis of Defence records a series of discussions with Anna Freud in the 1970s on her book *The Ego and the Mechanisms of Defence*, which was published in 1936. In one of the discussions, Joseph Sandler distinguishes between defences *against* painful realities and defences *toward*, which exist in order to gain or maintain a good feeling of security or safety (protective device) (p.19). In one of the later meetings, when they are discussing the fact that repression is developmentally a fairly late mechanism of defence, Anna Freud says that projection is used long before repression. Then Sandler says, 'Presumably because repression needs a considerable amount of strength on the part of the ego in order to work.' Anna Freud replies, 'Well, it needs structuralisation of the personality, which isn't there in the beginning.' Then she says, 'If you haven't yet built the house, you can't throw somebody out of it.' Sandler adds, 'Nor keep him locked in the basement' (Sandler and A. Freud 1985: 238).

Clearly, it is important to think developmentally about these matters: sometimes when the weekend or the summer break is imminent, one can interpret that the patient is really 'somewhere' upset about the coming break, and so is simply repressing it, when in fact he may have successfully split it off and projected it into the therapist. He doesn't feel 'somewhere he is missing her'; he feels *she* is going to miss *him*. Depending on the case, the feeling of missing may need to be contained and explored in the therapist for a lengthy period of time before the patient is ready to experience it as belonging to himself (see Joseph 1978: 112). In cases where the house isn't yet built, what may look like an attempt to throw somebody out of the house – to project the suffering infantile part into someone else – may really be a desperate attempt to find any house anywhere.

In their book *The Psychoanalysis of Developmental Arrest*, Stolorow and Lachmann suggest that it is important to distinguish between mental activity that functions principally as a defence and the superficially similar activity that is more accurately understood as a remnant of an arrest at a pre-stage of defensive development, characterized by deficiencies in the structuralization of the developmental world. Stolorow and Lachmann consider various 'defences' such as narcissism, idealization, grandiosity, projection, denial, incorporation, splitting, and compare the pre-stages of defence to real defences. They suggest, for example, that 'a functional conception of narcissism (i.e. one which sees it as fulfilling a need)' helps to alleviate the counter-transference problems that arise with narcissistic patients by enabling us to recognize that their narcissism is in the service of the survival of their sense of self. These ideas are important for work with deprived children who may present as very cut off and narcissistic and where an approach which is too confrontational may simply cause them to strengthen their defences. Stolorow and Lachmann also emphasize the difference between denial of something which is already known and 'denial' of something which is as yet not fully comprehensible. They write that 'when the analyst interprets as resistive what the patient accurately senses to be a developmental necessity, the patient often experiences the interpretation as a failure of empathy, a breach of trust, a narcissistic injury' (Stolorow and Lachmann 1980: 112). One is reminded here of Money-Kyrle's stress on the urgent importance of distinguishing between a projective identification motivated by destructive impulses and one motivated by desperation (1977: 463). He thinks analysts ignore this distinction at their peril, and surely in real life mourning is a gradual process. But when analysts and therapists urge patients to face their fears, their yearning, their sadness, long before they have the resources and imagination to do so, they may be asking too much.

A CLINICAL EXAMPLE

Some years ago I was treating a little borderline psychotic girl named Judy who suffered from asthma. She had never had an asthma attack in my presence, but one day she came in with a slight shortness of breath and said, in a very anxious voice, that she was having an asthma attack. I tried to show her that she seemed very frightened, as though she thought she was going to die. Her panic and breathing grew worse and I realized that, instead of helping her, my interpretation had escalated her anxiety. I thought quickly, and finally said something about the fact that she didn't seem able to tell the difference between a big asthma attack and a little one. It didn't seem to me a particularly profound interpretation, but she said, with surprise and relief, 'Ye.e.e.ss...' and her breathing improved. I was struck by the fact that a less anxious patient would have heard the implications in my first interpretation (that is, that she would not die) but that this terrified little girl could not. She had an extremely anxious and fragile mother, and I think she heard my first interpretation as though I, too, thought she was about to die. Although she panicked at every parting, however brief, I could never, in the early years, say that she imagined something terrible might happen to one of us during a weekend break: I had to turn the idea around, and talk to her about her difficulty in believing that both of us might make it through and meet again on Monday.

THE PARANOID-SCHIZOID POSITION AS A DEVELOPMENTAL PHASE

Klein first outlined her notions of the paranoid and depressive positions in two papers, 'Psychogenesis of manic-depressive states' (1935) and 'Mourning and its relation to manic-depressive states' (1940). It is probably well known that Klein did at first make some attempt to think in terms of phases and dates for these two very different states of mind – that is, she was thinking in terms of a developmental theory, following the tradition begun by Freud with his libido theory (Freud 1905b) and continued by Abraham (Abraham 1927). Gradually, however, the phase concept left Klein's writings altogether and she stuck much more closely to the notion of position. The idea of a position is, of course, a spatial metaphor and, in Klein's theory, it implied not just a different bodily location for the libido, but was, by definition, a relational, that is, an object-relational term. In deference to Fairbairn, Klein added the schizoid concept to the paranoid position and the characteristics at the schizoid end of the position are thought to be excessive splitting and fragmentation, excessive projection (later, in 1946, she added projective identification), a consequent weak ego and a weak trust in a good object (Fairbairn 1952). Grotstein points out that in a pathological state various symptoms such as loss of appropriate affect and confusion may follow, whereas in the normal infant there is helplessness and relative unintegration (Grotstein 1981b). At the paranoid position, Klein describes excessive splitting into good and bad of both self and object, with therefore excessive idealization and excessive persecution. Klein described the excessive projection of bad parts of the self into the object and thus excessive phobic fears or feelings of a paranoid type. Feelings of persecution spiral and escalate, owing to projection into the object and re-introjection of the by now bad objects, producing the need to re-project and so on. It is important to remember, however, that in a footnote in that same 1946 paper, Klein also wrote of how good parts of the self may be projected excessively, with consequent weakening of the ego and feelings of being swallowed up by the excessive goodness and value of the object. This phenomenon is as much a feature of the paranoid position as is the one characterized by projection of the bad part. Constant projection of the good part also produces a vicious circle seen in some very delinquent children and certainly in many psychiatrically depressed children, who may feel incapable of meeting the demands of a needy or damaged object that is felt to be beyond their strength to repair. The blanket of despair seems much more total and all parts of the self and the object seem to be engulfed in it. It is also important to consider that in some very disturbed and deprived children, the good part and the belief in a good object may not necessarily be projected; it may, instead, be severely underdeveloped.

I have written elsewhere in this book about the fundamental theoretical and meta-theoretical advance in the Kleinian differentiation between processes designed to defend against and processes designed to overcome depressive anxieties. Klein made it clear that true reparation, as opposed to manic or obsessional reparation, was not a reaction formation against, or denial of, depression and guilt about damage. In Klein's and Bion's thinking, overcoming, as opposed to denial or defence, involves healing modifications, but not evasions or triumphs or denials. I have come to think that a comparable distinction needs to be made when discussing the persecutory anxieties of the paranoid-schizoid position. Love has to be stronger than hate in order to overcome depressive anxieties. But what has to be stronger than fear to overcome, as opposed to defend against, persecutory anxieties? Here Bion's container is important, and so possibly is a closer analysis of the various functions of the 'good' object. The good object at the depressive position is an object loved and respected and capable of evoking concern. At the paranoid-schizoid position its goodness may also consist of its reliability, its assuring qualities, its solidity, its substantiality – that is, its good intentions, its protective qualities, its capacity to ensure feelings of safety; in a word, what Bowlby has called a 'secure base' (Bowlby 1988). Perfect love casteth out fear, but so, sometimes, does perfect safety.

I shall try to show in following chapters that Bion's work on projective identification as a communication and the work of the developmentalists have a number of implications for the treatment of psychotic and borderline children: first, we need a general concept of overcoming to stand beside the concept of defence for the paranoid-schizoid position; second, we need specific terms such as potency to stand alongside that of omnipotence; a sense of agency to stand alongside narcissism; relief, joy and hope to stand alongside manic denial; order, structure and predictability to stand beside obsessional defences against fragmentation, and many others besides. I shall try to show that these positive states of mind should not be seen as defences and need not wait for the developments of the depressive position. They occur in much more primitive positions of psychological development where it is not so much a question of splitting between good and bad being marked, but where what is at issue is the adequate development of, and belief in, the good. When Robbie and Bruner's babies close their eyes against distraction and borderline children begin to hold to the idea that Monday may really come, they may be engaged in an act of precious conservation and preservation. First, as Anna Freud says, build the house; first, as Klein says, introject the good breast; first, as Bion says, you have to have an adequate container; first, as Bowlby says, have a secure base.

9

THE NECESSARY ANGEL
Idealization as a development

>... I am the necessary angel of earth,
>Since, in my sight, you see the earth again.
>
> Wallace Stevens

In this chapter I wish to explore the distinction between processes of idealization used as a defence against persecutory anxiety or depressive pain and processes of idealization which occur as necessary stages of development. Klein and her followers emphasize both functions, but it is interesting that both the Laplanche-Pontalis (1973) and the Hinshelwood (1989) dictionaries of psychoanalytic concepts refer only to Klein's views on the defensive function of idealization. I shall try to demonstrate that the first appearance of ideal objects in the phantasies of chronically depressed children may signal, not a resistive or evasive defence against depression, but an important developmental achievement. My interest in this subject was stimulated by a remark of Elizabeth Spillius concerning the fact that we know little about the growth of idealization.

In Chapter 2 I described the appearance, after Robbie's return after his breakdown, of his drawing of the conker with the two chestnuts nestled cosily within. This was accompanied by an emergence from his hopeless apathy and a new and arousing belief in the three-dimensionality of his objects. However pathological and inferior this state of perfect smoothness and boundedness was to a more reality-based condition where life is acknowledged to have its collisions and sharp edges, it was nevertheless a considerable development beyond his previous world of empty spaces and stark leafless trees, where the only substantial objects that did emerge were two-dimensional and inaccessible.

Laplanche and Pontalis define idealization in the following way: 'Idealization is the mental process by which the object's qualities and value are elevated to the point of perfection. Identification with the idealized object contributes to the formation [of the] ideal ego and the ego ideal.' They point out that Freud thought that the idealization of the loved object was closely linked to narcissism. Rosenfeld has made a similar link (1964). Klein, in 'Some theoretical conclusions regarding the emotional life of the infant' (1952), states that 'It is characteristic of the emotions of the very young infant that they are of an extreme and powerful nature. The frustrating bad object is felt to be a terrifying persecutor, the good breast tends to turn into the ideal breast which should fulfil the greedy desire for unlimited, immediate and everlasting gratification. Thus feelings arise about a perfect and inexhaustible breast, always available, always gratifying.' She adds, 'in so far as idealisation is derived from the need to be protected from persecuting objects, it is a method of defence against anxiety' (p.64). But she also says 'While in some ways these defences [splitting and idealization] impede the path of integration, they are essential for the whole development of the ego, for they again and again relieve the young infant's anxieties. This relative and temporary security is achieved predominantly by the persecuted object being kept apart from the good one.' She goes on to say that object relations are shaped by love and hatred, and permeated on the one hand by persecutory anxiety, on the other by its corollary, which she calls the 'omnipotent reassurance derived from the idealisation of the object' (pp.70–1). Thus, Klein seems at some times to be stressing the defensive function in idealization, at others the fact that it is essential for the whole development of the ego. Perhaps a better phrase for the non-defensive essential function of idealization would be 'potent assurance' rather than 'omnipotent reassurance'. And it may be more helpful to think of states which are ideal rather than idealized (Deborah Steiner, personal communication): the verb tends to carry the implication of an active or intentional changing of one state into another, whereas the noun need not.

In 'The psychogenesis of manic depressive states' (1935), Klein again stresses need rather than only defence. She points to two preconditions for the eventual integrations of the depressive position to occur, which are 1) a strong libidinal relation to part objects and 2) the eventual introjection of the whole object. Again, in the 1940 'Mourning in its relation to manic-depressive states', she says 'The shaken belief in the good objects disturbs most painfully the process of idealisation, which is an essential intermediate step in mental development. With the young child, the idealised mother is the safeguard against a retaliating or dead mother and against all bad objects and, therefore [perhaps an 'also' would have been better than a 'therefore' to stress the element of need] represents security and life itself' (p.355).

Hanna Segal emphasizes something even closer to the notion of need in her *Introduction to the Work of Melanie Klein*, where she underlines the element of the strength of the ideal object and of the ego. This raises the issue of quantitative considerations, to which I shall return. She writes:

> If the conditions of development are favourable, the infant will increasingly feel that his ideal object and his own libidinal impulses are stronger than the bad object and his bad impulses. He will be able more and more to identify with his ideal object and because of the physiological growth and development of his ego, he will feel increasingly that his ego is becoming stronger and better able to defend itself and its ideal object. When the infant feels that his ego is strong and possessed of a strong ideal object, he will be less frightened of his own bad impulses and therefore less driven to project them outside.
>
> (Segal 1964: 54)

Rosenfeld makes a technical, but also an implied theoretical and quantitative point, too, when he says that the analyst should not break down the idealization too quickly with 'very vulnerable' patients who may need to idealize the analyst in order to create a benign atmosphere (Rosenfeld 1987: 271).

IDEALIZATION AS A DEFENCE: CLINICAL ILLUSTRATION

Alice, a 12-year-old girl, was referred for fairly mild depression, some difficulties with friends and working slightly below par at school. She had been born with a huge purple birthmark, an angioma, which covered the whole side of her face. It is inoperable while she is still growing but can be operated on when she finishes growing. Very little else can be done for it in the meantime, although her parents have taken her all over the country for various sorts of treatment. In this session she had been waiting for weeks to be given an appointment in London, not her home city, for laser treatment. The best the treatment could offer was to create a few tiny white spots in the purple mass. To the outside observer it would make very little difference, but similar minuscule improvements from other treatments seemed to mean a lot to Alice and to have kept her hope alive.

The session I wish to mention took place shortly before the Christmas break and after several postponements by the laser clinic in London. Each time the therapist tried gently to help Alice see that she was feeling frustrated by all the waiting and postponement of her hopes, and by the coming interruption to their relationship. Alice would momentarily acknowledge it, and then hasten to speak about the Alpine skiing she was looking forward to and how well she remembered it from last year and how beautiful were the whiteness of the snow and the brightly shining sun. It seemed to the therapist that, although Alice's feeling for the purity and beauty of the Alps was genuine, she was clinging to thoughts about them in order to avoid the painful dark thwartings of hopes and the irritation with her therapist for leaving her at such a time.

Alice, I suggest, had a well-developed capacity for idealization and appreciation of beauty. She took great personal care and was an attractive girl with lovely shining hair, which she arranged to fall over the discoloured part of her face. She had hope and strength and determination, and, instead of despairing apathy, a mild depression due, I think, to a difficulty in feeling permitted to acknowledge her own rage and impatience to be made to look normal. In her case, an already developed capacity for idealization was to some extent being used defensively, and she eventually obtained much relief from interpretations which freed her to feel the blacker feelings alongside the white. Her depression lifted and she became more alert and effective at school.

IDEALIZATION AS A DEVELOPMENT: TWO SEVERELY DEPRIVED BOYS

The point I wish to stress is that integration between the bright and dark sides of one's nature and of one's object is possible only when there is *adequate development of both the idealizing and persecutory strands*. There are quantitative issues here. Tiny increments in idealization in patients whose capacity for bright hope is severely underdeveloped should not be exposed to constant reminders of the very despair and anxiety they are finally managing, not to defend against, but to overcome.

I would like to illustrate the point by describing two severely deprived boys, a very depressed 12-year old-named Ricky, and a cut-off autistic 12-year-old named Andrew. Both boys seem, almost for the first time, to be conceiving of an ideal object, strangely enough, thanks probably to television, maybe even the same programme! I heard about the two sessions within a week of each other, and the two therapists dealt with the material in radically different ways.

Ricky had several separations from his mother in the second year of his life. She has had several different violent live-in partners. He is a passive boy who gives the impression of having been clinically depressed for all or most of his life. This session of once-weekly therapy took place after two cancellations, one by him, one by his therapist. When Miss J collected him and called his name, he at first did not respond, and then seemed surprised to see her. In the room he looked into his box and exclaimed 'Oh good, there's paper in it' and then he muttered a hardly audible thank you. For the first part of the session he remained quite withdrawn, ruling line after line on the page and insisting that these were 'just lines'. When at one point Miss J commented that he might have felt forgotten by her, he said: 'Mm, but you remembered the paper.' She acknowledged his pleasure at this, but, as he continued to be in general much less responsive than he had become prior to the two cancellations, she reflected that it seemed very difficult for him to talk to her today, as if he didn't know how or had forgotten how. She suggested that he was telling her that he had lost contact with her and felt out of touch and was now struggling to re-establish a line or link between them. He said, in an off-hand way, that he couldn't really talk while he was drawing, he needed to concentrate. Miss J persisted gently, saying that it seemed especially difficult today after such a long break. He then said, with more enthusiasm, that he thought he would draw a picture of a car he had seen on TV. It was 'an enormous car, ten times the size of this room and the same width. It had everything you could wish for in it, a swimming pool, TV, a telephone so you could phone someone. Also a bath, a fridge, food and a bed. Imagine having something like that all to yourself.' He wished it was his, he 'would never have to leave it for anything. It had everything. You could swim all day in the holidays.'

The therapist then made an interpretation which seemed to see this idealization as a defence. She said that she thought the car stood for her, that he wished he could move in lock, stock and barrel and have her to himself all the time and never have to leave, have a direct line to her (linked with the fact he comes only once a week). He said 'Mm' and then seemed to deflate. After quite a long pause, she commented on this and asked what he was thinking. He said he was thinking of his aunt. The aunt had split up with her boyfriend and had kicked him out. The boyfriend had arrived at their door asking if they could give him a bed for the night and if they could think of anywhere he could stay. He went on to show that he felt sorry for this man who had been kicked out, and remained deflated for the rest of the session.

This is a moving and disturbing account of the always difficult problem of getting the balance right in working with such disturbed children. I condensed the session considerably, but I hope I have conveyed the degree of devotion with which Miss J persisted in her attempts to understand Ricky's cut-off depression in the first part of the session. It was only after her efforts were rewarded, and his heart lifted, that she lost touch with him. She conveyed great understanding of his depression but not of his sudden burst of happiness. His hopes rose, I think, as her sensitive persistence gave him cause to believe that she really did have him in mind, and indeed probably had had him in mind and not forgotten him over the three-week gap: 'Imagine, something like that all for yourself.' He had, I think, a rush of belief in an object that was available, receptive and somehow full of resources. Looked at from the point of view of mature depressive position development where separateness is acknowledged and objects have to be shared with themselves as well as others, there may be 'defensive' elements in this ideal car. But surely the maternal object has first to be possessed before it can be shared? Dreams have to be dreamed first before they can be shed.

There is a further problem in this session which has to do with the power and reality of transference experiences in the here and now. The therapist took the story of the car to imply a *wish* for a state which was fundamentally unattainable. She could, instead, have acknowledged that Ricky had actually felt he *had just had* a surprisingly and unexpectedly good experience – that is, that he was not wishing for, but had in fact *found* a spacious and available object in her. The idealizing elements in this could then have been dealt with. But over-idealization of a state which is fundamentally good or ideal should not be confused with idealization of a state which is fundamentally bad. As it was, I think Ricky felt, like his aunt's boyfriend, kicked out of the new home in his therapist's mind that he had only just found.

The second patient, Andrew, was an even iller and more deprived boy, who as a baby had been left alone in the house without food for many hours and sometimes days at a time. His head was badly and permanently misshapen from hours of head-banging on his cot. Eventually he was fostered with very caring foster parents and began to emerge a little from a deeply withdrawn and animal-like state. At the age of 9, more civilized but still very strange and disturbed with autistic features, he was brought for treatment. After three years of three times weekly therapy with Mrs S, he became able to learn better at school and to be quieter and calmer, less frenzied and agitated. He had spent most of the sessions in the early years of treatment making strange high-pitched squeaking noises.

The session in question was an unusually quiet and peaceful one. The usual weird squeaks were absent. After some play with the Lego, Andrew began, for the second time ever, a long sequence of string play. He used the string to make a handle for himself to pull the door to and fro. (It is usually an important moment when autistic children start to conceive of links and, especially, of handles. It seems they have finally got both an object they can conceive of as graspable and holdable and a self that feels able to reach and grasp. Some useful research could be done on early reaching and grasping in autistic children and its connection with ego development. Clearly Andrew's early faith in the graspability of his objects had reason to be very limited.) Throughout this first part of the session Mrs S drew attention to Andrew's pleasure in his growing sense of control and agency. She also commented on the possessive and tender feelings that began to emerge.

Halfway through the session there was an unexpected interruption. Andrew seemed very annoyed, and Mrs S commented on his feeling that she 'should' have prevented it and protected his time with her. She also commented on his anger and jealousy. Andrew laughed and began to draw for the first time ever a car from the inside. (I suspect that her use of the expression 'you feel I should' was more appropriate than a 'you wish I would' or 'you want me to' because the 'should' conveys the understanding that the patient is not simply demanding a reliable and faithful object, he actually needs one.) In the early years of his treatment, Andrew's drawings of cars had always been of empty two-dimensional vehicles with no people inside. Gradually they had got some three-dimensionality and, even more gradually, a few people, but never before had he drawn one from the inside. The therapist wrote,

> It was as if drawn from the back seat: two comfortable front seats were seen in the drawing, the steering wheel, the lights. I had the impression that he was allowing me to look at the inside of his world. I said it seems that Andrew is feeling in a very comfortable luxurious place and he is proud of it. He wants to share it with me. He nodded happily. I said Andrew seems to be waiting to be driven, this drawing is from the back seat, where it seems that he has plenty of space for him and a good protected view from outside. He added quite quickly two details. 'It has a sun roof, look.' I said, 'Yes, the sun is able to come in, light and warm for coming into the car where Andrew is. Perhaps he is able to see well and to feel more comfortable now'. He then drew a Rolls Royce, handed it to me and said: 'What about this?' The Rolls Royce was drawn from outside the front.

She commented on his feeling comfortable in the room with her today, and on his feeling of well-being over being understood. She added that he was feeling great, like a Rolls Royce. He nodded, and as it was the end of the hour, he asked her to keep the drawings in her drawer.

Clearly Mrs S has handled the roomy spacious car in a manner different from Miss J. Both therapists, by careful sensitive work in the first part of the session, enabled their patients to get to the point of conceiving of a spacious, protective and available object which was felt to be specially for them. The difference is in their understanding of its meaning when it finally arrived on the scene. I think what enabled Andrew to get there was probably the combination of both Mrs S's exploration of his possessive tender feelings in the first part of the session and also her exploration of his possessive angry feelings in the second part. I think it was the fact of Andrew learning that such a wide range of feelings could be understood that gave him the conception of an object that had a great deal of room for him and that shone a kindly light on his experience. He could then go even further to impress her with his Rolls Royce potency.

There is an interesting technical dilemma here with autistic children or, for that matter, with any patient with inadequate development of imaginative capacities: this is when simply to describe the patient's pleasure in a phantasy and when to link it with transference meanings. There are moments when a Winnicottian respect for the play itself is important, and when a too premature transference interpretation would interfere with the very process of formulation the child is trying to achieve. But there are other moments when a comment which links the play with the relationship to the therapist may underline the experience and place it on firmer and more lasting ground. What is important about Mrs S's technique is that she allowed Andrew actually to have his ideal object in phantasy. She did not take it away from him by making it sound like an unattainable object that he was only wishing he could have. I suspect, however, that she could have made a transference interpretation which would not have interfered with the new hopes and the new development of idealization or, to be more precise, of an ideal object. On the contrary, if, for example, she had pointed out that he was beginning to feel that she had plenty of room for him in her mind, such an interpretation might have both underlined his growing contact with live human objects, and also prevented a too idealized state of mind which could otherwise lead to a crash and disappointment at the moment of the session's ending.

In *Listening Perspectives in Psychotherapy*, Hedges supports Kohut's theory and technique as related to idealized parental imagoes. Hedges discusses the weak egos of borderline patients, and says: 'It should be stated that with borderlines therapy is known to be ego-building, but this does not mean that the therapist should or needs to be building anything.' He believes that the analytic work can continue without 'support' or suggestion in direct or guiding forms from the therapist, but that an ego can none the less grow (Hedges 1983: 136; Kohut 1985). The argument of this chapter is to suggest that the process of introjection of an ideal object is a long, slow process. It depends, according to Klein, on whether the child has developed previously a strong positive relationship to part objects, and therapists should ensure that their interpretive work is tuned to the appropriate level, so that it does not stand in the way of this process.

10

CLINICAL DEPRESSION AND DESPAIR
Defences and recoveries

My subject in this chapter is depression and recovery. In his novel *The Unbearable Lightness of Being*, Milan Kundera explores the opposition posed by Parmenides and Nietzsche between lightness and weight. Kundera says that, of all oppositions, that between lightness and weight is the most mysterious and the most ambiguous. He agrees with Nietzsche that the heaviest of burdens is created by the weight of unbearable responsibility – of compassion in fact – yet the heavier the burden, the closer our lives come to the earth and the more real and truthful they become. On the other hand, he says, the absolute absence of a burden causes man to be lighter than air, to soar into the heights, take leave of the earth and his earthly being, become only half real, his movements as free as they are insignificant. The novel proceeds to explore this ambiguity (Kundera 1984).

I would like to explore this ambiguity too, by considering the distinction between 'depressive position' depression and clinical depression or despair. I would also like to explore the distinction between the manic defence and the 'manic position', that is, between states of mind which signal denial of unhappiness and those which signal escape from or emergence from such states into something like happiness. Robbie's flight and the flight of all his loved ones up out of the well signalled a recovery from the kind of apathy that goes beyond even despair.

As the editors of *The Writings of Melanie Klein* noted in 1975, Klein used the term 'manic position' in her two early papers on depression, 'A contribution to the psychogenesis of manic-depressive states' and 'Mourning and its relation to manic-depressive states', but does not mention it thereafter (Klein 1975: 433). She also uses the term 'obsessional position', which she does not use again. About the manic *defence*, Klein has the following things to say. She points out that Freud shows that it has for its basis the same contents as melancholia and is, in fact, a way of escape from that state. She offers an explanation of the cyclical nature of manic depressive illness by pointing out that the mania does not work as a permanent escape because its torturing and perilous dependence on its loved objects drives the ego to find freedom, but its identification with these objects is too profound to be renounced (Klein 1935: 277). Segal subsequently went into this question in much more detail. She suggested, for example, that mania was not simply a defence against or escape from depression, but that it also acted as a cause of depression, because of the triumph and contempt expressed in the desire to deny the significance and power of the object (Segal 1964). Klein had also added a further point about the manic defence: she not only linked it with depression, as Freud had done, but she also pointed out that it served as a refuge from a paranoiac condition, which the ego is unable to master. Thus, the dread of bad objects may fuel the need for mania. This is clearly an important issue for clinical technique. Therapists have probably all had the experience of feeling that a very driven, high, arrogant patient is trying to make them feel small and stupid in order to deny his deeper knowledge of their value to him. In fact, he may be doing no such thing. He may be trying to make the therapist feel small and stupid because he feels the minute he relaxes his grip the therapist will demonstrate her true badness and power and make him feel small and stupid. It is quite easy to think that a manic patient is denying depression, but often what he is denying is paranoia. The feeling state which, according to Klein, is most specific for mania is the sense of omnipotence, and it is utilized for the purpose of controlling and mastering objects. A second mechanism is that of denial, particularly of the dread of internalized persecutors and of the id. She declares that that which is first of all denied is psychic reality, and the ego may then go on to deny a great deal of external reality. Klein also describes the mastery over the internalized parents and, in addition to attempts at (what was later called by Segal in 1964) manic reparation, one other defence mechanism characteristic of the depressive position: this is the introjection of good objects, which Klein says leads in mania to the hunger for objects, as in the 'cannibalistic feast' described by Freud (Klein 1935; Freud 1917). (See Appendix 2 for further discussion of the 'manic position'.)

It has been pointed out by many authors, among them Meltzer

and Spillius, that the Kleinian view of the normal depressive position
has shifted considerably over the years, that, although Klein stressed
the difference between it and pathological depression in this very
first paper, in fact the difference has been enlarged since then and
is stressed more strongly nowadays (Spillius 1988a:4; Meltzer 1978:
10). I am suggesting that the work with borderlines, particularly
clinically depressed children, might require us to take much note of
that difference, but also to make a similarly clear distinction between
the manic defence and the manic position.

At some moments, Klein refers to the normality of the manic
position; at others, she stresses its defensive quality and even its
pathological nature – for example, when she uses an expression such
as 'cannibalistic feast'. The depressive position is stimulated by loss
of the loved object; the manic position, she suggests, is stimulated
at any time that the child finds the breast again after having lost
it. Here the ego and ego ideal coincide (Freud) and cannibalistic
phantasies are set going. Klein says, 'No doubt the more the child
can at this stage develop a happy relationship to its real mother, the
more will it be able to overcome the depressive position.' There is
some evidence that she is still thinking of the depressive position as
something to be overcome, as though it were pathological and still
coloured by paranoid phantasies. It tends to be thought of now not
as something to be overcome, but as a state to be lived in and lived
through for most of one's life, if one can manage to stay there. I
would like to suggest that the more modern notion of a healthy
depressive position implies by definition some development along
the lines of a manic position, too. The word 'depressive' stresses
the elements of sobriety, freedom from illusion and grandiosity, but
it may carry dangerous implications for those patients who have
been sunk into states of deep despair and are beginning to move
towards a little hope and to feel a little light hearted. There is no
loss without a previous experience of something gained, and surely
it is this lifelong rhythm of gain, loss, gain, loss, reunion, parting,
reunion, parting which is what human relationships and human life
are about. There is an interesting chapter in Tustin's book *Autistic
Barriers in Neurotic Adults* where an ex-autistic adult, who had
returned to treatment but had recently had a very long parting
from her therapist, gets her back again after the break and has a
dream, saying: 'It's the oddest thing that I have discovered – I have
discovered a rhythm of safety.' Her use of the word 'rhythm' rather
than 'position' of safety seems particularly apt when one considers

that it is never a static 'position', and Klein in fact stressed this herself (Tustin 1986: 272). Professor Ravetto of the University of Turin suggested on one occasion that it might have been called the 'manic-depressive' position, and Bion has stressed the movement between the paranoid-schizoid and depressive positions (Bion 1963).

The work of mourning is connected with the depressive position and this has been well documented in the psychoanalytic literature. But what about the other work, what Stern has called the infant's 'slow and momentous discovery that his experience, which he already senses is distinctly his own, is not unique and unparalleled, but is part of shared human experience' (Stern 1983: 77). This may be work which has to do with learning about gain and enrichment, not loss. It is well known that the process of having a baby requires enormous adjustment: new introjections, new identifications in the mother, not only, I think, because of the loss of her previous identity and because of the loss of her baby from her inside, but also because of the process of digestion, of taking in the fact of birth, which in its way is just as shocking as death. Wonder, joy, awe may be as humbling and maturing experiences as disappointment, frustration, grief and loss, and just as sobering. The important thing is the unprepared-for, unexpected change which is not designed by ourselves. Many people, not only those with a history of deprivation and not only those with considerable envy, have just as much difficulty with moments of gain as with the moments of loss.

In her discussion of the paranoid and the depressive positions Klein is careful to show the differences between the pathological paranoid and depressive states and the normal ones. Segal and Meltzer have also documented the difference between the two sets of states quite carefully, yet the manic position has disappeared from Kleinian literature (Segal 1964; Meltzer 1978). Anna Freud and Joseph Sandler speak of normal narcissism (Sandler and A. Freud 1985). Bion distinguished between pride and arrogance (Bion 1957). But how do these link with the fundamental core of Kleinian theory, the theory of the development towards the depressive position?

In a 1935 paper entitled 'The manic defence', Winnicott declared that his own widening understanding of Klein's concept of the manic defence had coincided with a gradual deepening of his own appreciation of inner reality. He described the omnipotent manipulation, the control and the devaluation characteristic of this defence, yet he seemed disturbed as to how to account for the degree to which it is employed by everyone in normal life:

> It should be possible to link the lessening of omnipotent manipulation and of control and of devaluation to normality and to a degree of manic defence that is employed by all in everyday life. For instance, one is at a music hall and onto the stage come the dancers, trained to liveliness [this is 1935]. One can say that here is the primal scene, here is exhibitionism, here is anal control, here is masochistic submission to discipline, here is a defiance of the super-ego. Sooner or later one adds here is life. Might it not be that the main point of the performance is the denial of deadness, a defence against depressive death-inside ideas, the sexualisation being secondary?
>
> (p.131)

Certainly, this is a defence against deadness, but why is it not also an assertion of, an expression of, aliveness? Is death any truer than life, loss any truer than gain, or are both not part of the fundamental ambiguity of human existence? Winnicott goes on to ask about such things as the wireless which is left on interminably: 'what about living in a town like London with its noise that never ceases and lights that are never extinguished. Each illustrates the reassurance through reality against death inside and the use of manic defence that can be normal.' Here he is stressing the defensive function in the manic response.

Winnicott then explores, quite brilliantly, the use of opposites in reassurance against certain aspects of the feelings of depression. His list of opposites includes two categories, the one depressive, the other 'ascensive': chaos versus order, discord versus harmony, failure versus success, serious versus comic. Winnicott goes on to discuss the defensive aspects of mania and finds a new word for the totality of defences which act against the depressive position. This is the word 'ascensive', which he seems to prefer to 'manic'. It is useful, he says, in indicating the defence against an aspect of depression, which is implied in such terms as 'heaviness of heart', 'depth of despair', 'that sinking feeling', etc. He goes on: 'One has only to think of the words "grave", "gravity", "gravitation" and of the words "light", "levity", "levitation", each of these words has a double meaning, a physical relationship to weight, but also the psychological meaning' (p.135). Psychologically it is seriousness

131

against devaluation and joking, so the latter, he continues, can be seen to be a defence against depression. He goes on to say that even the Easter Resurrection and Ascent following on the Good Friday despair is clear evidence of a manic phase. He calls this evidence of recovery from depression; yet surely there is a big difference between the notion of defence and the notion of recovery, and this is well documented in Klein's discussion of mourning and reparation (Winnicott 1935).

The distinction between manic states which are a denial of depression and states which signal a recovery from depression is absolutely vital, and if the therapist confuses the two she may really succeed in killing hope for her depressed patients. There are many notions in everyday speech, such as 'the heart lifting', 'spirits rising', 'hopes soaring', which should alert one to the non-defensive life-assertive aspects contained in what Winnicott calls ascensive feelings. The fountain of life as portrayed in literature and painting, the Resurrection itself, and indeed all mythology and spring rituals of rebirth, may represent notions of recovery from depression and new faith, new life, new hope. The 17th-century poet, George Herbert, described this beautifully, in his poem to God entitled 'The Flower'.

> How fresh, O Lord, how sweet and clean
> Are thy returns! ev'n as the flowers in spring;
>   To which, besides their own demean,
> The late-past frosts tributes of pleasure bring.
>   Grief melts away
>   Like snow in May,
>   As if there were no such cold thing.
>
>
> Who would have thought my shrivel'd heart
> Could have recover'd greennesse? It was gone
>   Quite under ground, as flowers depart
> To see their mother-root, when they have blown;
>   Where they together
>   All the hard weather,
>   Dead to the world, keep house unknown.

The penultimate stanza reads:

> And now in age I bud again,
> After so many deaths I live and write;

I once more smell the dew and rain,
And relish versing: O, my onely light,
    It cannot be
    That I am he
On whom Thy tempests fell all night.

(Hutchinson 1953)

I do not know whether Herbert's recovery of greennesse involved a recovery from depressive position depression or a recovery from a more pathological state, but either way what he is talking about is a recovery from, not a manic defence against, depression. Klein herself, in the paper on mourning, makes it clear that the child's wish to grow up is motivated not only by rivalry with his parents and a wish to triumph over them, but also by his wish to grow out of his deficiencies. She says this wish ultimately to overcome his destructiveness and his bad inner objects and to be able to control them is an incentive to achievements of all kinds. She adds that every step in emotional, intellectual and physical growth is used by the ego as a means of overcoming the depressive position. 'The child's growing skills, gifts and arts increase belief in the psychic reality of his constructive tendencies, in his capacity to master and control his hostile impulses, as well as his bad, internal objects' (1940: 353). In her *Narrative of a Child Analysis* Klein frequently refers to the growth of Richard's confidence in his gifts and his hope about future 'potency', which she clearly sees as very different from omnipotence (1961: 465).

A CLINICAL ILLUSTRATION OF THE DEVELOPMENT TOWARDS THE 'MANIC POSITION'

The improvement in the capacity to think in a 10-year-old autistic girl seems to have arisen in a situation where a loss followed by a gain led to a sense of new powers, but not, I think, to mania. Sally's previous week's session had had to be cancelled suddenly by Mrs R, her therapist. The session began with the theme of Sally's preoccupation with the problem of falling off an object that was so smooth there was nothing to hold on to. (Her parents did seem to be in fact quite hard and insensitive but well-meaning people.) Mrs R commented that perhaps she hadn't felt she could keep a grip on her therapist with the cancellation last week. Sally then drew a picture of a man, and then began to worry about the distance between his chest and the ground. She said 'It's very deep', then added firmly 'But he is very tall, so he is not going to fall all the way'. (At times her thinking was still very concrete.) At moments she spoke as if the man were herself. Suddenly, she got up and went to the windowsill and said that the wall came up to under her chin and 'One can jump up. I have got arms. Luckily I do', she said. 'At least I have arms so I can jump up.' The therapist suggested that this was connected with her power to grip on to herself mentally. It might have been helpful to have added something about the fact that the child felt as though now she had arms and they were so powerful that they got the therapist back again. However, it seems as though the child had somehow understood this anyway. She had already made great strides in her therapy. After a game where she pretended to escort a little child, she said, 'That was pretend.' Then she turned and said, 'But what is real is I have arms.' The therapist again acknowledged the feeling of achievement. At the end of this session, Sally did something she had never been able to do before. As she was leaving, she hesitated – stopped in fact – and said in a direct and thoughtful manner, 'I'm afraid'. Mrs R asked 'Of what?' and Sally said she didn't know. What was new about this communication was that this expression of anxiety was not couched in her usual autistic, geographical, concrete and physical terms, but in mental and emotional ones. She would in the past have instead complained about the shape or texture of some object in the room. I would suggest that she had discovered two things: first, that her object after all need not be so smooth, that her good object was grippable and her bad object escapable; second, that she herself had arms for gripping, and that this bodily awareness may have implied a corresponding awareness that she had interpersonal and mental means of holding on to the therapist's attention and of getting something across to her. She showed that she could make her therapist wait while she formulated and then communicated her feeling of fear without even having to produce or make up a reason or justification. In later sessions, she spoke of hanging on with all her might and, in fact, became much better able to come out of and stay out of her state of autistic withdrawal.

Segal points out that the three essential features of the manic defence are triumph, omnipotent control and contempt. I would suggest that in this piece of clinical material, what may look like triumph over the object and omnipotent control of it may, in fact, demonstrate a growing and delighted realization in a depressed child that the object is, after all, within reach, within one's grasp. This may imply pleasure about potency rather than triumph about omnipotence. Sally's discovery of the power of her arms to pull herself up (and of the corresponding ego functions) is not dissimilar to Robbie's pride in the discovery of the bones and muscles inside him that made him move. Both autistic children had felt helpless and immobilized and confronted with an inaccessible object. Their discovery of new powers and a sense of agency and control may not involve triumph over the object, as in the manic defence, but a pride shared with an accessible and pleasable object, possibly indicative of the manic position. A 'Hallelujah' is very different from a roar of triumph.

So far I have not dealt with the third feature outlined by Segal (1964): contempt. Winnicott's term was 'disparagement' and Klein's 'devaluation'. I would suggest that, for some chronically depressed deprived children, an analysis of their object relations may imply the need for an additional term, one which conveys a lack or deficit in the capacity to value, not a refusal or defence. In some of these cases the child's depression is of the type where the object is over-valued and his self is under-valued. One little deprived boy, for example, was very identified with an ugly slimy slug. He was tremendously relieved when his therapist finally understood that he felt she felt that he was ugly. After that, he ceased drooling and dribbling, became much more tidy in his dress, and began to talk about a snail whose little house had magnetic powers which enabled it to attract the therapist to him. He had begun, I think, to feel valued by his object and by himself, but this new valuing of himself was not accompanied by any particular desire to devalue others.

In other cases, the blanket of depression and deficit in the capacity to value is even wider: the child values neither himself nor his object, not necessarily because he desires to devalue something previously recognized as good, but out of a more chronic sense of emptiness and lack of worthwhileness, meaning or point. When such children perk up, this may be either because they are excited to discover an ideal object (see Chapter 9) or because they are thrilled to discover new powers and valuable qualities in themselves. Such discoveries of a new self should not be confused with pathological narcissism or with states marked by envy and contempt. The children may want, at such moments, not to show off their new achievements, but to show them and share them. They often need help in making the distinction between showing to give pleasure and showing off to stimulate envy and cause pain.

Sometimes the child who is emerging from the state of being swallowed up by the object as described by Melanie Klein and Paula Heimann – that is, from impotence and helplessness - does feel a great sense of relief when the super-ego load lightens a little (both in Klein 1946). A depressed, obsessional, inhibited patient of mine named John decided one day not to start one of his usual and what he called 'unoriginal' obsessional rituals in the session. He decided simply to say something that he called 'original'. He meant that he was going to take a chance and free associate. What came into his mind was that the other day he had been playing football with a friend. They hadn't had their usual leather football, they had had to use a lighter plastic ball. When they kicked it into the air, he said, 'You couldn't even tell where it was going to come down, because the wind kept catching it.' Strangely enough that had been 'fun' (he practically put the word in quotes). It is a word, I think, I had heard him use only once before. The story conveyed exactly the way in which he himself had managed to let his thoughts take wing and go where they would, and I was struck by how unusual that was for him. This is clearly not what Winnicott called 'contemptuous levity' nor 'defiance of gravity'. It is more like a beginning light-heartedness that can free the child from his over-valuation of the object and from being overburdened by it. A few months before, after a comment I had made about his obsessional rituals and defences, this same boy said in a lively way, 'Imagine, I don't have much homework tonight!' That, he said, was a very nice feeling. He kept going over this fact in a rather surprised way. I pointed out that he seemed to feel less burdened this evening, that his burden seemed lighter. A moment later he went over and measured himself against the box in my room to show me how tall he had become. I said that it seemed he was suddenly feeling big enough and strong enough to cope with this thing called homework, instead of feeling, as he usually did, that it was too big and overwhelming a burden. (He had seemed, quite literally, to stand taller when he had suddenly felt his load lighter.)

John was a neurotic child, but it is probably the case that many autistic and deprived children, or any child who has been clinically depressed for most of his life or despairing about his own goodness or his own ability to get in touch with a good object, may discover that, after all, his shrivelled heart has recovered greenness. He is able to reach out to light and warmth, to take heart, take courage and even, sometimes, to walk on air. The child may develop an increasing sense of his own psychological powers, exactly in the way the baby learning to grasp, sit up, stand and walk gets an increasing sense of his bodily powers. In the psychological realm it is important to ascertain when such a sense involves much needed respite from burdens and gravity and when it involves, or is in danger of becoming, a dangerous heady flight which may lead to a crash. The distinction, though important, is often difficult to make.

11

SOME PRECURSORS OF REPARATION IN THE HARDENED DESTRUCTIVE CHILD

In Chapter 3, I mentioned the session where Robbie began to mourn the normal childhood he never had and to complain about other people who never sorted stale things from the fresh. The session followed his development of 'backbone', and both, I believe, followed my developing a much firmer attitude towards his perverse and repetitive preoccupations. Although the autistic child is very different from the psychopathic child, the apparently conscience-free addiction to the child's own preferred way of doing things is similar. The indifference is similar, as are some of the technical problems for the therapist.

Robbie's perverse addiction to his beloved repetitive sickening words and phrases has, strangely enough, something in common with the psychopathic child's addiction to cruelty and cruel power: before they can get in touch with more caring concerned parts of themselves, they have first to take other people more seriously. Robbie hardly knew they existed; the psychopathic child may know they are there but view them as beneath his contempt and interest. I am oversimplifying greatly, but in general, with a certain sort of hardened grandiose destructive child, it is useless for the therapist to appeal to the child's better self until he has developed some capacity for respect. Such respect for the object seems to have to do with its capacity to look evil in the eye without retaliation or moral outrage, and also without blinking (see Symington 1980). The moment when the child finally feels he may have gone too far does not betoken depressive-position concern, but it may indicate a sobering down from a grandiose destructive state where anything goes. This may be connected with a new-found respect for, and possibly even a productive fear of, the object. This does not mean

138

one should try to frighten one's patients, but it is important to understand that the more conscious and sobering fear of having gone too far with some destructiveness is preferable to the unconscious split-off terrors he was undoubtedly prey to before. It is a hard and disturbing education to treat such children, and I think that therapists who have had very sadistic or perverted patients either change or go under. They do not emerge unscathed.

The Hinshelwood *Dictionary of Kleinian Thought* points out that, long before Melanie Klein formulated her theory of the role of reparation in the depressive position, she had noted the significance of children's distress over their own aggression, of their pity for wounded and damaged objects, and of their desire to restore and help such figures (Hinshelwood 1989). When eventually formulated, the theory stated that the move from the paranoid-schizoid position to the depressive position signalled both a change in the type of anxiety to which the individual was prone and in the quality of his relationships with his objects. In the paranoid-schizoid position, it is fear on behalf of the self; in the depressive position, it is concern on the object's behalf. In the paranoid-schizoid position, love for the good object and hatred for the bad object are separated and split apart; in the depressive position, the person becomes aware that both sets of feelings belong to one whole object (Klein 1935). Klein stressed that such integration was an achievement, that it was different from ambivalence and from confusion, and that it arose only when loving feelings were strong enough to overcome hatred. She also seems to have distinguished two different parts played by the love in its encounter and struggle with hatred: first, a preventive and sparing one, where it acts as a check and restraint on hatred, and second, a reparative one, where there is a wish to repair damage already done and not prevented (1937; 1940).

To my mind, the concept of reparation involves a huge advance both in the theory and in the meta-theory of psychoanalysis. I wish to explore some implications of this theoretical and meta-theoretical advance, and also to consider the possibility of some developmental and psychological antecedents of reparation.

Reparation has been seen as inextricably bound up with the developments of the depressive position, but I would suggest that reparative activity can be found to have precursors of a 'pre-reparative' or, to use a better word, 'pleasing' or 'pleasure-giving' (or, for that matter, even placating) kind in the paranoid-schizoid position. Hinshelwood suggests that Klein distinguishes between three types of reparation: 1) manic reparation which carries a note of triumph over the damaged object (the person may repair an object felt to be damaged by someone else, so there is no need for guilt, for example), and this does not achieve real reparation; 2) obsessional reparation which has more to do with the placating of a bad object than concern for a good one; 3) true reparation grounded in love and respect for the object which results in creative achievements. Clearly, the distinctions between the three types are vital, but Klein's need to draw her readers' attention to the differences between false and true reparation may have led to a situation where manic and obsessional reparation tend to be regarded as defences against, and therefore somehow inferior to, the true reparation which occurs at the depressive position. The danger, in my view, is that they may not be seen as capable of being developmental achievements in their own right (see Steiner (1979) for an exception). I would suggest that these 'false' types of reparation may, especially in the case of borderline psychotic, deprived, egoless or delinquent children, involve important transitional stages in the development towards true reparation. I would add that they may draw some of their strength and power from something which has little to do with guilt, or even with love's reaction to hatred, but simply with love's wish to express itself by giving pleasure to the loved object. This implies some growth and development of idealization in the paranoid-schizoid position. I shall return later to this pre-reparative, pre-guilt function of love.

Hanna Segal elaborates Klein's distinction between types of reparation: she discusses the difference between the dreams of one patient manically denying his depression about a damaged object and another patient acknowledging the damage and attempting to repair it. The first patient dreamt he saw a house on fire and collapsing, but he drove past it, thinking it had little importance. The second patient dreamt that she was putting together a jigsaw puzzle representing a house in a landscape. The associations led to many past situations, particularly in her parental home. The putting together of the puzzle stood, says Segal, for the analytic process which was restoring and recreating a shattered internal world. It also stood for some creative work the patient was undertaking in her outside life. Segal says:

> The working through of the depressive position in normal development depends on the capacity to make reparation. When the infant feels that in his hatred he has destroyed his good external and internal object, he experiences, not only an intense feeling of guilt and loss, but also pining and a longing to restore the lost, loved object externally and internally, and to recreate the lost harmony and wellbeing. He mobilises all his love and creativity to that end. It is this reparative drive that, in the Kleinian view, is the most important source of mental growth and creativity.
>
> (Segal 1964: 15)

Segal seems to be speaking of the drive or urge towards reparation in two ways here: one as arising out of guilt and loss, that is, as an effect; the other as a causal agent facilitating a further working-through of the depressive position. Klein herself, in 'Love, guilt and reparation', also refers to the way in which the drive to make reparation helps in situations of despair. She writes: 'Normally the drive to make reparation can keep at bay the despair arising out of feelings of guilt, and then hope will prevail, in which case the baby's love and his desire to make reparation are unconsciously carried over to new objects of love and interest' (Klein 1937: 342).

Psychoanalysis has taught us that we can deal with the problem of guilt in a variety of ways: by denying it, projecting it, obsessionally undoing the guilty act; or we can repair an object not damaged by us as a means of avoiding guilt; or we can become so overwhelmed by guilt that we fall into a state of despair and give up; or we can repair and try to put right and restore the damaged object itself. All of these strategies for avoidance and evasion – all but the last, that is – are in a way perfectly consistent with a mechanistic view of the psyche. I am thinking here of a mechanism as something which is self-limiting, something which produces, say, alterations in the geographical position or in the means of expression of an energy source, but nothing more. Energy, that is, may be transferred from one place to another, but the amount of energy none the less is constant. Repression, denial, projection, manic reparation and, for that matter, sublimation do not resolve guilt, they avoid it. They produce no fundamental change in the personalities concerned. Real reparation is a truly different concept which, unlike these others, allows for development, growth and, most important of all, genuine change.

Klein herself insisted that reparation was not a reaction formation – not, that is, just the other side of a reversible coin like denial or undoing (1935: 265). She listed the various phantasies which represent the attempt to repair the disaster created through one's own neglect or destructiveness: for example, preserving the loved object from the attacks of bad objects, putting the dispersed bits of it back together again, bringing what has been killed back to life. Money-Kyrle suggested another type, 'negative reparation' – in other words, ceasing to do the bad thing one has been doing repetitively. This is very important with delinquent or very sadistic patients, and I am certain it is an important pre-stage of reparation (Money-Kyrle 1977).

In real reparation, certain consequences of reparation follow which may not be reducible to their prior elements. A mechanistic change such as obsessional undoing is different from the changes of state that occur where processes (even chemical processes) are concerned. An object restored after acknowledged damage is not the same as before the damage was done, nor is the subject. The re-introjection of the repaired object, where acknowledgement of damage and guilt is real, is different from any previous introjection of an undamaged object. A repaired object, however perfect and accurate the restoration, is fundamentally different from an undamaged one. I believe there is apparently disagreement between the Florentine and Sienese schools of art restorers as to whether it is better to try to restore the painting exactly as it was when it was made or to try to restore it so as to include some of the ageing and fading processes that people in the last century or two would have been familiar with. It is an interesting controversy, and it is remarkable how touching and beautiful damaged frescoes may be.

It is also interesting how different are biblical descriptions of the Deity's relation with his righteous children from the descriptions of his forgiveness of the sinner. Money-Kyrle distinguished between the type of persecuting conscience or god who demands penance and propitiation and the more depressive god, who speaks more in sorrow than in anger and who is felt to grieve at his children's moral failure rather than threaten punishment (Money-Kyrle 1978). Where the sorrowful object can become the repaired and restored object, the possibility of real change and growth can take place. This is not simply a question of two types of morality nor even only a question of two different types of object relation: the theory of reparation as a means of working through the depressive position brings a different meta-theory in its train, a theory based on process rather than mechanism, and on change and growth rather than diversion and fundamental sameness.

This problem of reductionism in science, especially in speculation about the nature of mind, intelligence and the brain, and in the relation between them, has been brilliantly tackled by Douglas Hofstader in his book *Gödel, Escher, Bach*. Hofstader is a mathematician trained in theoretical physics, who is also a linguist and a music lover. He lectures and researches in computer science and is particularly interested in the subject of artificial intelligence, although one gets the impression from the book that his work on AI has only increased his respect and awe for the complexity of the mind and brain. He begins with a fascinating dissertation on Bach's *Musical Offering*, paying particular attention to the *Canon Per Tonos*:

> It has three voices, but what makes this canon different from any other is that, when it concludes or rather seems to conclude, it is no longer in the key of C minor, which is the key it began in, but now is in D minor. Somehow Bach has contrived to modulate, change keys, right under the listener's nose, and it is so constructed that this ending ties smoothly onto the beginning again. Thus one can repeat the process and return in the key of E only to join again to the beginning . . . .
> One would expect after successive modulations, which seem to be leading the ear to remote provinces of tonality, to be hopelessly away from the starting key, but, in fact, magically, after six such modulations, the original key of C minor has been restored. All the voices are exactly one octave higher.
>
> (Hofstadter 1981: 10)

This is the first example of what Hofstader calls 'strange loops'. He says the strange loop phenomenon occurs whenever, by moving upwards or downwards through the levels of some hierarchical system, we unexpectedly find ourselves right back where we started. He believes the work of the Dutch graphic artist, Escher, contains the most beautiful and powerful visual realization of this notion of strange loops. Later in the book there is another example, the Central Dogma of Typogenetics: he points out that strands define enzymes via the typogenetic code, the DNA code; in turn enzymes act back on the strands which gave rise to them, yielding new strands: 'An enzyme is a translation of a strand and contains, therefore, the same information as a strand, only in a different form, in particular, in an active form. New information gets created by the shunting of symbols in strands' (p. 513). He also points out that this two-way street which links upper and lower levels of typogenetics shows that, in fact, neither strands nor enzymes can be thought of as being on a higher level than the other, because they each act upon the other in this kind of spiralling way, like in the ever-rising canon.

Melanie Klein makes clear that, in conditions where love is stronger than hate and there is guilt about what hate has done to the loved object, the patient who feels capable of reparation wishes to change the damaged object into a repaired object by some healing method or other. The point I wish to stress is that the re-introjection of that repaired object changes the self and changes the internal world and the love is then strengthened even more. Klein herself remarks again and again on the strengthening of the ego and the growth that takes place in the internal world as a result of this kind of reparative activity.

Much has been written concerning the sorts of conditions in the self which interfere with the initiation of this benign circle: excessive hatred and persecution or excessive defences against them, excessive guilt or defences against guilt. Of equal importance are the qualities and conditions in the object itself which may facilitate or prevent the initiation going through this benign circle or strange loop. What precisely do we mean, for example, when we speak of an irreparable object or irreparable situation? The balance of love and hate and guilt in the self must be considered, but so, too, must certain qualities of the object connected with its reparability. Does this factor of reparability in the equation have any agent power? The wish to make reparation somewhere is also coloured by the belief in, if not the probability of reparability, nor even the hope of reparability, at least the possibility of reparability. I think that, where the situation is clear-cut and love and belief in goodness well established, the condition of reparability may seem irrelevant simply because it can be taken for granted. But in many iller patients such considerations do sometimes seem to tip the balance between whether the child makes a move forward into some kind of benign circle, however tiny its beginning, or settles for the old, repetitive, pathological patterns.

I am reminded of an extremely sadistic, grandiose and ruthless boy, who was riding roughshod over his whole family and was also violent, delinquent and awkward with his therapist. Shortly before the summer break, the parents told the consulting psychiatrist that the child wanted a kitten to play with during the summer. The psychiatrist and parents came to the conclusion that the boy was not ready for this, that he might do damage to the animal and so produce guilt in himself, and they decided not to let him have one. Now there was, as I remember, no evidence whatever that he had ever been cruel to animals and, of course, no-one can say whether or not that was the right decision clinically for that patient. It would have been a gamble either way. But what I want to discuss is the somewhat dangerous theoretical notion that sadism in one situation implies sadism in another. A good theory of splitting should leave room for the possibility that the impulse to reparation has to start somewhere, and if it starts small, even towards the 'wrong' object, yet meets with success and is nurtured, it may set going one of the benign circles I have been describing.

In 'Love, guilt and reparation,' Melanie Klein points out that school life may provide a field for new experiments in relationship to people. With the large choice of children available to select from – larger than the number of siblings in an ordinary-sized family – the child may find one or two children who respond better, she says, to his special make-up than his brothers and sisters do. These new friendships may give him an opportunity to revise and improve the early relationships with the brothers and sisters which may have been unsatisfactory. Klein goes on to point out that the actual relation to the brothers and sisters may then improve. Now, one could speak of the child's wish to care for the kitten as a type of manic reparation, in the sense that it might have been better for charity to begin at home and for him to begin treating his family better. This might even be an accurate description of the manic mood and state in which the new activities might begin. But if they succeed and the outcome is successful, then it may make it easier for the child to return more hopefully to a new relation to the original object. In fact, Klein adds that 'the new companionships prove to the child that he is able to love and is lovable, that love and goodness exist, and this is unconsciously felt also as a proof that he can repair harm which he has done to others in his imagination or in actual fact' (Klein 1937: 328).

A very demanding child told her therapist that, when she had

145

been behaving particularly horribly at home, her mother would say, despairingly, that she herself would probably end up in a psychiatric hospital if this went on. It is interesting to speculate whether this mother ever really felt able to invite reparation, rather than simply try in an impotent way to increase the child's guilt – a strategy, which, of course, led nowhere. She could stimulate guilt, but seemed unable to deal firmly with her child and to set the kind of limits and make the kind of demands that would have helped her daughter to develop some restraint. The object's reparability in the sense of its receptivity to the reparative impulse, in however minimal or disguised or displaced form, is especially important for work with borderline patients where there is despair, conscious or unconscious, about this issue.

I would like now to enquire into some possible further sources of the impulse to reparation. So far I have been suggesting that the balance between love and hate in relation to guilt are not the only relevant conditions. Klein writes in 'Some theoretical conclusions regarding the emotional life of the infant', 'Since the tendency to make reparation ultimately derives from the life instinct, it draws on libidinal fantasies and desires' (1952: 74). Now, in what way may the tendency to make reparation derive from the life instinct? I would suggest that, if the tendency to make reparation implies the wish to make good a damaged object, this impulse may, at an earlier stage of development, be partly nourished by and based on the tendency to make better an already good object. A useful model for this notion is the baby's early smile. It is well known the delight this brings to the parents. Workers such as Brazelton and Stern have studied the intensity contours in mother's and baby's reciprocal interactions over time, and the positive feedback loops which describe the way each contributes small increments to the mounting intensity, how it decreases, mounts again, decreases and so on (Brazelton *et al.* 1974; Stern 1985). I do not know if they have studied the baby's smile as a cure for the mother's depression, but it is a phenomenon well known to close observers of infants. However, they seem to be describing the smile that is used not to cheer up a depressed mother nor to bring to life a dead object, but to give additional pleasure to a possibly already pleased and alive object. It is these moments of 'pleasing' or 'pleasure-giving', which so many borderline and deprived patients seem to be unable to conceive of as being within their powers. When the normal child, for example, takes his first solid food, or uses the potty for the first

146

time, or uses the spoon, or learns to walk, or in the early weeks simply returns his mother's gaze, or gets a good hold on the breast, I believe he senses in the meeting not only his capacity to receive goodness and pleasure, but his capacity to give it.

I used the destructive boy and Klein's schoolchildren as examples of situations where reparation may begin in a split-off area of the mind, even entailing reparation of a manic kind, but which can nevertheless start a strange loop or benign circle or positive feedback that may eventually enable real reparation to be set in motion. I would now like to describe situations of an even more pathological nature, where reparation and its conditions, love and guilt, hardly seem to be in evidence anywhere in the material. It is easy with very destructive patients to miss moments which may actually represent not the type of positive precursor or reparation I have just described in the normal infant, but perhaps a pre-precursor. Sometimes, the simple fact that the patient has begun to try to be like the therapist in some way is an important precursor. It does not seem reparative in any obvious sense, but the beginnings of an attempt at identification may signal some belief that the object is receptive to development, receptive to being given pleasure. Often when a patient plucks up courage to reveal his disturbed baby self, it is partly because he is humble enough to be in touch with dependency. But it may also be because he is brave enough and confident enough to feel he can give someone the pleasure of seeing him let go a little.

An even earlier precondition for reparation may have something to do with the sense of the going-on-being of the self in time and, for that matter, of the object in time. A very destructive embittered child, Lee, born prematurely and brain-damaged to a drug-addict mother, lived most of the first year of his life in hospital. He had numerous nurses for caretakers and was always on the edge of death, with frequent resuscitations and other intrusive medical interventions, such as lumbar punctures, into his tiny being. He has right side hemiplegia and major learning and behavioural problems. Until recently, he has destroyed everything he has ever made, and particularly enjoys destroying his own and other people's hopes. He has mild epileptic fits and, although his life has been saved, his psyche has seemed profoundly ruined. He has an extremely cynical, hardened, but at times superficially charming approach to other people, which is a way both of expressing and hiding his deep despair about whether or not anyone could stand him. He sometimes manages to charm strangers, and he plays upon his physical

147

disability. But those who know him well often feel profound disgust at his lies and tricks, cruel mockeries and contempt. Recently, he has shown signs of the faintest respect for his therapist who has begun to be aware both of his perverse mockery and also of his genuine despair – the result of major work on her counter-transference feelings of disillusionment and hopelessness about whether or not she could ever get through to an undamaged part of him. He has masturbated less in the sessions and been less frenziedly destructive. He has even begun to colour a picture with agonizing care not to 'go over the lines'. This has taken six days, and the therapist has interpreted his change in behaviour and his wish not to go 'over the line' with her too. She has seen his obsessional reparation not as a defence against true reparation but, instead, as a development beyond a despairing abandonment to destructiveness.

On the day when the colouring in of the drawing seemed nearly finished, Lee could not bear the suspense and began rocking his chair more and more violently against the table, saying 'Look what I am doing!' He ended up by falling forward, and cutting himself (his disability leaves him very vulnerable to imbalance). Although clearly frightened, shocked and in pain, he kept insisting, 'I don't care'. He seemed to have felt himself to be in great danger as he neared the end of the drawing, partly because he was terrified that he would ruin it as usual, partly because he was even more terrified about what would happen if he didn't. Finally, after recovering from his bump, he returned to the picture and finished his colouring. He then ran wildly about the room shouting, 'I've finished', in an over-excited but also genuine way. The therapist felt that his satisfaction was genuine and poignant but that his exultation was joyless. She and I discussed the possibility that this was not so much because he was denying depression, but because he could hardly take in, and certainly not express, genuine relief, genuine pride and genuine joy. He said, wonderingly, that he had never finished work at school and it was clear that this experience had been both very important and very strange and depersonalizing. He could not really believe it himself. He was, after all, a child whose very breath of life, his oxygen supply, had been in doubt many times in the first year of his life; the idea of continuity, flow, completion, satisfaction on that elementary level was probably foreign to him. Both his sense of his object and his sense of his self seemed to be infinitely interruptable. I think something a little more solid started to grow as he began to sense the steadiness in his therapist's refusal to be seduced by his cynical charm, her refusal to reject him for his destructiveness, and also her willingness to be alert to his despair and his tiny beginnings of straightness, directness and hope. Lee's colouring within the lines is different from reparation in a less desperate and more mature child, but even in its obsessionality, and the later wild confused exultation, it may well have signalled an important precursor: the sense of continuity and steadfastness of both self and object.

I said at the beginning that Klein's wish to show that manic reparation and obsessional reparation were quite different from true reparation may have led to a situation where they tend to be seen as defences against the need for true reparation, rather than as being developmental achievements, of however limited a nature, in their own right.

A highly destructive, cynical boy, Jasper, had autistic features of a particularly perverse and maddening kind. He was a child who took a cruel relish in driving his family and schoolmates and therapist crazy with frustration, disappointment and boredom. He could time the moment of a destructive act so perfectly that it would have emotional impact on someone just at the moment either when their hopes of his meaning well had begun to rise or when their patience was at absolute breaking point. One day, after about fifteen minutes of the usual sadistic treatment of his therapist, someone knocked on the playroom door by mistake, and startled them both. The intruder withdrew before being seen and the session continued, but with a difference. Jasper began frantically to try to repair a previously broken window frame that, in fact, really required the skilled hand and tools of an expert. He insisted that he 'knew how to do it' with sellotape. In one way, this can be seen as a piece of manic reparation, because the child may feel somewhere that it is not the window that needs repairing, it is his relationship with his therapist and other human beings subjected to his torture. But suppose we consider what it means for this boy to move from a cruelly grandiose and contemptuously sadistic state of mind to one where a moment of shock and fear has sobered him a little, then a piece of manic reparation is indeed a development. It may not achieve the depressive position, but it may signal a step on the way towards it. The child had had a shock and perhaps had felt that someone was feeling he was going a bit too far with his destructiveness, and someone had had enough. He may have had a sense that something needed mending but had not been ready to know exactly what. Thus, although the repair has both an obsessional placating element and a manic denial of dependence, it is less carelessly grandiose and less manic than the previous total abandonment to destructiveness earlier in the session. The patient's feeling that 'something better get mended fast' – a cross between fear and guilt – needs to be noted so that the patient's fleeting moment of awareness does not get lost. Such patients can return all too easily to the old hardened state.

I have tried to suggest two things in this chapter: that the Kleinian theory of reparation has both major theoretical and meta-theoretical implications, and that, although it is usually seen as inextricably tied to the depressive position, it has its precursors in the paranoid-schizoid position – in, for example, the belief in the continuity of being of self and object, and even in certain types of 'false' manic and obsessional reparation. Attention to such precursors is important in the work with autistic, borderline and psychopathic children.

12

CHILD SEXUAL ABUSE
The need to remember and the need to forget

Robbie's deep unwillingness and total inability to forget his endless stories and favourite phrases have given me a belated but healthy respect for processes of forgetting. I am aware that I paid far too much heed to his repetitions in the early years of his treatment, especially when he was talking about an experience that I knew had been disturbing to him. I told myself he really needed to go on talking about it. But his particular manner of talking did not involve a real or useful remembering. Nor was he really processing the experience or digesting it. The process of coming to terms with pain, loss, trauma or abuse is complicated, lengthy, not always visible and certainly not necessarily verbalized. Robbie, of course, was not an abused child, but he was extremely traumatized by the two abrupt separations at a young age. Whereas the more mildly traumatized patient, whose disorder is affecting his personality on the neurotic level, may need to remember the trauma in order to forget, the more damaged children whose trauma is more severe and more chronic may need to forget the trauma in order to be able to remember.

I would now like to explore some of the steps in the process of recovery from child sexual abuse. Recovery can be a long slow process, particularly for the children who have been abused chronically at a young age. Disclosure should lead to protection from abuse, but the treatment, and for that matter the disclosure itself, may be being undertaken with a child who has hardly got a notion of non-abuse. Society's feeling that something is changed and resolved by the disclosure may not be shared by the child. What the abuse has meant for him and meant to him may be very different from its meaning for us. He may, for example, be too emotionally and cognitively blunted for anything much to have any meaning at all. Or he may have been corrupted himself and have become fascinated with abuse or an abuser himself. He may fear the abuser far more than he fears the abuse. Or he may feel deep love for the abusing figure and this love may be stronger than his fear or distaste for the abuse. Or he may have all of these difficulties. In any case, our notions of protection, of justice, of care, may be quite unreal to him. It is surely the right of every child to take such concepts for granted, if only in the depths of his mind, but the psychotherapy may sometimes have to begin at the beginning by taking note of their absence.

In thinking about possible stages in the recovery process, I want to begin with some of the literature on Post-Traumatic Stress Disorder. In his classic book *The Nightmare*, Ernest Hartmann has suggested two major paths by which post-traumatic nightmares may or may not develop into the sometimes debilitating condition of PTSD: 'The first is the path of normal healing and resolution. Here, although the traumatic material stands out as distinct and disturbing for a few weeks or months, it is gradually thought about, fantasized about, and dreamt about; it is handled by the usual integrative process', which he likens to 'knitting up the ravell'd sleeve of care'. The second major path is that of encapsulation, where the traumatic material does not merge with ordinary dream content and does not become integrated into the remainder of normal life. Both Hartmann, and Pynoos, whose work with children who witness catastrophe is of some relevance, stress that therapy or counselling should be offered during or soon after the acute phase. Pynoos notes that a year or even less may be too late (Hartmann 1984: 215; Pynoos and Eth 1985).

However, the very notion of trauma assumes some degree of previous trauma-free development, and, in the case of abused children, some notion of non-abuse, of self-respect and self-valuation. There is, unfortunately, a third major path which is far more serious than encapsulation: this is where the trauma begins to colour the whole of the personality. Pynoos suggests that one of the subtle ways in which exposure to extreme violence may affect children is through traumatic influences on ongoing developmental processes, such as memory, cognition, learning and, of course, personality. As I said, both writers stress that the therapy should be given at an early phase. For the type of reconstructive, short-term, cathartic and uncovering type of therapy they mostly have in mind, I am sure they are right. The fact is, however, that many of the chronically sexually abused children arrive in therapists' hands long after the event. Their condition may require a rather different kind of treatment, one which is more closely related to modern psychoanalytic definitions of the curative factors than to older theories which depend on reconstruction and uncovering of lost or repressed memories (Strachey 1934). I am suggesting almost a theory of forgetting, as opposed to a theory of remembering, although I am aware that this is a gross and indeed false over-simplification.

I have already sketched these newer ideas in earlier chapters. The older theory of the curative process arises from the notion of defence, conflict and resolution. Grandiosity, say, could be seen as a defence against insecurity, manic states a defence against depression, bravery a defence against fear. Painful truths needed to be 'faced'. The notion that we must help the abused child to 'come to terms with his abuse' by helping him to remember it, derives in part from this set of ideas. Psychoanalysis owes a good deal to what one author has called the 'unmasking trend' in the late Romantic movement, and such unmaskings have afforded huge relief and freedom to many inhibited and withheld people. Yet in the work with abused children it is usually they who succeed in unmasking the workers. Their rescuers often have little to teach them about human evil, selfishness, greed and lust. Their task is somewhat different.

I would suggest that a thought becomes thinkable often by a very slow gradual process, a process which cannot be rushed. The implications for the question of how the abused child may be helped to come to terms with his abuse may be that the 'remembering' may involve a million tiny integrations taking place, each one under conditions where other aspects of the abuse, other integrations, can afford to be forgotten. The abuse may have to be explored one aspect at a time; for example, what does it feel like to be told to lie down and have to do something when you have no say in the matter? What does it feel like to be told to undress when you don't feel like it and have no say in the matter? What does it feel like to be able to issue those instructions to someone else? How do they take it? All this may be explored via a doll's experience and, in many instances, that is exactly where it should be allowed to remain.

The trauma may colour a multitude of different aspects of the patient's personality. What does it feel like, for example, to be told you have to do your homework when you don't feel like it? The child's irritability and sensitivity to the least sign of intrusiveness may seem as though it were a 'displacement' from the original trauma. But is, in fact, 'displaced' the right word, if 'displace' is used to imply (it need not) that the material is appearing in the wrong place and should be interpreted back to its rightful place – i.e. in discussion of the trauma or abuse suffered by the child? The new, apparently innocent and non-traumatic place may be a safer place if it enables the child to think about his trauma in manageable digestible portions or what Strachey called 'minimal doses' (1934). Should the therapist be trying, in the treatment, to get her patient to think about the experience in its totality, or should she stick more closely to the child's own pace? Freud said of the work of mourning that each single memory had to be dealt with and mourned and relinquished (1917). In the same way, maybe each single aspect of the abuse, the bits and pieces of the experience, particularly if it was chronic, may need to be digested one step at a time. My guess is that this is particularly true for the children who have been abused at a very young age and have also suffered mental and cognitive damage. Such shattered, blunted children may need the pieces of themselves to come together in order to have a sense of I, of YOU, of HE long before they can comprehend: 'He – someone – did that to me, and I felt he shouldn't have.' That statement itself requires an enormous degree of mental development. At the very least, it requires the existence of mental equipment with which to think about experience. The treatment may have to start by facilitating the building up of this equipment.

In the same way, ideas concerning the need for the analyst to contain unwanted feelings for the patient for long periods of time are important for the dealing with powerful projections (Joseph 1978). A more mechanistic view of 'defences' such as projection, reversal or displacement sometimes tended to carry the implication that that which was projected needed, almost by definition, to be returned to its rightful home, and so did that which was reversed or displaced. Yet when should the move away from the original experience be treated as a dangerous evasion (which it often is) and when should it be respected as an attempt to explore the experience in a safer, more tolerable context? When the abused child starts abusing us in the counter-transference, when does the therapist remind him it is his abuse he is fleeing, and when does she remain silent, and comment only on the fact that he seems to be relishing doing this nasty thing to her? I do not, of course, mean literal sexual abuse of the therapist, although many children do try to invite abuse or to practise it on their therapist. I can think of several who have looked their therapist in the eye and said, coolly, 'Go on, do it to me! You know you really want to!' But I was also thinking of the children who masturbate in front of the therapist, not because they are any longer really absorbed in the excitement of the masturbation, but because they wish to push into someone else the shock and outrage they were not allowed to express, nor even to feel. In the past, I think the psychoanalytical therapist might have felt it necessary to remind the child that it was his own outrage he was projecting. Now there is greater understanding that the child may need that experience contained by someone else who can stand it better than he can. This may have to go on for some time, months or even years perhaps, until the experience is less overwhelming and less indigestible.

I would like to give some clinical examples of children who are at what seem to me to be progressively more advanced stages of development. I should make it clear that I am not suggesting that all abused children go through this progression, for in fact many are not as ill as the ones I shall begin with. I am describing not stages but what I suspect may be necessary conditions for some degree of normal development to get going. Occasionally, these conditions that clinicians talk about do follow in orderly progression in a single case, but the human mind is so complicated, with so many factors at work, both internally and flooding in from the environment, that there are leaps and regressions and sidesteps which disturb and disrupt any concept of orderly progression. I am suggesting these simply as a possibly useful ordering principle.

The first child is a 6-year-old girl, Sandra, who, at the beginning of treatment, was thought to be retarded. She had the mental functioning of an 18-month-old baby. She had had a difficult birth, and was born floppy and blue. She had been a passive quiet baby. She possessed very few words when she started three times weekly treatment. She had been sexually abused anally and genitally – mostly anally – for a long period of time when she was 4 by a cohabitee of mother's. She was still in nappies. This child's play was extremely fragmentary and fragmented: for example, she would take out and look at particular dolls or objects, sometimes attempt to name them, but even when she succeeded, she simply put them down again. There was no sequential symbolic play. Nothing really happened to the dolls, nor did they make anything happen. But one theme did begin to recur: the dolls kept being told, 'Lie down!' That was all; nothing followed – just that. Early on it tended to be the little girl doll who had to lie down; later, it was the man doll. She began, instead of simply breaking the plasticine into pieces, to push it, make marks on it and push into it with her finger. She was nowhere near using the plasticine to make something, but what she was doing was making a mark, her mark, on it, and in it, and this seemed to delight her. She had also begun getting a bit rougher with the man doll. I should mention that she had shown considerable improvement at school where there was a move to change her diagnosis from retardation to autism, and that was being investigated.

What was interesting to me was the notion that such a fragmented child could maybe explore only the fragments of her experience, a fragment at a time. First, 'Liedownness'. Perhaps, also, she had to explore the feeling of what it was like to be able to push into plasticine, long before she could get hold, mentally, of what it had really felt like for her, how horrifying and infuriating, to have her body penetrated. At the moment, she may not have been able to allow the fragments, 'lie down' and 'be penetrated', and, for that matter, 'me' to come together. I believed the therapist should follow her pace, but explore each fragment with her by paying very close attention to what the child felt when she carried out this bit of play, and what she felt the doll felt. That way a real coming together could take place. I do not believe we can surgically stitch bits of the mind back together. Occasionally, we can assist the process, but mostly we have to let them grow back. The condition Sandra illustrates has to do with the problem of the degree of integration, or cognitive capacity, or, in psychoanalytic terms, ego and introjective equipment, a child has with which to think about the experience. This child had a long way to go.

Mr P had been treating a borderline schizophrenic boy named Alan. He lived in a children's home. He may have been sexually abused by his brother, but was very violent himself, so much so that, when he was fostered, he had to be sent back to the children's home. The school was finding it difficult to hold on to him. He had not yet been violent with his therapist, but talked to Mr P about the 'evil blighter' side of himself. Almost all of his communications were delivered in a dead, detached voice. He also had some very strange clang associations: a 'hole' can become a 'halo' and the 'halo' can become 'holy'. A few months into treatment, his weekly session began with his talking about God brainwashing and imprisoning the devil, and speaking as though he himself was this cruel God. The therapist's notes continue:

> Later on, he took an old drawing from his box and told me that, if I wanted to carry on filling it in later, then I could do so, that I was 'free as a bird', an expression that he used several times. He went on to explain to me, when I said something about this, that it was a *metaphor* and that a metaphor meant that a person *didn't really mean what he was saying*. He was trying to define a metaphor: he gave as an example that, if I were to hit him, he would say: 'You'll be dead for that', but he wouldn't actually mean that he would stab me. I said that I thought perhaps he did feel like stabbing me, but that also he might feel it but wouldn't necessarily do it. Also I said that feeling it didn't necessarily make him into a horrid person as he seemed to think . . . . A little later on, he talked of how he would fight his enemies at school (he gets into a lot of very vicious fights at school), and he would sort them out. I got the impression that, if somebody came along, he would feel frightened of them and then he would fight them. They would be angry, he would say to them: 'You can't take a joke' and they would then go off.

I want to draw attention in particular to the notion of metaphor and the idea of others who 'could not take a joke'. I think it would be quite important with such material to interpret *not* the child's wish to stab (not that Mr P did), but the child's *fear* that he will stab and, furthermore, his fear that not only he but his object, too, doesn't know the difference between a thought and an action. It seems to me that this boy certainly had a problem with his own violence, but even more of a problem with his *object*'s. He had said that his enemies couldn't take a joke. He was, I believe, searching desperately for an object that can contain and transform violent action into violent metaphor. Interpretations of an uncovering and unmasking type (which fortunately Mr P did not make), which tried to reveal Alan's violence to himself, would, I believe, have been heard by him as an amplification, escalation and accusation, rather than as a receptive containment of his wish to scale down his violent object relations.

Later he took the green car, which had previously always been full of baddies, and suddenly decided to place each of the three baddies in one of the three other cars, so that they could be controlled there. Then they could throw the green car over the cliff and get rid of it. It was an interesting model for some attempt to encapsulate and get hold of, through fragmentation or splitting or division, the overwhelming problem. In a later session, he drew a map of Bristol, full of boundaries which he then decided were too thin. He went over them and changed them to borders, which 'would be much thicker'. He made them much thicker, particularly the border between Avon and Gloucestershire. This was because 'in Gloucestershire crazy things happened. For example, three seconds could be ten minutes. People drove on the wrong side of the road. The bridge between Avon and Gloucestershire opens and closes very very fast.'

Alan seemed to be trying to strengthen the barrier which kept the crazy things out because he felt that they could come in and out with amazing unregulated rapidity. If the patient's symbol-forming function and alpha function is very weak, and if these functions are also inadequate in his internal object, it may be important for the therapist not to make interpretations which encourage symbolic equations, but rather interpretations that enable vital longed-for distinctions to be made. Then, maybe, real symbolic development may eventually begin to take place.

Kanter has pointed out in *The International Review of Psycho-analysis* (1984) that, with the increasing emphasis on the out-patient treatment and the rehabilitation of the schizophrenic patient, the concept of 'resocialization' is frequently utilized, but rarely defined or clarified. Perhaps, he suggests, this is the result of the lack of dialogue between the field of psychoanalysis and psychiatric rehabilitation. His paper attempts to bridge that gap, using a psychoanalytic developmental perspective that examines what he calls the 'unfolding intra-psychic and intra-personal processes' in adult chronic schizophrenics on a day unit. The developmental perspective focuses on the deficits in the patients' personalities, deficits which arise from 'inadequate negotiations of latency era tasks, especially as regards ego skills in relation to the extra familial social environment'. Kanter also insists that, when the schizophrenic from his day unit begins to have phantasies and shares phantasies with other people on the ward, even phantasies of the sick-joke type, this is a considerable step beyond hallucination. This seems not so far removed from Bion's idea of the process by which a beta element can become transformed into material suitable for dreaming or thinking. Kanter believes the boundary between a hallucination and a joke, however sick, needs to be respected.

In Sandra's case, I am suggesting the child cannot remember the abuse until she knows how to remember. In the case of Alan he may need to build up a sense of an object who is not a retaliating abuser and who knows the difference between a phantasy and a deed, before he himself can even begin to think about the real abuse and violence done to him. The child may have to begin the remembering in tolerable and safe conditions while he himself begins to forget a little and build up a non-abused aspect of his personality. One child was able to talk about the abuse for the first time, and really remember it, as well as his fear and finally even his outrage, only after some months of therapy when he realized his therapist protected him and enabled him to 'get past' some dangerous boys in the corridors leading to the school therapy room (Sinason 1986). While the abuse threatens from every side, remembering in the cathartic sense that Hartmann and Pynoos describe may be impossible.

A third condition or stage arises with the children who may indeed have begun to build up faith in a non-abusing world, or in children who anyway had a better start before the abuse and whose confidence has never been completely destroyed. But for this non-abused side to be strengthened, the child may have to be permitted at moments to forget. This may relate to some of the psychoanalytic thinking on the latency period. Dealing with children who have been awakened sexually during their pre-school years gives one a new respect for the 'calm' of the latency period. It is interesting to consider what happens when abused children begin to develop an interest in the non-sexual, non-abusing world. Like many of the improving psychotic and improving borderline psychotic children, as they become saner, they seem to have to be excessively defended against phantasy and symbol. Unlike the normal latency child who delights in jokes which make puns on words with toilet or sexual connotations, one child who was trying to give up his preoccupations with anal masturbation, could not see the joke. He had been anally penetrated regularly at the age of 2 and had, before treatment, become very perverted himself. Yet later, in treatment, he was almost sobbing the day he tried to tell his therapist about a 'bun' and the word 'bum' kept slipping out. At such moments, it is my view that the part of the personality that is trying to forget about the abuse may need more attention than the part that can't help remembering it. I do not mean that therapists should ever collude with attempts to deny what has happened, but they should try to distinguish between attempts to overcome and attempts to deny. It is easier said than done.

A little girl from a family of child prostitutes who used to describe herself as belonging in the gutter, after many years of treatment and much improvement, told her therapist that she was going to put her tadpoles into the pond in order that they should make some babies. The therapist asked how, and she said: 'well, they go there with their mate'. The therapist started to interpret the sexual content, but the child corrected her, and the therapist realized that the child was using the Cockney word – mate – to mean friend (Hunter 1986). It seems to me that that child had achieved a very important development, in that she was able to conceive that friendship and friendliness might have something to do with making babies. At that point, perhaps, the last thing she needed was sexual enlightenment and thoughts about physical intimacy. Concentration on a thought, a task, or a subject requires the focusing of attention, but it also requires the capacity to ignore other thoughts, tasks and subjects, the capacity to put aside those others. It also seems to require the willingness of thoughts, tasks, subjects to remain in the background and wait their turn, so it is also a sort of object relation with one's own thoughts.

The fourth stage or condition I want to describe concerns a situation where remembering and forgetting seem to occur side by side. Hartmann described carefully how the traumatic content gets handled by the usual healing integrative process, and so gets integrated into the rest of normal life. I wanted to give what seems to me an evocative and thought-provoking example of this by describing some drawings by a child who was abused once by her father at the age of 4 and several times again at age 8. The father regularly placed his penis in Catherine's mouth while stimulating her between the legs. Both parents had had periods of psychiatric hospitalization. However, the mother had managed to care for the children quite well during some of the periods when they were not in care. This child did not seem as damaged as the others I have described. In her early pictures in the first few months of treatment there were signs of a kind of irritable tension. Lines of force emanated, for example, from a dog's wagging tail as he stood tensely waiting for a cat to come down from a tree. The dog did not look particularly frightening, but the sense of urgency in him was palpable. On another occasion, Catherine drew a huge lighthouse, with rays of light coming from it, rising up between two steep hills. A ship was out at sea, and the picture was well executed and impressive. There were several noticeable features about the lighthouse: first, it looked extraordinarily like a phallus, dominant and compelling. But, whereas in the dog pictures the light came from the ceiling and the urgency came from the dog's tail, now, instead of wagging physical urgency and tension, the force field emanated from a light source – a very powerful, powerfully important and valued light, a protector of ships at sea. There may have been some integrative process at work here: perhaps some of the therapist's understanding and intelligence had been introjected and admired, perhaps the parents' love and determination to stay in contact with their children. It remained, however, a very phallic lighthouse and the hills seemed to resemble thighs. Remember that Catherine had been orally abused. At the time I first saw the drawings, what interested me was the technical point concerning latency: I thought the therapist should let the lighthouse be a lighthouse and not draw attention to its phallic properties. If Catherine developed a fascination with lighthouses that was a lot better for her than becoming a prostitute. But what about its phallic quality? Two other sexually abused children have spoken in ways which seem to imply that there can never be complete forgetting, not only because of the evil of the experience, but also because of its power. One child spoke about a flower that had been opened too soon (Sinason 1988). There is perhaps an awakening, sometimes to a powerful sensual experience which the child cannot help but remain in awe of. The situation is especially complicated where there remains deep love for an abusing parent. One would have to work with great delicacy at such moments to help the child to distinguish love from sexual perversion, and both from an almost worshipful attitude to sensuality. Chronic or regular abuse may come to permeate the child's whole being in ways that are highly complex and in no way easily, if ever, expunged. That lighthouse leaves many unanswered questions in my mind.

I have tried to suggest four possible conditions for the process of recovering from child sexual abuse. First, in order to remember usefully, it is necessary to be able to think and remember, and to put at least two thoughts and two feelings together. Second, the child may need to remember from a safe and protected and hopeful perspective, which may involve necessary 'displacements' and 'projections', or rather, replacements and perspectives. It may also involve first finding a non-abusing object and an object capable of keeping firm boundaries between deed and phantasy, action and metaphor. Third, while this non-abusing world is built up, the therapist may have to respect the child's need to keep out both abuse and the past. Fourth, even when much needed digestions, integrations and healings occur, we may need to respect the child's latency development. But we should not be surprised to discover that the abuse still plays a powerful part even in the healthiest of symbolizations.

13

BEYOND THE UNPLEASURE PRINCIPLE
Play and symbolism

In Chapter 2, I described how the urgency in my voice on a certain day seemed to waken Robbie from his long sleep of autism, and how, as he surfaced, he greeted me like a long-lost friend, with a surprised and loving 'hello!'. Although we were in fact due to part that day, I believe it was not so much his awareness of the separation but rather my obvious alarm about his seeming so close to psychic death that brought him to life. I think he suddenly saw me as real and as really there for him. It was not so much the prospect of my absence as the evidence of mine and his own presence that woke him up. This was followed by his therapeutic breakdown and my subsequent increase to intensive treatment, and then, a few months later, the lifeline session. I have suggested in previous chapters that I have come to think that the object's availability can be as alerting and thought-provoking – especially in children whose object has been too remote – as is its unavailability in children who have taken its presence too much for granted. I now want to discuss these ideas in relation to theories of play and symbolism.

Milan Kundera once said that Laurence Sterne's novel *Tristram Shandy* asserts, by its rambling and free associative form, that real poetry lies not in action but in the place 'where action stops, where the bridge between a cause and an effect is ruptured, and thought wanders off in sweet lazy liberty' (1986). Kundera is referring to what seems to be the playful element in poetry. It may be instructive to compare some of the psychoanalytic theories of play with the theories and findings put forward by the researchers in child development. The psychoanalytic theories have tended to concentrate more on the serious elements operating in play, and the child development workers more on those elements which have to do with what my surprised obsessional patient, John, once called, wonderingly, 'fun'. It is not surprising, of course, that child analysts and child psychotherapists are more sensitive to the serious motives in their patients' play, considering the level of illness and trouble they tend to see in their patients. I once saw a picture drawn by a very deprived little boy – it was not an unusual sight in the caseload of the therapist concerned – of a child buried alive in a grave, his arm pushing out of the coffin and reaching skywards. In some ways this groping arm seemed to indicate a breath of hope, but the trouble was that the graveyard above was mostly filled with evil-looking old crones and witches. Not much sweet lazy liberty and fun there.

In fact, many chronically depressed, deprived children have great difficulty in using their imagination at all; some are hardly able to draw or play and many are quite unable to imagine, even in their play, that life could be different or that they could exert much control over their fate. It is essential, I think, that we become alert to their moments of emergence from depression, and that we distinguish carefully between the narcissistic identifications of the genuinely manic patients, based on omnipotence, and the first beginnings of new identifications and new internalizations, based on fantasies of potency, in children who may have been clinically depressed all their lives. Both motives, of course, may coexist in a single patient at any one moment, but they should not be confused.

As early as 1921, Klein became interested in how learning, a supposedly intellectual activity, could be interfered with by blocks caused by unconscious phantasies and fears. She then became interested not only in the blocks to learning, but in the activity of learning itself, and declared that everything a child did in his play was an expression of his unconscious phantasy. In those early years, it was particularly his unconscious sexual phantasies and their symbolic expression that she saw in the material. So, for example, the way a child added numbers or had problems with subtraction could be seen to relate to his phantasies about what happened when people came together, or when people were separated (Klein 1921 and 1932). This is not the whole story, of course. Oliver Sacks has described how, for mathematicians or those amateurs who love numbers, numbers can involve a recognition involving warmth, emotion, personal relation. He quotes the mathematician Wim Klein as saying 'Numbers are friends for me, more or less. It doesn't mean the same for you, does it – 3,844? For you it's just a three and an eight and a four and a four. But I say, "Hi! 62 squared."' (Sacks 1985: 198).

I have described elsewhere in the book the modern psychoanalytic ideas which have gone beyond the early findings of oral and sexual meanings to an exploration of more mental phenomena. I have also described some of the research findings that suggest that newborn babies begin life as little abstractors and pattern perceivers. It is interesting that Michael Fordham, who has done so much to bring Jungian theory down to earth into the world of the infant and young child, seems to stress bodily experience even more than some of the modern Kleinians who have been influenced by Bion's ideas (Fordham 1976). My impression is that while the Jungians have been coming down to earth, the Kleinians have been trying to make their way to heaven, and the two groups have recently crossed somewhere in the middle! What all the analytic orientations have in common, however, is a belief that play has meaning, and that even play of the most meaningless kind has meaning.

The first detailed example of observation of a very young child's play and a discussion of its significance is in Freud's *Beyond the Pleasure Principle*. He describes a game invented by his 1 1/2-year-old grandson, who was a 'good boy' who did not disturb his parents at night and never cried when his mother, to whom he was very attached, left him for a few hours. Freud had observed that he often played a game with his toys, which Freud became convinced had to do with goneness and his mother's departures. One day, Freud made an observation which confirmed his view. The child took a wooden reel with a piece of string tied around it and threw it over the edge of his cot, so that it disappeared, exclaiming 'o-o-o-o'. He then pulled the reel out of the cot and hailed its reappearance with a joyful 'da' ('there'). Freud suggested that the complete game – disappearance and return – was 'related to the child's great cultural achievement – the instinctual renunciation . . . he had made in allowing his mother to go away without protesting. He compensated himself for this, as it were, by himself staging the disappearance and return of the objects within his reach' (1920: 15).

Freud pointed out that it was no use pretending that the enactment of the joyful return was the main part of the game, because the first act, that of departure, was staged as a game in itself and far more frequently than the episode in its entirety. He emphasized that it is the unpleasurable experience of the departure that was being played out, but that the pleasure principle still played a part because a passive experience was turned into an active one. Note that the element of pleasure does get into this early psychoanalytic theory of play, but the pleasure in the joyful return of the object, and in the control over the departures of the object, is seen primarily as a defence against unpleasure. Freud, in his customarily thorough and intellectually honest manner, raised the problem that the joyful return might seem to be a major part of the play, but he insisted that it was not. In a way, perhaps he could not help seeing it as a less significant part, because of the nature of his view of 'reality' as something which was fundamentally frustrating, painful and disappointing, and which therefore had to be 'faced' and come to terms with. This emphasis and this theory is helpful in understanding the play of a child functioning at a fairly well or neurotic level who has confidence in the accessibility of his object, but who needs to work over and play out the gaps and breaks in this security. Such an emphasis and such a theory may require supplementing, however, for work with the type of child who lacks, and therefore needs to work towards, another type of 'reality', one which contains hope, security and even pleasure.

Susan Isaacs also discussed the reel game, but in a somewhat different language based on object-relations theory. Isaacs refers to the child's 'triumph in controlling feelings of loss' but she also says his play 'consoled' him for his mother's absence (Isaacs 1952: 73). What is, nevertheless, missing from her account is the important, but at that time still fairly recent, Kleinian distinction between processes which are defensive against pain and depression and those which are designed to overcome it and foster growth. Much, therefore, would depend on the child's inner state of object relations as he played the reel game: whether he was playing it mainly in order to deny his mother's absence and, more important, her significance (playing on the level of what Segal has called a symbolic equation), or whether he was playing it to gain some control and make her absence more bearable (playing at the level of what Winnicott has called a transitional object), or whether he had no doubt about either her significance or her absence, but was exploring and trying to learn more about the properties of absentable objects in their own right (playing at the level of what Segal has described as real symbol formation). These three possibilities are related, as I have indicated, to the theory of symbolism put forward by Hanna Segal in 1957 and Winnicott in 1958. A fourth possibility may be worth consideration.

Segal is responsible for the distinction in psychoanalytic theory between a symbolic equation and a symbol (1981). She had noted the difference between the difficulties a neurotic patient might have in playing the violin and those of her schizophrenic patient, who explained that he no longer played the violin because he couldn't be expected to masturbate in public. In the latter case, that of a symbolic equation, she pointed out that the substitute's own qualities, its violinness, are not recognized or admitted. 'The symbolic equation is used to deny the absence of the ideal object or to control a persecutory one. It belongs to the earliest stages of development. . . . The symbol proper, on the other hand, is felt to represent the object. . . . Its own characteristics (that is, the object's) are recognized, respected and used. It arises when depressive feelings predominate over the paranoid-schizoid ones, when separation from the object, ambivalent guilt and loss can be experienced and tolerated' (1981: 57). The symbol is used (at the neurotic or normal level) not to deny but to overcome loss. Tustin has drawn attention to the technical implications of her own suggestion that the autistic objects of autistic children should be seen as symbolic equations not as symbols: that is, the therapist should not treat such autistic objects as symbols standing for the real object, but rather as the opposite, as a turning away from a living human object. The autistic object is seen by the patient not as a poor substitute for but as far superior to the human one (Tustin 1981).

Winnicott's concept of the transitional object is placed developmentally between the symbolic equation and the true symbol. He describes this as an intermediate area of experience between the pure narcissistic illusion that everything belongs to oneself, and the mature awareness of separateness and indebtedness, where true symbolic functioning is possible. Thus, if the child uses his teddy as a transitional object, the child partly recognizes that the teddy is different from the primary object (breast or mother) and partly doesn't recognize this, nor, according to Winnicott, should he be made to do so too soon. Winnicott stresses that the transitional object may be the child's first Not-Me possession, and says this is an area that must go unchallenged and should exist as a resting-place, a paradox which is necessary and should be respected. He meant, I think, that the therapist should not be continually reminding the patient that the teddy isn't mummy and is only a defence against loss and separation and dependence. He seemed concerned that this would neglect the other half of its meaning – that is, that the transitional object is the child's first major experience of independent possession – and neglecting this could interfere with the child's creativity and development. The teddy, after all, is the child's own. Winnicott's stress on the child's *possession* of the not-me serves to remind us that what Segal was really describing in her theory of symbolism was two different kinds of object relation. So the child in the intermediate or transitional stage has an experience of an object which is his very own, but he also has an experience of himself as an owner. The final stage where symbolism is achieved, that of differentiation, was regarded by Segal as more mature than the first, where all is equation and possession, and this would apply, if, as Winnicott also believed, the infant moves from a state of illusory possession to a state of weaning and loss.

For the deprived child, however, the situation may be different. He may have had few such illusions; he may have started from a quite different direction. His symbols may be as bleak and desolate as Beckett's *Endgame*. A ball, or a doll, or a teddy may not have acquired and been lit up by symbolic meanings at all. Such a child or baby will play, even with the newest of toys, in a desultory and empty way. The child may not have an illusion of oneness, he may be starting from a vision of empty desolation and nothingness – ash. His first steps towards a phantasy of possession, of winning a longed-for object, pleasing it, attracting it, getting together with it need to be greeted with interpretations which acknowledge not omnipotence but powers and potency, not reassurance but the rightful need for assurance. The deprived child may, with help, arrive at the transitional level in transition from a place different from and, in a way, prior to the one described by Segal and Winnicott. He may then be in the process of learning not about the properties of absentable objects, but about the properties of objects which return, and about his own capacities to make them return. We need symbols for sunsets, but also for new mornings. This is the fourth possibility which may need to be added to the theory of symbolism. The deprived child may be moving not from a symbolic equation through a transitional stage to true symbol formation, but from a symbolic emptiness through a transitional stage to true symbol formation; in the latter case and on the latter flight path, a different emphasis in the therapist's interpretations may be required.

THE REALITY PRINCIPLE

Many psychoanalytic theories assert that it is the negative experiences in life that are the great teachers, the great stimulators, that pleasure soothes and feeds illusion, and unpleasure awakes and alerts us to the great outside world of 'reality'. The most concise formulation of this idea occurs in Freud's paper 'Formulations on the two principles of mental functioning'. Here Freud suggested that it was the pressure of internal needs, followed by disappointment of their satisfaction, followed by the inadequacy of hallucinatory wish-fulfilling dreams to gratify these needs in any long-term way, that eventually drove the mental apparatus to form a conception of the real circumstances in the external world and to endeavour to make a real alteration in them. 'A new principle of mental functioning was thus introduced; what was presented in the mind was no longer what was agreeable but what was real, even if it happened to be disagreeable. This setting up of the reality principle proved to be a momentous step' (1911b: 219).

The identification of what the negative stimulators to thought really are has been enormously refined since the days of Freud's insistence on the frustrations of sexual longings. For example, the Kleinian notion of the reality that has to be faced for maturity and character to develop is more private and in a way more tragic than the one Freud's little Oedipus must suffer: it is not the brute force of the power of reality which forces awareness upon the growing child; it is, rather, the force of his love and its influence over, and restraint upon, his hate that enables him to tolerate and accept, rather than submit to, loss. Instead of renunciation, there is relinquishment. Instead of control, there is acceptance. Thus a child may play the reel game in the paranoid position in order to control and triumph over his mother's departures; in the depressive position, he may, in playing the game, be coming to terms with them.

Yet many of the theories, including Winnicott's and Bion's, come together in a tendency to stress the experiences of loss, separation, separateness, or what Winnicott calls disillusion, as the great stimulators of learning and intellectual growth and development. It is only fair to point out that it is the balance between illusion and disillusion that Winnicott stresses, not simply the disillusionment and pain in the equation (1958). It is also true that Klein, read carefully, also stresses balance rather than just the negative, although her positive is less about merging fusion than about a loving and more alert relation. She certainly stressed over and over again that the introjection of the good breast was the fundamental foundation for future development (1937). But is it only a necessary condition for development, or is it sometimes sufficient in itself?

To move from the psychoanalytic literature on play to the child development writings is almost comic, because the emphasis is so different. In a book on *Play* edited by Bruner, Jolly and Sylva (1976), Bruner's introduction begins by somehow taking for granted the playfulness of play, and he cites the common finding that young chimpanzees seem to be able to play most freely when their mother is nearby to provide a buffer against distraction and pressure. Corinne Hutt points out that 'Play . . . only occurs in a known environment, and when the animal or child feels he knows the properties of the object in that environment; this is apparent in the gradual relaxation of mood, evidenced not only by changes in facial expression, but in a greater diversity and variability of activities. In play the emphasis changes from the question of "what does this *object* do?" to "what can *I* do with this object?"' (Hutt 1966: 211).

Since Freud, psychoanalytic theory has been much preoccupied with the notion of the absent object (O'Shaughnessy 1964). Many clinical studies and detailed observations of infants have suggested that a person's capacity to have confidence in the durability of the loved object when it is out of sight is extremely important for cognitive and symbolic development, for the ability to endure and survive life's painful losses and crises, and for mental health in general. Some experience of separateness, loss and pain seems to be a vital ingredient in this development. Yet the child development research on the cognitive problem of 'object constancy' has suggested that the whole issue of when 'out of sight' implies 'out of mind' and when it does not is highly complex (Bower 1974). There would seem to be other vital ingredients besides the experience of loss. Babies around one year of age who were unable to find an object hidden before their eyes in an inverted cup (a famous Piagetian experiment) had little difficulty when the cup had a picture of a smiling face stuck on it. They also found the task much easier if the experimenter leaned forward, caught the child's gaze and said, 'Go on, you find it, then!' The researchers point out that this seems to remind the child that the experimenter really does want them to find the toy, that she was not hiding it away, just hiding it for them (Freeman *et al.* 1980). Clearly, an object which is too available might never stimulate curiosity and intellectual interest, but it seems to me that one which is too unavailable may have the same effect.

CLINICAL ILLUSTRATION

Mrs H had been treating a 9-year-old girl called Molly referred by the educational psychologist because of learning difficulties and withdrawn behaviour at school (daydreaming and rocking). Her mother had collapsed and died very suddenly when she was 2, just four months after the birth of her baby sister. Molly was black, had a loving and devoted father and close and caring older brothers and sisters. They moved to London to be in contact with warm and helpful members of father's family there. However, there was a period when the family lived in another city, and the father had a permanent relationship with a woman who was extremely cruel and neglectful to the children. The father is now separated from this woman. So I am considering Molly to be a deprived child because of her early bereavement and maltreatment, but it will be clear that she was by no means as despairing and cut off as some institutionalized children or those who have had numerous changes of caretaker. She began to weep in her third session and it seemed as though she might go on weeping for ever.   In a later session, she asked whether, if she jumped out of the window, Mrs H would jump out after her to save her.

The session I want to discuss followed an unplanned half-term break. This sort of situation can easily stir up older dreads, older depression and feelings of being let down. This was some months into treatment and although her hope and trust were precarious, she was certainly no longer withdrawn.

The therapist writes:

> Molly came quickly with me from the waiting area, then delayed in the corridor some 10 feet from my door. She threw out 'Don't speak! You're not my friend.' I commented – from the rear – that it had been a long gap, and that she was wondering if we were still friends. 'You're not my friend.' She motioned roughly with her arm for me to go past her in the narrow passage. I said that I felt she would like me, as usual, to be in my room for her when she came in, and that I would do this. I went in and, sitting in my seat, was at an angle of 60 degrees or so to the door. To face her when

she enters is both persecuting and terrifying, so ambivalent is her attachment.

The session continues with the child being very defensive and bitter, rejecting the therapist but gradually moving towards her.

> She climbed on to the little table and balanced with her feet on the door handle, hands on top of the open door (a quite dangerous position). Looking down on me, she laughed, 'Are you scared?' She moved the door. 'Did I make you scared?' I developed it, saying, 'Did you scare me to death?' I can make you die' she asserted in quiet, convinced seriousness. I said that sometimes it was hard to hope that we wouldn't be killed – or our time together – when she was angry with me.
> 'Come on!' She bounced down. 'Let's play hide and seek.' I turned my back while she hid four times. Each time there was great delight in being discovered and I offered the obvious interpretation about being lost (each out of sight) and found, linked to the half-term just past and the holidays to come. [The therapist then comments in the notes, not to the child, that, interestingly, this was an enactment of her ACTIVELY seeking Molly, which of course hadn't happened in the half term break.] It was time to finish and she seemed content.

This piece of material is interesting partly because of the development which follows the therapist's acceptance of the child's doubts about her goodness and trustworthiness. But it is the dangerous play on the door and the hide and seek game that I wish to look at from the theoretical and technical point of view. Considered in one way, the session can be seen to be about coming to terms with loss. But from another, Molly may be seen to be gradually trying out, playing out more and more clearly, the idea that this woman seems to have returned and that she, Molly, seems to have had the power to bring her back. Certainly she may be partly getting rid of an experience of powerlessness, but she may also be having an experience of pleasurable power – the power to make a maternal object seek her out. Should the therapist interpret to the child that she is denying what happened last week – i.e. loss and departure and let-down – or should she say that Molly seems to want to be sure that her therapist is really looking for her, really concerned about her and really has returned? (Note that in fact the therapist was careful to interpret both lostness and foundness, and in the live clinical situation, it is rarely a question of either–or.) Would the second interpretation offer reassurance and denial of more painful realities? I think not. I suspect for some people who have suffered very early in their lives, or very much in their lives, joy and fun and the power to pull the object to one are elements of 'reality' which take as much digesting and learning about as their opposites. Mrs H described Molly's 'delight' in the game, not her manic triumph.

All children, except the most anxious, love to play hide and seek. Their pleasure usually involves a complicated mixture of emotions, and probably the fact of the mix itself is pleasurable. There is played out fear, excitement, anxiety about loss, but also joy at finding and joy at being found. The child's pleasure and delight in discovering a person who seeks him out when he is hiding or lost and who *wants him and wants to find him* need not arise from narcissistic or defensive motives. It is a natural and necessary part of normal development, and Molly's therapy seems to have had an exceedingly healing effect on her.

To conclude: I have looked for a word or concept that might stand opposite Freud's great theory of the 'work of mourning' and carry the same weight and dignity. Words such as rejoice, celebrate, give thanks, do not convey the lengthiness and slowness of the process – akin to mourning in its slowness – of the birth and development of hope in a child who may have been clinically depressed all his life. The nearest I can get is something like the 'work of regeneration', or, to paraphrase Daniel Stern and George Herbert, the 'slow momentous discovery that his shrivelled heart can contain greenness'.

14

WILDEST DREAMS AND LIES
Aspiration and identification
in depressed children

INTRODUCTION

One of the things that perpetually astonished me about Robbie's mind was the complete absence in it of any concept of the future. In the early years, he was completely immobile and lost, without any sense of moving time at all. Yet, even when he finally began to stir and to emerge from what he called his deep freeze, he seemed to be like someone walking backwards into the future, his mind totally preoccupied with the past. If there was a thing called the future, he neither knew nor cared. It was something far iller than denial; there seemed simply to be a blank where the future should have been. It was years before he came to use the future tense in his speech and, as I shall show in Chapter 16, even more years before he used the subjunctive or the conditional. I do remember that once, when he was still speaking with some feeling about the hallucination or dream of falling off a cliff down into the evening, he spoke about being able to see a single star. It seemed to be very faint and far-off, but I suppose that was a beginning. There was some glimmering of an idea that there could be life and light ahead. But what was utterly foreign was the idea of an open future, a certain future, a place which pulls one on and towards which one moves with some momentum. I have been struck subsequently by the absence of this concept in other, more paranoid, psychotic children, and by its inadequate development in depressed children. Psychoanalytic technique has moved a long way from its original emphasis on the past to a greater interest in transference events of the living here and now of the patient's present relationship with his analyst. It may be necessary, however, particularly in work with chronically depressed children, to consider also the importance of these other phantasies.

The prospective, forward-looking and aspiring element in human nature has always been important in Jungian analytic theory, in Margaret Lowenfeld's ideas and in Vygotsky's psychology.

Klein suggested that mourning and reparation were central to the process of overcoming (as opposed to defending against) clinical depression. In the present chapter I would like to suggest that the capacity to dream dreams may also be an important step on the way to overcoming clinical depression. Dreams of glory or nobility are of course often a defence against painful losses or shames in the past or present, but at other times they are something else: they are, I have come to think, an essential and vitalizing component of normal development and of the normal child's phantasy life and play; they are, I mean, a developmental necessity.

The deprived or severely depressed child, however, may not be able to have such phantasies, or barely be able to conceive of having them. Thus it may not be enough for the psychotherapist, functioning as a parental object, to be prepared to be receptive to, or to share, such phantasies, for the depressed child may be lacking in them. When they do emerge, they may have to emerge first not in the mind of the child but, via a particular kind of projective identification (which I suggest deserves another name), in the mind of the therapist or teacher or caretaker. The child may *seem* to be having grandiose phantasies at such moments because the *content* of the phantasy is grandiose, but in fact he may be actually too depressed to be grandiose. He may lack conviction but be trying out the phantasy on someone else, tentatively and possibly for the first time, to see if they are prepared to have it for him, on his behalf. The process may resemble, but in fact be very different from, genuinely grandiose communications from a genuinely manic and narcissistic child.

What I am suggesting is that certain apparently quite pleasurable and grandiose boastful phantasies, even lies and manipulative pressures, may contain a seed of hope of a tentative and modest kind. This may require a receptive containment by the therapist which need not involve collusion with lying or betrayal of truth. Such 'lies' may be an expression of a defective development in the area of the child's aspirations and in his relationship to a parental object which, in the case of the normal child, would be able to have aspirations for him. Such lying or confabulatory communications to the therapist, although often termed projective identifications, might better be termed anticipatory identifications, to give due weight to the prospective and forward-looking element in human development, especially in the development of a human being who is still a child. The notion of anticipation, which I have borrowed from some late work of Bion's (1980), also refers to the tentativeness of the identification, a tentativeness which may easily be masked by the apparent grandiosity of the content.

I shall also suggest that this prospective element is an important dimension in normal play and in the development of symbol formation. Segal pointed out that the symbol or representation stood for a reality which was once, but is no longer, possessed or possessable, and which is mourned (Proust the adult remembering his lost childhood for example). But, in the case of the child (especially one recovering from depression), the symbol or representation may sometimes stand for a hopeful reality which does not yet exist but which could actually come to pass in the future. It may, that is, be one day possessable, or, at the very least, in cases of injustice and abuse, it can be seen and said that it should be so. Too much stress by the therapist on loss and absence and relinquishment in such cases may interfere with important developments in symbol formation. The grammar of play may need extending beyond the past and beyond the present to include the future and conditional tenses and the subjunctive mood – that is, to include that which shall be, that which may be and even that which ought to be. Such a grammar may have interesting implications for a psychology of the will.

In the previous chapter I drew attention to the existence, in the theories of symbol formation of Segal and Winnicott, of three possible ways of playing the reel game. I also pointed out the possibility of a fourth way of playing the game, where the child is not playing out the issue of loss and departure and separateness, but the issue of gain and return and a coming together. I now want to suggest a fifth possibility: I would like to go beyond the notion of the child who, playing the reel game, senses his power to make his mother return, and suggest that he may sometimes be dreaming of even greater future powers. I would also like to suggest that he has been aided in this by his parents' phantasies for him and about him: this may be an important element in the theory of the function of the parent as container of the infant's projective identifications. The mother, in addition to containing and transforming her baby's or child's frustration, and even his delights, may also much of the time function as a container for his aspirations. Bion suggested that a child's dream of heroic achievement, therefore, need not imply only a denial of childish impotence; it might be, said Bion, an anticipation of future grown-upness and future powers.

Surely the same may be said of day-dreams and of the child's play. We need the psychoanalytic perspective to help us see the acorn in the oak tree, the baby in the child or the lost breast in the child's cuddly soft teddy. But we may need the developmentalists' and Jung's perspective to help us to see the oak tree in the acorn, the man the child will become and is *in the process of becoming*. The teddy bear may be, therefore, not only a transition from the actual mother to a proper symbol for the mother, but also a transition between the lost actual mother to the anticipated future wife. A child contains more than his present and his past. A child, more than any adult, is filled with a sense of his future – provided, of course, he is not severely depressed. Clearly, mothers and fathers may assist this process of development or obstruct it. Mothers and fathers carry for the child not only a sense of the baby that he once was and in part still is, but also a sense of the man or woman that he will become, and *is becoming*.

Some years ago a little boy patient of mine named Tommy came into a session with a mask, a Marine sergeant's mask with a big square jaw – this was just before Hallowe'en – and he put it on straightaway. I said that he seemed to want me to see him as strong and powerful today. I then added that I thought that we both knew this was because he was actually scared to death because his treatment was ending prematurely at Christmas when he and his family were due to move to the North of England. We had been talking about it a great deal lately, and he feared not only the cold, but violence, horror and poverty of a nightmarish kind. When I implied, however, that the mask was a defence against his anxieties and fears of weakness, he simply shouted 'No' with terrible desperation. I thought about some of the books I had been reading at that time on the subject of defence, and a few minutes later, when he put on the mask again, I repeated that it was clear that I was to see him as a very strong, brave, tough fellow today. But this time, I left out the second part; I did not add that underneath he was really terrified. He listened tensely, and then said slowly and with great relief – 'yesss'. Then, after a little while, he said that in fact he was worried sick about the move.

Since then I have thought a lot about that mask. At first, I implied that Tommy wished he were strong, but that of course we both

177

knew that he was not. This was an idea consistent with a theory that play attempts to control reality, or evade reality, or triumph over reality. And some play, much play, does precisely that. With a less ill patient with more ego and more confidence to fall back on, such an interpretation might have been appropriate. It may have helped him to feel he could talk about his fears. But supposing Tommy needed his object, not to remind him of the current sad, frightening, pathetic reality, but of the possibility of one day being strong? The little 2-year-old wearing his new cowboy hat is not greeted with a reminder that he is not yet really grown-up. The parent says 'Wow, what a tough guy you are today.' She contains, not only his disappointments, but also his aspirations. She plays the game not by colluding with a symbolic equation and agreeing that he *is* a Daddy or a cowboy, but by considering the possibility that, although this is pretend, it is not 'only pretend' in a reductive or belittling way. She may contain in her mind the belief in the possibility of his eventual grown-upness.

Klein wrote two classic papers about the process of projective identification. In one paper (1946) she described how a person may rid himself of unwanted bad parts of his personality into someone else – or, alternatively, unwanted good and valued parts in the same way. She showed how the ego may be impoverished by such splits and projections. But she also wrote about another kind of projective identification (which I wish had a different name) whereby a person may go into someone else's identity in an intrusive and invasive way and take it over almost completely (1955). Everyone has met the student who does not simply echo the teacher's teaching; he begins to walk like him, talk like him, use his mannerisms; and the phenomenon is a source of irritation and discomfort to those who witness it or are the object of it. The teacher can feel quite denuded in such circumstances. Kleinians distinguish carefully between this type of identification and a healthier kind, sometimes termed an 'introjective identification' where the person may identify with an admired object, but where differences are recognized and respected. In 'introjective identification' the new identity is not stolen, but earned or even received as a gift from a friendly well-treated object.

But what about the *process of development* from the more uneasy and total state of projective identification to the healthier one, the development from stealing another's identity to using it gratefully? What about the stages in between? Or what about the development, in a child, from the state of being too despairing to imagine he could ever be like admired or idealized figures, who simply seem too remote and unattainable, to a state where he begins to imagine the possibility? Such a child may be moving from a state of projective *unidentification* through a transitional state of tentative trying on of a new identification. What about identities which are not stolen, only borrowed and tried on for size?

Bion suggested, as I have said, that we should not see dreams as only attempts to rewrite the past. We should see them as living life events, life experiences. He said, however, that we could also see them as in some ways anticipatory of the future. I had a little boy patient who dreamt he had found a fossil in his garden and woke up so sad that it was 'only a dream', because, he said, he'd always wanted to touch a piece of history. Bion thought that my patient's dream, and others like it, were not 'only dreams', that is, not necessarily denials of childish impotence; instead, they could be seen as anticipations of future grown-upness. This prospective element is important in the thinking of Jung, who wrote about this long before Bion (see Storr 1983). In two books which make reference to Jung, masks were used not as disguises, but as experiments with, attempts to try on, a new identity (Muir 1987; Wells 1985). It might be useful to use Winnicott's term 'transitional' for identifications of this type. It may even be necessary to go slightly further, and underline the element of the future – and of possibility – by using a term such as 'anticipatory' identifications.

Before I turn to some more clinical material, it may be useful to consider the relevance of the work of the great Russian psychologist Vygotsky. He pointed out that 'In play, a child always behaves beyond his average age, above his daily behaviour, in play it is as though he were a head taller than himself. As in the focus of a magnifying glass, play contains all developmental tendencies in a condensed form and is a major source of development' (1978: 102). Bondioli, Achinto and Savio have pointed out that in this sense Vygotsky sees in play the creation of a *potential* development. (Bondioli, Achinto and Savio 1987). Vygotsky does leave out the fact that there is also regressive play – play, that is, where the child behaves a head shorter than himself, and plays at being a baby – but his stress on its forward-looking quality is interesting. In the field of learning, he points out that most tests measure functions which have matured, the fruits of development, but that we should also measure the buds or flowers of development. The former measure characterizes mental development retrospectively, the latter prospectively. The latter 'takes account of processes that are currently in a state of formation, that are just beginning to mature and develop'. He insists that the state of a child's mental development can be determined only by clarifying its two levels: the actual developmental level and the Zone of Proximal Development (Vygotsky 1978).

Betty Joseph, using Bion's notion of the analyst as a container for parts of the patient's self, has suggested that the analyst may be made to hold even the patient's intelligence. I myself still find it amazing to ask a patient what he is thinking, hear him say that his mind is utterly empty, and then, if I have the wit to ask him what he thinks *I* am thinking, discover that his mind is buzzing with ideas. Such a child may have intelligence and an active mental life, but may unfortunately have split it off into others. But what of the even iller children, those who have never properly developed certain aspects of their personality – the chronically depressed, or chronically abused? Such children may need an object which can carry hope for them, or belief in them, not because they are projecting something which once belonged to them, but because they have never really developed much hope, and cannot as yet tolerate hope themselves. Such children may have very little sense of a future; they may see closed doors and grey skies everywhere. Becoming like their heroes may seem an impossible dream. They often see themselves as very stupid or very ugly. We dare not offer false promises or blind reassurance, but we must be alert to, and aware of, the first moments of light, for the child may need to discover whether such awareness can take place in us first, before he can allow it in himself.

A second clinical example: a deprived institutionalized adolescent girl named Carol was referred for psychotherapy because her rude behaviour to various foster parents had left her quite unfosterable. Her rejections by the foster families were very painful for her because she had been the only one of her brothers and sisters to be rejected by her natural family. However, she was not a hardened child and her hopes rose when her therapy began. One day she brought a photograph of herself with someone whom she maintained was her 'uncle'. The therapist realized that this must be an uncle in one of the foster families who had rejected Carol. Miss B, feeling that her task was to help this superficially cocky but empty and deprived child to come to terms with her life-long depression and sense of loss, said in a kindly manner, something like, 'I think you would like me to think that is your uncle, but we both know the sad truth is he is probably an uncle from your foster family.' Her interpretation is very similar to my first comment to the little boy with the mask. But suppose we take note that behind Carol's cocky brazenness a highly tentative *question* was being asked: i.e. 'Can you conceive of me as a person who could ever have an uncle?' So the therapist could say, 'I think today I should see you as a person who could have a close family' or 'You feel you and I are getting to know each other, a bit like family'. I do not think she should say, 'You *want* me to see you as . . .' for the idea of wanting pushes too much responsiblity back on to a child who may not yet be strong enough or hopeful enough to do his own wanting yet. The child may need the therapist to carry that hopeful phantasy for him. Three years later, Carol was finally capable of being fostered: she said, not only that she realized she would miss her key worker at the children's home, but that they had 'got very close'. Her external circumstances could change when her internal relationships had become more friendly. The imagination is the great healing ground and the great area of potential development for that which can be and that which ought to be. This potential can be respected, I think, without colluding with denials of reality.

A third clinical example: Danny, a little boy of 8, was referred to me for failure to learn at school, effeminacy, aggressive behaviour and a worrying fascination with lighting fires. His parents felt that he had missed a lot as a baby and young child because they had been preoccupied with a life-threatening illness of his elder sister. The sister has since recovered, and the family has begun to pull itself together, aware of the damage to their younger child. Danny presented as a pompous, boastful, but also dead and depressed boy who made long, detailed speeches about things that had happened to him recently – always in a very wooden voice. He had no idea how to play. He confabulated and told boastful lies, but if I made the mistake of asking too careful questions which revealed suspicion of their truthfulness, he clammed up defensively. I gradually realized that he was terribly hurt by my questions and that, although he seemed an arrogant child who assumed his listener would swallow anything and became outraged if they didn't, arrogance and outrage and defensiveness were not the whole story.

Danny was a fat softy, a mama's boy who was despised and disliked at school and had few friends. After about a year's treatment, he had learned how to restrain his aggressive outbursts, to be a little less boastful, to lose weight and to make a few friends. He came in one day and said that he and a group of boys at school were playing a new game. They were having jousts; he was the horse, and his friend, one of the smallest boys, was the rider. He was the horse, he explained proudly, because he 'had the strongest shoulders in the class'. He and his friend were the best pair in the group. I commented on his pleasure and pride in being able to show me a friendly strong side of himself, and he then went on, excitedly, to say that sometimes his friend called for him at home in the mornings, and the friend would leap off the balcony on to his shoulders, just like in the TV programme of the *Three Mousketeers*. He added, watching me, 'Sometimes I gallop him all the way to school!' I knew, and I am sure he knew I knew, that this was a lie, but the pressure and significance of the phantasy was so powerful that it seemed important not to challenge it at that moment. I had seen him deflate hopelessly too many times before. I think the important thing was that *I was to see him* as heroic, dashing, masculine, and this is how I put it to him. I did not say, 'You *want* me to see you as . . .' A few days later, when he seemed in a more solid state of mind, I was able to comment on the fact that he does exaggerate, and he agreed. But at the raw and vulnerable moment of his sharing his wildest dreams with me, such a 'sobering' comment would, I think, have been wrong. And I found that on the occasions when I managed to be sensitive to the tentative, anticipatory quality which lay hidden in the boasts, Danny became more, not less modest.

In conclusion, I have come to think that we may need a grammar of play. Winnicott (1971) said that play took place in the great intermediate area between total phantasy and absolute reality – one could add, between that which is not and that which is. Play, therefore, may be thought to concern that which may be, that which ought to be (a sense of justice is essential for the mental salvation of chronically abused children), that which could be and even that which will be. The reel game played for the first time by a chronically abandoned and hopeless child may involve a question about the possibility that some objects may return: the child may be beginning to develop the notion that one day he will have the power to draw them back. A mask, or a photograph, or a lie, may involve an offering which contains, not necessarily a denial of past reality or current pain, but a tentative question about the possibility of a new version of the present and even a new view of the future. The therapist's, or teacher's, or parent's mind may sometimes have to provide the proving ground where such ideas are tried out. In theoretical terms: whereas the manic child may develop from pathological projective identifications to introjective ones, the depressed child may develop from inadequate or non-existent identifications to introjective ones through processes which may be termed anticipatory identifications. Goethe wrote about something like this in Mignon's song, in *Wilhelm Meister*:

> So let me seem, until I am
> Strip not my white robe from me
> from the lovely earth I hasten
> down into that sure house.

The translators (Bird and Stokes 1976) say that the literal translation would be: 'Let me remain attired as an angel until I become one.'

15

AUTISM
The controversies

Scientific observation is not merely pure description of separate facts. Its main goal is to view an event from as many perspectives as possible.

Alexander Luria

I now want to examine some of the growing areas in which some non-psychoanalytic organicist theories of autism overlap with the psychoanalytic. In some ways, the ideas of the opposing camps have moved a little closer, although there are still major and serious differences. Certainly, both groups have developed and modified their earlier, very divergent positions. The bridge between them, I think, may lie in the study of infant development and infant–mother interaction, and in the concepts of modern British psychoanalytic object-relations theory.

Organicists and psychodynamicists originally divided over both the issues of aetiology and of treatment: the organicists advocated biochemical and neurological causation and drug or behavioural treatments; the psychodynamicists, particularly in America, blamed the environment and recommended therapeutic communities or psychotherapy (Bettelheim 1967). (British psychoanalytic writers have throughout been much less environmentalist.) Much confusion, I think, could be avoided if the argument over treatment were not so frequently coupled with the issues of aetiology: it is, for example, perfectly possible for neurologically damaged patients to be helped both emotionally *and cognitively* by psychoanalytic therapy (Spensley 1985; Sinason 1986). The work of the psychoanalyst Betty Joseph implies that even an endowment as apparently native as intelligence needs to be defined, not only in terms of a one-person psychology, but in terms of object-relations, a two-person psychology (Joseph 1975). For example, two borderline psychotic patients of mine, who for many years were thought by their parents and teachers to be retarded, were framing their thinking and their remarks stupidly in part because they consistently imagined themselves to be communicating with a stupid person. Some of Sinason's patients suffered from secondary handicap in part because they were speaking to people whom they imagined expected them to be stupid. Successful outcome using the psychoanalytic method with autistic children does not necessarily prove that the original condition had no organic elements. Giannotti and others in Rome have shown that psychotherapy improves autistic children's electroencephalograms (cited in Tustin 1990). Successful outcome may, however, provide evidence concerning the interpersonal and intrapersonal elements in the psychological state that eventually emerged at a secondary, tertiary or much later stage in an interacting chain of causality which is leading the child down an autistic path. Autism may often start with some neurological dysfunction, but its subsequent particular form of psychological deficit may need description and exploration and even cure in terms which take account of object relations and of the stage of development in object relations and in the child's capacity for emotional communication.

AETIOLOGICAL ISSUES

Both the organicist and the environmentalist aetiological theories of autism claim to derive their authority from two seemingly contrasting conclusions in the original landmark paper by Kanner identifying the syndrome of Early Infantile Autism (1944). The paper described eleven children who presented a combination of features: an extreme aloneness from the beginning of life, an inability to use language meaningfully and an anxiously obsessive insistence on the preservation of sameness. On the one hand, Kanner implied an environmental aetiology when he noted that there was a great deal of obsessiveness and preoccupation with abstractions in the family background, and added that there were 'very few really warm-hearted fathers and mothers' in the group. This led to over-enthusiastic theories of refrigerator mothers and of simplistic psychogenic causation, particularly among American psychodynamic thinkers (Bettelheim 1967). It also led to much heartache and guilt for the parents of such tragic children. On the other hand Kanner also added that the accounts of the children's aloneness from the beginning of life (the failure to reach up when expecting to be picked up and the failure to mould their bodies to the posture of the people who held them) argued against the parents as the prime causal agents. He came down on the organicist side and concluded that the children had been born with an 'innate inability to form the usual, biologically provided affective contact with people, just as other children come into the world with innate physical or intellectual handicaps'. There is now a considerable and growing body of evidence demonstrating brain abnormalities in autistic individuals (Dawson and Lewy 1989b; Frith 1989; Gillberg 1990).

Many writers, both organicist and psychodynamicist, tend now to assume multiple causation, although for many organicists this so-called multiplicity is purely medical. Yet Gillberg quotes research which shows that the behaviour of autistic children with demonstrable neurological dysfunction *does not differ* from that of autistic children without such dysfunction (1990). The organicists (Hobson 1990 excepted) sadly seem unaware that psychodynamicist writers in Britain such as Tustin, Meltzer and Reid do not hold to a strictly environmentalist view but also assume multiple causation of a complex and interactive nature. Their multiple causation would, however, include psychogenic factors (Tustin 1981; Meltzer 1978; Reid 1990). Tustin, for example, suggests that the same picture can arise as the result of very different precipitating circumstances and reactions. She points out that the organic handicap could prevent the child from making 'adequate use of early nurturing, so that pathological autistic compensations will have come into play. These, combined with neurological impairment, result in the child's being grossly out of touch with reality. Thus organic factors can lead to the same external appearance as psychogenic factors' (Tustin 1981: 18). I would add, for example, that a baby with mild neurological dysfunction and a limp and flaccid or disorganized approach to life, born to an already depressed mother whose depression worsens at her failure to cope with her apathetic baby, may then become even less engaged, producing more depression in the mother. And so on. Very severe impairment, on the other hand, can tax the relatedness of even a healthy happy mother (see Fraiberg (1974) on the difficulties the mothers of blind babies may have in noticing their babies' responsiveness to them). No neurological impairment at all in a baby with all the normal readiness to engage in relationships might be met with depression or withdrawal in the mother to such a severe degree that the baby may *reluctantly but slowly and surely give up* trying to engage her attention, with devastating implications for his emotional and cognitive development. These ideas are not fanciful; they are based on clinical observations and research from a variety of sources in both Britain and Italy (Di Cagno *et al.* 1984; Miller *et al.* 1989; Murray 1991) and from the Under 5's Counselling Service at the Tavistock which works to turn such vicious circles into more benign ones. An interactional feedback model applied to the first days and weeks of life – where both nature and nurture are given their proper due, but so too is *the awesome power of an effect to become a cause of itself* – should be a promising area for prospective research into the aetiology of autism. Many clinicians and observers have seen the consequences of a feedback system where each partner in the infant–mother relationship may become more and more insensitive to the other's ever more minimal cues, with grave implications for the baby's emotional development, and, I suggest, for his intelligence. (See Bronwyn Hocking's courageous and moving account of how this happened between her and her baby (1990).) The growing body of clinical observation and scientific research into the baby's responsiveness to environmental forces in utero makes the situation even more complicated, but should serve as a necessary warning against simplistic linear aetiological theories of autism (Piontelli 1987; Liley 1972). (This interactional model has something in common with the mathematical theory of chaos which makes use of non-linear equations for the study of weather, earthquakes, cotton prices, heart failure, and fluid dynamics. According to chaos theory, tiny differences in input can quickly become overwhelming differences in output, a phenomenon given the name 'sensitive dependence on initial conditions'. Gleick explains that, 'in weather, for example, this translates into what is only half-jokingly known as the Butterfly Effect – the notion that a butterfly stirring the air today in Peking can transform storm systems next month in New York' (Gleick 1987: 8).)

Perhaps if we are to understand the way innate factors interact with environment, we do not need a single causal chain with two factors contributing at the beginning; we need, instead, a double helix where heredity and environment twist around each other in interacting spirals like Hofstadter's 'strange loops'. Cognitive impairment, at the end of such processes, can be out of all proportion to the original weak heredity or original inadequate environment or even to both. The severity and profundity of the condition of autism does somehow lend itself to strong reactions and powerful but all-too simplistic explanations. Something so terribly inhuman in a human child seems as if it must have an equally terrible and powerful single aetiology.

THE PSYCHOLOGICAL FEATURES OF AUTISM: THE NEED FOR AN OBJECT-RELATIONS THEORY

Discussing the aetiological issues, Uta Frith, an organicist, draws attention to the example of an enzyme deficiency disease, where introduction of the remedy *at the wrong point* in the chain of causal events produces no beneficial effects. She concludes that until a full understanding of the aetiology of autism is achieved, 'it will be necessary to take account of the psychological symptoms of Autism, over and above any hopes for a biological cure' (1989). Although I shall suggest that the psychological descriptions are limited by the use of a one-person psychology, perhaps this is better than no psychology at all where descriptions are given only in terms of brain functioning. Whether or not this psychological being has any connection with the child studied by the psychoanalytic method is a subject to which I shall now turn.

One of the major findings of the huge 1979 Wing and Gould study of 35,000 Camberwell children was that the three features previously considered to be typical of autism did indeed form a triad. Since then, many organicists have attempted to explain why these three features should be so linked, what underlying characteristics they might have in common, and what might be the binding force between them. The three features – 1) severe social impairment (note the change in wording from Kanner's 'severe autistic aloneness'); 2) severe communication difficulties, both verbal and non-verbal; 3) absence of imaginative pursuits including pretend play, with the substitution of repetitive behaviour – all imply a notion of impairment. Looked at from a purely descriptive and somewhat superficial point of view 'severe social impairment' may seem to be the equivalent of 'severe autistic aloneness'. From another point of view, what the child is *not* may be taking precedence over what he *is*. Aloneness is more personal, is closer to the subjective experience of a human being, and may open the way to further questions about the subjective state of the child: does he feel alone? Are there different ways of being alone? Is something invisible keeping him company? What might it feel like to be him? What does it feel like to be with him? And, perhaps most important of all, under what interpersonal conditions are there variations in this feeling of aloneness? Does it vary with changes in the therapist's feelings about the child, for example? Such questions about the state of the child's internal world of self–object relations cannot even arise when the debate is closed by the concept of neurologically caused social impairment. The notion of impairment is, in a way, even stronger than deficit, in that it carries strong aetiological implications of damage. In any case, Rutter, reviewing the research literature (1983), proposed that all of the symptoms could be accounted for by a cognitive deficit basic to them all. He stressed that this involved an incapacity, rather than a disordered usage, and he criticized Kanner and Tinbergen for viewing autistic withdrawal and desire for sameness as being driven by psychological motives such as fear or need for security. It is a pity that Rutter and Frith, so deeply critical of what they regard as the psychodynamicist tendency to explain autistic symptomatology in terms of resistance, avoidance and defence against anxiety, are unaware of the psychodynamicist literature in Britain, which makes use of a far more complex psychology, that of depressive collapse. Tustin's concept of 'compensations' of a pathological autistic kind, for example, is different from a notion of defence *against* something; it seems to involve more the idea of 'making do' with less than enough. In her more recent book (1990) she stresses that the autistic 'shell' is not only compensatory; it also has a protective function. Tustin writes as much about problems of despair and ecstasy as about panics and rages. (Daniel Stern's distinction between defence and *coping* or *executive* mechanisms of the gaze-averting normal infant responding to an intrusive over-stimulating mother (1977: 110–14) raises interesting questions for me about how a perfectly normal mechanism can become, over time, rigidified, and how we may need different names and different mechanisms to describe the quality of the absence of contact at different stages of the process. A piece of coping, in the form of a withdrawal from too intense or disturbing a contact, can begin to become a defence against over-stimulation, for example, or a compensation for under-stimulation; with time, either can eventually become an addictive, or even a perverse, way of life.)

The clinicians in fact seem as interested in distinguishing sub-types of autism as in outlining its general features. Tustin has tackled this problem in more than one of her books, and Reid of the Autism Workshop at the Tavistock Clinic will outline her views on this subject in her forthcoming book. Tustin (1981, 1990) distinguished the 'shell-type' child who may use his autism in defensive or protective ways from the 'amoeboid' children who are much more defenceless. My patient Robbie presented as a very amoeboid child; later, as he began to make some contact, he became very 'entangling' – another Tustin sub-type – and later still, as he toughened up, quite able to use his autistic withdrawal in shell-type resistive ways. Thus I do not wish to claim that the notion of defence has entirely disappeared from the psychoanalytic clinician's thinking: rather, that it has had to take a much more modest place. The clinician knows nowadays that he must work with a deficit which is both emotional and cognitive (see Chapter 7).

Tustin's description of psychotic depressive *collapse*, then, is very different from withdrawal as a defence against fear. Meltzer strikes a similar note when he insists that the 'internal spacelessness of self and object in the post-autistic personality is a *continuous defect* unrelated to stress of anxiety'(Meltzer 1975: 19, my italics). Meltzer states firmly that the autistic states proper are 'not to be understood as derived by mechanisms of defence against anxiety, but tend to be brought about by bombardment of sensa in the face of both inadequate equipment and failure of dependence' (p.21). Tustin also implies a concept of deficit when she refers to the child's difficulties in filtering experience. (Neither author claims that the filtering problem or the bombardment problem is purely psychogenic.) Both also go on to discuss the effects of the original autistic withdrawal in producing deficit (or perhaps one should say progressive deficit). Tustin is clear about the way in which the autistic 'plug' or 'shell' actually does prevent the child from introjecting new experience, and Meltzer differentiates between the autistic state proper and the autistic residues. He also refers to the cumulative function of the amount of life-time missed during the child's states of mindlessness. It should be clear, then, that in no way are either of these authors making use of simplistic linear causality by suggesting that autism is caused by defensive strategies against environmental insult.

But the great difference between their writings and Rutter's and Frith's is in the model of the mind which involves what is, by definition, a two-person psychology. That is, the mind contains not just a self with particular qualities and orientations and possible deficits; it also contains a relation to and relationship with what are called 'internal objects' or 'representational models' (Klein 1936; Bowlby 1988). This view, of course, carries the implication that human beings are born object-seeking and object-related (that is, born to seek and need relation with other human beings), an implication shared by interpersonal and intersubjectivist analysts in the USA (Sullivan 1953; Stolorow *et al.* 1987). The particular emphasis from object relations theorists, however, is on the internalization of these relations with people, and on the fact that phantasies about and experiences with, or lack of experiences with, these living, human figures are as much a part of the human mind as is the sense of self. To paraphrase Bion, there is always at least a preconception of a living (and thinking) human object. Without an adequate realization in experience to meet this preconception, an adequate concept of this living thinking human object may not emerge. But the preconception may still be detectable. So the question of deficit in the self would have to be accompanied by the question of what sort of deficit might exist in the object. (The internal object would never be seen as identical to the external one. It is thought to be shaped in part by elements in the baby's nature and phantasy life.) It is the descriptive psychology, not the aetiology, that is so different in a two-person psychology which considers the internal sense of twoness as not wholly dependent on external experience (Bion 1962).

So, although from a behavioural or external point of view Robbie's behaviour was the most un-object-related I had seen outside the back wards of psychiatric hospitals, the question I asked myself was: towards what kind of object or near-object or no-object is he relating or failing to relate? His answer when he was eventually able to put it into words was 'a net with a hole in it'. When Bion speaks of his schizophrenic patient projecting into a space so vast as to be almost infinite, he is still using an object-relations model, which I believe has compelling explanatory and descriptive as well as therapeutic power. The therapist has to understand that people talk and converse with a conception of a listener in mind; their words are aimed and if there is felt to be nowhere to aim them, why talk? Autistic children occasionally talk *at* someone, but almost never *to* someone. My puzzled question concerning Robbie's net had been, 'How was I to become dense enough, substantial enough, condensed enough to provide him with something, or someone who could concentrate his mind?' Simply waiting receptively and too passively for him, in his infinitely dispersed and flaccid state, would have taken a life-time. Until I belatedly got clearer about my task, it did.

THE ORGANICISTS' VIEW OF THE
PSYCHOLOGICAL DEFICIT

Rutter's conclusion (1981) was that autistic children's social abnormalities must stem from some kind of 'cognitive' deficit, in the
sense of a deficit in dealing with social and emotional cues. He
made it clear that the research did not indicate a deficit in the
processing of stimuli in any particular sensory modality, but rather
the stimuli that posed difficulties were those that carried emotional
or social meaning. There are now different theories, supported by
some extremely ingenious experiments, which attempt to identify
the precise nature of the underlying deficit. They all, to my mind,
take too narrow a view, because they tend to define the deficit in
terms of a one-person psychology of a very limited nature. Dawson
is an organicist who sees the children as suffering from a difficulty
in modulating states of arousal, and I shall discuss some problems
with this explanation in the chapter on stereotypies (Dawson and
Lewy 1989a).

Frith's (1989) view of the deficit is somewhat different from
Dawson's. She follows Leslie in arguing that what the autistic child
lacks is a theory of mind, and this arises, she suggests, from a deficit
in higher brain functions concerned with meta-representation. She
argues persuasively that the strange peaks in the intellectual perform-
ance of autistic children – the so-called islets of ability and the
rote memory skills of the *idiots savants* – are signs of dysfunction
due to an overgrown capacity to ignore context. The autistic
individual, says Frith, lacks a 'central cohesive organizing force'
which she likens to a strong flowing river 'which pulls together
large amounts of information (many tributaries)'. This particular
metaphor, to which Frith returns at several points in her book, is
an interesting example of the limitations, I suggest, of her use of
a one-person psychology. For surely it is not the river which pulls
together the tributaries? It is the force of gravity which is the central
organizing force that pulls the water from the hills to the tributaries
to the mighty river itself and eventually down to the sea. Just as
the geographical metaphor is incomplete without some attention to
the laws of the physics of motion, so is a one-person psychology
which ignores the caregiver's role (first as an external object, later
as an internalized one) in encouraging, focusing, channelling and
enhancing whatever degree of native capacity, drive for coherence
and object-seeking capacity the neonate starts with. In any case,

the evidence for the newborn child's social capacities suggests that it is born with a drive for coherence which is by no means purely cognitive. It also leads one to question Frith's view that a theory of mind is a late-maturing mechanism, i.e. that it matures in the second year of life. The central cohesive force is, I suggest, our innate potentiality for human relationship and its eventual realization in interactions and in the internalization of these interactions. We are born, possibly even conceived, as object-seeking.

There are, however, some vestigial correspondences between the cognitivists' idea that autistic people lack a theory of mind and Meltzer's stress on the mindlessness of the autistic states, and also Tustin's on the meaninglessness and asymbolic quality of 'autistic objects'. But there the similarities end. For example, Tustin and Meltzer both stress that there *are* moments of mindfulness in their patients, and they are consistently alert to the child's potentiality for what Bion called a *preconception* of mind, if not a fully developed conception (1962: 91). In any case, the psychoanalytic writers mean more by 'mind' than do the cognitivist theorists. What is so markedly absent from the cognitivists' descriptions is the idea of a mind as an inner world full of living objects, memories, thoughts lit up by meaning. A mind is a vast panorama of thought-about feelings and felt-about thoughts which are constantly in interaction with one another. They are dynamic and energetic. Thoughts have their own power of existence: we can think about them, we can chase them if we seem to be losing them, we follow them up where we can. We can shut them out and push them down. Sometimes they turn on us and chase and nag us in their turn. Sometimes we succeed in putting two of them together, sometimes they get together on their own without our permission. Sometimes they haunt us, often they elude us. In contrast, Frith's and also Baron-Cohen's concept of what a mind is seems dry and barren, narrowly defined in terms of the experiments on which the theory is based (Baron-Cohen 1988).

The experiments themselves however, lacking as they are in attention to the emotionality and dynamism which fuels and accompanies thought, are nevertheless ingenious and imaginative. Baron-Cohen, Leslie and Frith used an experiment devised by Wimmer and Perner for the study of the development of a theory of mind in young children. They used two dolls, Sally and Anne. Sally has a marble which she puts into her basket. She then goes out. Anne takes out Sally's marble and puts it into her own box while Sally is away. Sally comes back and wants to play with her marble. The experimenters ask the watching child, 'Where will Sally look for her marble?' Most of the non-autistic children, already giggling at Sally's plight, get it right, and point to the basket. Most of the autistic children get it wrong and point to the box which they themselves (but not poor Sally) know the marble to be in. Frith's explanation is that autistic children do not understand that to see is to know, and that not to see may involve not knowing (Frith 1989: 159ff). She believes that what Kanner and, more recently, Hobson, take to be an affective (emotional) disorder is better explained by the lack of a central cohesive factor in the brain – that is, by a deficit which is cognitive. Psychoanalytic observers of such a piece of research, while not ruling out organic factors, would be far more detailed in their investigation of such a phenomenon. They would, I think, be interested in the inability of some autistic children to *identify with* Sally. This involves a leap from one's own self to the other. The capacity to identify with the state of mind of another person, or with that of an imagined other person, is seen as neither purely cognitive nor purely emotional; it is thought to partake of both but to involve very particular processes which cannot even begin to be examined in a one-person psychology. The clinician would also suspect that some of the more developed 'shell-type' children may not want to know that to see is to know (Hobson 1989).

Baron-Cohen, another proponent of the cognitive theory, seems at first glance to be taking a position similar to the psychoanalytic in considering that what is central to autism is the autistic child's difficulty in understanding other people's mental states. But by 'understanding other people's mental states' he means a purely cognitive, and in fact very complicated, activity, for he imagines the whole thing having to work logically and inferentially. And of course it would do so if our cognitive understanding of what others feel and believe were never fuelled and shaped by empathic or projective identifications, by the ability to feel with or for other human beings. What Baron-Cohen does is to make what I suggest is a false distinction between the understanding of *mental* states and the understanding of emotional states, which he thinks is much easier. He thinks that mental, unlike emotional states, are not directly observable and have to be inferred, 'an inference that requires a complex cognitive mechanism'. He says that to understand what someone believes is more complicated than understanding what they are feeling, because beliefs and desires are always *about* something. Yet one does not get the impression that the

194

normal children who were giggling at Sally's plight were engaging in a complicated series of Sherlock Holmesian-type inferential calculations. Projective identification with another person or an imaginary person can happen instantaneously; once you have thus taken the other person's vantage point, working out how things look and seem from over there is easy; once you are in Sally's shoes, you know immediately that she thinks the marble is still in her basket. And anyway, I suggest, you already know a little about how it feels to lose something, because lost and missing objects tend not to pose purely cognitive problems to their losers and missers. Baron-Cohen also seems to be grossly oversimplifying when he suggests that emotional states such as happiness, sadness, fear and anger do not necessarily have content, and as such may be of less use in predicting and making sense of social behaviour.

As a clinician, I am used to trying to puzzle out the many different ways in which an autistic child can be withdrawn. I feel I have witnessed hundreds of different ways in which they can fail to use their minds. So I am struck by the researchers' almost monotheistic search for a single explanation and a single description in the Sally–Anne experiment. For example, I would suspect that some of the autistic children failed the test because, in their mindless way, they gave the answer they expected the experimenter wanted of them: what they had heard was not the details of the question – 'Where does Sally think the marble is?' – but 'Where is the marble?' They often latch on to just a bit of a phrase; they seem to grasp lamely, ineffectually, limply and sometimes desperately on to the tail end of sentences or phrases, not in the hope of its making a big difference, but as though believing anything is better than nothing (clutching at straws, like Robbie's grasp on a piece of grass when he felt he was falling down off the cliff into the evening). Identifying with Sally would be beyond them, but so too would pausing, confidently, to think about the question. Their apparent mindlessness has many determinants, some earlier in the causal chain, others later and more derivative. It need not always be because of an organic defect; it may be the result of a massive relinquishment of the use of their minds (possibly the result of chronic depressive collapse with subsequent mental atrophy of mental functions) or because of a massive projection of their thinking functions into other people. Robbie, for example, at certain times was simply beyond believing in the existence of mental life anywhere; at later, somewhat better periods, he did feel somebody could think and had answers, but it certainly could not be him. So if I asked him a question, he would look into my eyes for the answer, even though he knew it perfectly well himself. I have seen other autistic children give any answer simply to get the questioner off their backs.

Hobson, the major proponent of the affective, as opposed to the cognitive, theory of autism draws quite close to a psychoanalytic object-relations perspective in a paper 'Beyond cognition' (1989) in which he insists that, contrary to Baron-Cohen's view, feelings are always *about* something or someone. His research, based on a series of experiments with photographs of faces displaying varying degrees of emotion revealed, has shown that autistic individuals have a specific abnormality in the way they perceive emotion in people's faces. He argues that they have a biologically based impairment of affective-conative relatedness with the environment. He suggests that they seem to lack the co-ordination of sensory-motor-affective behaviour and experience that is a usual feature of intra-individual, as well as inter-individual, mental life. He thinks it may be due to a neurological dysfunction, but not invariably. But he does insist that the cognitive deficits – for example, in language, in symbols, in the failure on the Sally–Anne test – follow from the inability of autistic children to participate in the affective life of the other and 'so to construe a knowledge of persons as persons'.

A MODIFIED OBJECT-RELATIONS THEORY

In a subsequent paper, 'On psychoanalytic approaches to autism' (1990), Hobson goes even further. He states that a psychoanalytic object-relations approach, preferably a 'circumspect and self-critical' one, may have an important place in the study of autism. He thinks there can be mutual enrichment between the organicists and the psychodynamicists, and believes that the study of autism may demand modifications in object-relations theory and indeed some rethinking both of the innately determined underpinnings and of the very early experiential underpinnings for object relatedness. I would suggest, however, that some of the necessary modifications are already in existence, and that there is also already available to us some rethinking of the kind he implies. These developments make the seemingly impossible task of applying an object-relations theory to children who seem by definition so clearly *un*-object-related, somewhat easier. Robbie, for example, who can be described on

196

one level as totally un-object-related, can be seen as in fact relating to an object, but an object of a very minimal type, a net with a hole in it or a tenuous piece of grass holding him from falling off the edge of a cliff.

Since the work of Klein in the 1930s and 1940s the idea of the object in psychoanalytic theory has been evolved and modified from that of the whole human person represented in the mind of, say, the normal 3-year-old, the whole person so obviously not related to by the autistic children of 3 and upwards studied by Rutter, Frith, Baron-Cohen and Hobson. Klein (1937) stressed the importance of part-objects such as the breast, Winnicott (1960) the holding function of the mother, Bion (1962) the mother's containing function. Further major modifications resulted from Rosenfeld's work (1987) on the object of identification in narcissism, Bick's study (1968) of the two-dimensional object, Meltzer's study (1978) of the dismantled object, Tustin's work (1981) on autistic objects and Bollas's theories (1989) of the alternative object. I would like to add my own suggestion of the importance of the reclaiming object (see Chapters 4 and 5). Subsequent theorists have gone on to use a more consistently mental language, and have modified the definition of the maternal 'object' even further: Stern's study (1985) of maternal attunement, Trevarthen's research (Trevarthen and Marwick 1986) on the 'motherese' language, Bion's stress on the mother's function as a transformer of her baby's communications and projections, all involve significant reformulations in the description of what 'knowledge of persons as persons' might involve. In addition, the work of Klaus, Kennell and Brazelton, and, I would add, the powerful image of Robbie's lifeline, provide evidence for the enlivening, alerting, claiming and reclaiming functions of the caretaker figure (Klaus and Kennell 1982; Brazelton et al. 1974).

Thus a circumspect and self-critical psychoanalytic object-relations approach is already available to us and may be of considerable use in providing the student and researcher in autism with better tools for the description of its psychological condition. Cognitive deficit or affective deficit or even cognitive-affective-social deficit, all of which are seen in one-person psychology terms, may be better described and better understood in terms of a deficit both in the sense of self and also in the internal object. The first symptom in the triad, the social impairment, could thus be seen to include an impairment or deficit in the 'sociality' of the internal object. The child may not only lack interest in the object, he may expect it not to be interested. In the same way, the second major symptom, that of communication difficulties, may need to include in its description and definition a description of the communication (expressive, receptive and alerting) difficulties in the internal object. (I shall leave a discussion of the third symptom, that of stereotypy, for the next chapter.)

But the enrichment may certainly be two-way: the study of autism may, as Hobson implies, lead also to even further modifications in object-relations theory. It has certainly taught me to look as closely at the deficit in the autistic child's self-representations as at the deficit in his object-representations. Bion's model of the mother as container implies a baby full of as yet unprocessable emotions or unthinkable thoughts, projected outwards for her to contain and process. The baby's self, however burdened and unreflective at such moments, is seen as *full of something*. But in Brazelton's model, and in many ordinary observations, the self of some newborn babies can be seen as much more loose and flaccid and dispersed – an altogether emptier picture of a self but nevertheless a self which is *capable of being gathered together by a mother concentrating on him and offering herself (concentratedly) as a focus of concentration.* I shall return to this interesting problem of the deficit in the sense of self in the last chapter. If one says 'you' to an autistic child, he sometimes looks over his shoulder, seeming not to be able to find himself. Such children need special help in doing so.

Another important modification in the concept of the object is the distinction Bion makes between a concept and an innate preconception. The baby is born, according to Bion, not yet with a concept of but at least with a preconception of a breast. His own view that the baby was born with a drive 'K', the need to make contact with psychic quality, or, in simpler terms, the need to get to know someone, implies that the baby is born with more than a preconception of a breast; it is also born with a preconception of what O'Shaughnessy called, in a personal communication, a 'psychological object' or, to paraphrase Trevarthen, 'live intelligent company'. What Bion calls a preconception seems somehow more on the way to being a concept than anything I have witnessed in some of the flatter, emptier babies I have observed in infant observation studies and in the course of infant–mother psychotherapy. Perhaps the babies Bion observed were made of stronger stuff than at least some of the ones Brazelton, for example, describes. Certainly, the stronger, more alert neonates do strike one as having much more than a preconception of an object; they seem already to have a concept, and they can surely be called object-seeking or object-related, or, to try out another formulation, intelligence-seeking and intelligence-related. For the weaker, more flaccid, still unawakened neonates (whose brains may be unimpaired; this is a discussion of the descriptive psychology, not of the aetiology of autism), perhaps the most we can say is that they do have a preconception of an intelligent object in the sense that they are object-prepared and object-requiring. That is, they are innately *prepared for*, and innately *requiring*, a relationship with an intelligent being, and able to respond *when this being creates the right preconditions*. The preconception may, in these less alert babies, need a very specific kind of realization in experience if it is to turn into a concept of an intelligent being, of a mindful, interesting, interested and attentive mind. The specificity may have to be exactly appropriate to the child's particular developmental deficit, possibly to problems in development during the first days and weeks of life. I shall attempt to discuss some of these specific realizations during psychotherapeutic treatment in the next chapter.

SUMMARY

I have tried in this chapter to find a way through the minefield of controversies which surround the tragic condition of autism. In a discussion of its aetiology, I have sought to avoid the limitations of any aetiological theory based on a linear causality and offered an interactional model which takes account of the awesome way in which an effect can become a cause of itself. I have discussed some of the psychological features of autism and suggested that these might better be studied in terms of a two-person, rather than a one-person psychology. A modified object-relations theory with an understanding of primitive or minimal objects, or pre-objects, and with distinctions between preconceptions and concepts is, I point out, already in existence in the work of Klein, Bion and infant development researchers.

16

RITES AND RITUALS
IN AUTISM
The use of the counter-transference
Robbie at 30

THE COUNTER-TRANSFERENCE USED FOR
PURPOSES OF DESCRIPTION

There is no doubt that autism is a condition which provokes
extremely powerful reactions in its students. Perhaps it is the
depth and profundity of the withdrawal, and the seemingly cold
determination to stay withdrawn, which is so unnerving and
which calls forth these extreme reactions. In the organicists, it is
a reaction which a clinician would regard as excessively, possibly
even defensively, detached. In the clinicians, at least in my own
case in the early years, it was a reaction which led to too great
an engagement, in the sense of a determination and insistence on
finding meanings where meaninglessness so clearly ruled. There
have been major differences, not only over aetiology, but in the
language of description. I have already commented on the change
from Kanner's description of the first major symptom as one of
'extreme aloneness from the beginning of life' to Wing's 'severe
social impairment'. Yet the differences between Kanner and Wing
over the description and definition of the third symptom are even
more dramatic. Kanner's 'anxiously obsessive desire for sameness'
(1944) becomes, in Wing's hands, 'the absence of imaginative and
pretend play, with the substitution of repetitive behaviour' (1979).
The later descriptions seem careful to eschew Kanner's assumptions
of human motivation, desire and human meaning. But a purely
behavioural description leaves out important descriptive features.
Is repetitive behaviour simply repetitive behaviour, or can we allow
ourselves the freedom to see the deadliness in it, the emptiness
and possibly something even worse? Do the emotive adjectives
necessarily involve a reading in, or should they perhaps be a

careful part of the description of the behaviour? For what is left out, even in Kanner's somewhat more emotive account, is the horror, disbelief and tormenting boredom engendered in the mind of anyone who is willing to *sit for long enough* with an autistic child engaged in his particular autistic ritual, to attend fully to what this feels like and to examine, reflectively, the quality both of the child's behaviour and of the feeling states engendered in himself by such behaviour. These emotions in the counter-transference towards the autistic child may, of course, lead the clinician astray: he may, for example, be tempted to read meanings into meaninglessness. But used properly and circumspectly, they may be not only the lifeblood of the therapy, but a vital instrument for the accurate and detailed *observation* of autistic symptomatology. I shall therefore leave in the emotive language, partly because I am aware that it was only when I allowed myself to feel my profound boredom in the face of Robbie's repetitive behaviour, and, moreover, to acknowledge the full horror I had been denying about Robbie's own lack of boredom and lack of urgency about the passage of time, that I got anywhere at all, first, in understanding his state of mind and, second, in helping him to come to life. Neither scientific detachment, nor pseudo-neutrality, nor even receptive containment in its more passive forms were adequate. Is our normal human desire for and expectation of aliveness and novelty, and the reaction of horror at the deadness and boring quality of the rituals necessarily a 'reading in', or is the sense of human alarm and urgency essential to lend our statements adequate descriptive power?

There are further reasons why a more emotive clinician's language is appropriate for purposes of accurate description. It has to do with the clinician's perceptions of the qualitative nature of the rituals themselves at each moment: that is, his perception of some very disturbing and unpleasant qualities attached to the rituals. These have little in common with the more respectable motives that the organicists imagine the clinicians believe in, such as avoidance of anxiety. I am thinking instead of the perverse excitements, the bathing in thrills and frenzies, and also of some of the more sadistic and destructive motives which may attach themselves to the rituals and may play a large part in their perpetuation. I suspect that the real insanity of autism is at times so disturbing that organicists and environmentalists all search for single explanations or causes which are sufficiently separate from the psychological *being* of the child to spare the onlooker the task of looking too closely. Perverse or

201

addictive motives do not always accompany the rituals, but most clinicians consider it a more worrying prognostic sign for the therapy than when the rituals are more purely compensatory and also not too fixed. But even without these perverse elements, the *degree* of withdrawal, the degree of refusal or inability to respond to our overtures, evokes powerful feelings of rejection, incomprehension, despair and also rage. Many professionals prefer to view such a black hole in a mind from a great professional distance. Others, in their desire to get close, may neglect the importance of the conditions under which such distances can be bridged.

If Hobson (1989) is correct in asserting that autism should be counted a social-affective deficit which derives from faulty empathic interactions with others, then the instrument for study may need to be not only scientific description of quantifiable units of behaviour but a study of the method of empathic interaction itself. To examine the autistic child while ignoring the interpersonal dimension *between us* is like listening to music while tone-deaf or comparing the scent of two roses without a sense of smell. The musician buying a new cello insists on playing it first in order to assess its tone and resonances. To judge its responsiveness to his playing he has to engage with his instrument in a highly skilled way. Hamlet, mocking Guildenstern for imagining he can play *him*, says of himself, 'and there is much music, excellent voice, in this little organ, yet cannot you make it speak'(*Hamlet* III, ii). The psychoanalytic observer of autism studies not only the child's responses to him in the transference, but his own counter-transference responses to the child, and then the child's responses to his responses. He studies reponses *in the context of their relationship and in sequence* and studies how changing context affects responses from moment to moment. What is studied is a relationship, a duet, not a solo. Two of my autistic patients do certain things only when my attention has wandered for a moment, never when my attention is fully on them. I have to monitor my responses as well as theirs. Intersubjective analysts in America have pointed out that if an archaeologist unknowingly dropped a wristwatch into a dig, it would be dangerous to assume that everything found in the dig must have been there beforehand. As Stolorow, Brandchaft and Atwood put it, psychoanalysis is unique among the sciences in that the observer is also the observed (1987).

This attention on the part of the therapist/observer to changes in the state of his own mind can shed much light on the autistic child's apparent lack of interest in other people. Frith stresses that anyway this is not a lack of awareness of other *people* but rather of other minds. Frith goes on to discuss the autistic child's lack of interest in creating shared attention: for example, Curcio (1978) has shown that young autistic children never exhibited proto-declarative pointing. I once heard Trevarthen give a wonderful example of the effectiveness of this for 'social referencing' in a 10-month-old baby girl, who was brought into his experimental lab by her mother for the first time. She apparently pointed with astonishment and a somewhat agitatedly curious 'uh!?' at the video camera up on its stand. Her mother replied confidently and reassuringly, 'That's a video camera, dear', and the baby gave a satisfied 'uh' and turned her attention elsewhere. The baby clearly did not understand the words 'video camera', but she did understand that her mother felt that strange contraption was a knowable thing. Frith takes Curcio's finding to be evidence of an (innate) inability to recognize other minds. But suppose we specify, instead, a *developed deficit* (a development beginning in early days and weeks of life) *in the ability and/or will to recognize other mindful minds, that is, minds sufficiently undepressed or undisturbed to share in delighted recognitions and capable of attending to and attuning to oneself.*

My own clinical experience with autistic children leads me to think that, although they do not *declare* an interest and invite one to share it in normal open ways, they do find their own methods of *eliciting* interest and attention, and not always interest and attention of a ₁ ₋rely need-satisfying type; that is, they seem to elicit mindful attention. One autistic patient, Mark, can go on engaging in his repetitive rubbing of the table, walking in circles, rubbing the table, walking in circles again for half an hour at the far end of the room while my gaze is on him. The minute, probably the second, my mind and probably my gaze wanders away from him, or the quality of my gaze changes, the circle changes to an oval. This brings him into my field of vision and he gets my attention back! Then, and only then, does he return to his circle. If I was only studying his behaviour and not also monitoring my own state of mind, I would miss this connection and miss his responsiveness to my lack of responsiveness. Robbie, even from his position on the couch where he could not see me at all, always seemed to know the moment my attention wandered and sometimes would then introduce one of his most annoying verbal rituals, a permanently effective way of drawing anyone's full attention to him. Asperger, who identified what many people regard as a higher-level sub-type of autism, thought that the children seemed to take things in with short peripheral glances (Frith 1989). I suspect this is true of some of the iller autistic children, too. The problem is that the child may be using his apparently most un-object-related symptom, a stereotyped ritual, in highly indirect, but nevertheless powerfully object-related ways. I shall illustrate this later.

EXPLANATIONS FOR THE RITUALS

I want now to review some of the ways in which previous authors have discussed the problem of stereotypy, or repetitive behaviour. I have referred, in the previous chapter, to Dawson's view that the explanation for the autistic children's lack of habituation could be seen in their inability to modulate a state of arousal (Dawson and Lewy 1989a). This is an interesting observation, but not necessarily a causal explanation. Kanner (1944) himself did refer to actions and rhythmic movements, and noted that the accompanying ecstatic fervour strongly indicated the presence of masturbatory gratification, but this observation has, to my knowledge, never appeared again in the organicist literature. The understanding of perverse sexual acts, or perverse fantasies with perverse content, has a long history in psychoanalysis, but the understanding that perverse fantasies may express themselves more indirectly not through the content but through the *form* of verbal presentation is a relatively recent formulation (see Joseph's observations on 'chuntering' in 'Addiction to near-death', 1982; Hinshelwood 1989).

My own experience with Robbie suggests that a particular repetitive preoccupation could begin as a way of managing some state of disturbance or of emptiness, or, sometime later in his treatment, even as an object of genuine fresh interest. But the fuel which afterwards kept it going was neither the disturbance nor the emptiness nor the novel interest but something else. Perversions and addictions have a way, like bronze, of keeping their shape even after the cast is removed. The binding agents, once the mould is cast, may be of another order altogether and tend not to be amenable to being analysed away by simple explanatory interpretations referring to whatever causal agent may have set the activity in motion in the first place.

Dawson discusses the psycho-physiological evidence that autistic children have abnormalities of attention: that is, they do not habituate. The clinician treating these children may feel she is on the edge of death from boredom at witnessing a repetitive activity for the hundredth or thousandth time, but the child never seems to get bored! It is my impression, in fact, that a very close study both of the moments when the therapist gets bored – which can alert her to the fact that the child perhaps should also be getting bored by now – and of the subtle qualitative changes in the child's repetitive activity may reveal that he actually does seem to be getting bored, but does not show this in any obvious way. Sometimes he goes on because he doesn't know how to stop, sometimes he forces himself to go on because he cannot imagine doing anything else, sometimes he is driven to go on, sometimes he goes on because he likes producing boredom in us, and sometimes he goes on in a kind of frenzy because he finds this particular stereotypy thrilling. Or he may go on mindlessly in a desultory way, but he goes on. The lack of habituation needs, I suggest, to be studied in far more detail.

Dawson points out that autistic children also fail to turn to a new stimulus even when they do habituate. These moments when the child is suddenly tired of a stereotypy pose difficult but crucial technical problems for the therapist. Such moments, as I have said, are anyway difficult to detect and, because the child often does not know what else to do with his attention, are gone before the therapist can get in quickly enough to make use of them and help the child to see he might find some other object of interest. A lot depends on whether the child has simply lost heart or whether he is more coldly determined in his refusal to find new objects of interest. Dawson argues that the autistic individual suffers from a difficulty in modulating his state of arousal, and that this directly influences his capacity to attend to and comprehend both social and non-social information and, ultimately, to function adaptively in both of these spheres. Her research on therapeutic interventions shows that autistic children's attention to other people can be increased by sensitive interactive strategies that provide simplified, predictable and highly contingent responses and allow the children to control and regulate the amount of stimulation. This seems to me a promising area of thinking and of treatment and sounds close, in certain respects, to the developments in psychotherapy I have been describing in this book (Dawson and Levy 1989a). (And see the interesting broadening in the behavioural methods used by Howlin and Rutter (1987) in their home-based treatment of autistic children.)

Much work has now been done on the way in which the modulation of arousal is achieved and laid down in the early months of life in millions of repetitions of minute rhythmic and cyclical interactions between the baby and his living human responding caretaker. Stern and others have shown (Stern 1974), for example, that the maternal gaze and the constellation of vocal and facial behaviours that may accompany it exert a strong effect on both eliciting and holding the infant's gaze. Attention, as Meltzer (1975) said, has to be 'paid' and, as Klaus and Kennell (1982), citing Cassel and Sander (1975), put it, it is the face and voice and breast of the mother which act as the 'magnet which lines up the iron filings'. Later, once such experiences are internalized, the magnet's attraction is internalized and represented inside, so the normal child is drawn to seek contact with a living object which can produce novelty and which he now expects to find. In other words, it is *attraction* emanating from a living object which helps to combat distractibility. Until the organicists consider the effect of these early interactions in relation to, and together with, the factor of neurological dysfunction, their assumption of basic impairment in the brain as the only causative factor in autism has to be seen to be extremely partial. Dawson's theory suffers from the same problem as Frith's 'central cohesive force': both derive from a one-person psychology. Surely it is the mother in her focusing function (Lisa Miller, personal communication) who plays a major part in the central cohesive organizing function and a major part in modulating arousal. Much comes from the baby, but much comes from her, too.

Frith's explanation of the repetitive behaviour is somewhat different; it is that it is due to the child's lack of symbolization and his problems in processing sensations. She believes that the terrifying power of sensations, and the repetitiveness in autism are two sides of the same coin – the coin being the impairment in the central cohesive force. At one point she mentions the slow habituation to novel stimuli and adds that, although some research suggests that stereotypies occur among normal people in stressful situations in order to reduce the level of arousal, an extensive review shows that stereotypies often *increase* arousal. Again, this would not be difficult for the clinician to explain. A symptom may begin as a reaction to stress, and therefore would lower arousal; it may add secondary gains where it neither decreases nor increases arousal;

and eventually it may even gather perverse motivations to itself, thus increasing arousal. Years of observations of the changing use of a single symptom make the simple notion of a primary function, or even of secondary gain, far too simplistic. It may gather countless new motivations to itself. I have felt with some of Robbie's symptoms that almost the whole of his personality and a huge range of quite complex feeling could be caught up in a single repetitive series of phrases. Oliver Sacks (1985: 195) quotes Richard Wollheim who (in the *Thread of Life*) makes an absolute distinction between calculations and what he calls 'iconic' mental states. Sacks goes on to discuss the *idiot savant* calculating twins: 'They do not seem to "operate" on numbers, non-iconically, like a calculator; they "see" them, directly, as a vast natural scene.' Robbie's icons were far more limited, but he did seem to experience a synaesthesia similar to Luria's famous mnemonist, and sometimes, when Robbie repeated some of his favourite phrases or described someone who had 'a bright green velvety voice', his face would light up with joy. So the rituals were by no means always dead or always perverse, particularly at their inception (Luria 1968; Wollheim 1984).

ROBBIE'S RITUALS: THE NEED FOR MULTIPLE EXPLANATIONS

Robbie's repetitions often went through what finally became, for me, a familiar series of stages. At first they seemed to involve a reaction to anxiety, or an agitated but excited interest, and an inadequate attempt to control and get hold of and process such an experience. On one occasion, for example, long before Robbie could manage to cross streets and travel about London by himself, he escaped from his mother's car and arrived 15 minutes early for his session. I knew he had no idea of road safety and I couldn't imagine how he had arrived alone so early in this excited state. He was too mad in those days to be able to explain what had happened, so I had to remain in ignorance until his frantic mother arrived. My voice clearly betrayed the anxiety I felt for him (and for his mother) when I said, 'It's a bit too early, Robbie, could you wait for a while in the waiting room?' For years afterwards, he never entered my door without saying, 'It's a bit too early'. I am certain that on the first day he picked up my shock and for the next day or so was trying to come to terms with it – and also, of course, with his own. But for years I went on trying to understand what I saw as its meaning, when in fact the sentence had become ritualized. I thought his words told something about the fact he had sensed I wasn't ready for him and that there was a deeper sense in which he felt the world hadn't been ready for him. This may well have been the meaning in the first few days. But later the situation changed. Had I used my counter-transference honestly and acknowledged the terrible weariness I felt when I opened the door years later and he still uttered this dead phrase in a dead manner, I might have succeeded in not being as autistic with him as he was with me. I might have also been able to show him what we learned together years later, that somewhere he did know that this dead dullard's way of talking to people made them feel very unwelcoming and unreceptive to him.

There were many other verbal rituals which, responded to on the wrong level by me and others, would never have outlived their usefulness and become digested and processed in the natural way. After the first genuine use, they tended to go into a stale dead period where they seemed to have no meaning or life or motivation attached to them at all. Later, once I became alert to this, I interpreted it more vigilantly, and he became less repetitive – or else he used his repetitiveness for the provocative, irritating, but certainly very alive and hopeful motives I have described earlier. By then, the rituals were never desultory. But it is in relation to the desultory periods that I think Frith's observation is so instructive: she insists that 'what is needed by a central agency is switching off, not switching on'. Frith, of course, thinks this is done in the brain, but it may be that it is also partly learned in the early days and weeks of life, in interaction with an undepressed mother who helps the baby to switch *on* to new objects of interest by the animation of her face, voice and breast.

The problem was that if a symptom escaped my attention – or that of his parents, as they too became alert to this problem – it tended to go into a stage which was addictive, or even perverse and fetishistic. These are the rituals which may overlap closely with the iconic states described by Wollheim and Sacks, but they are far narrower in emotional scope. Robbie in anxious moments could lick the inside of his lower lip apparently for purposes of self-soothing; but at other times, he gave himself over to it, he did it with a masturbatory and highly sensual pleasure, and the expression on his face was sly, perverse, unpleasantly lascivious and somehow lewd and triumphant. Tustin (1981) and Meltzer, both writing from a psychoanalytic perspective, are the only authors after Kanner who refer to fetishism and perversion in autism. (Reid of the Autism Workshop at the Tavistock Clinic has a book in preparation which includes this topic.) Meltzer refers to the autistic child's favourite toy or ritual as a 'fetishistic plaything' (Meltzer 1973, 1975: 28).

Frith and Dawson give clear, if unemotive descriptions of the lack of symbolization in autism, but it is to the psychoanalytic clinicians one must turn for close observations of the ways in which and conditions under which the autistic child may move back and forth from the concrete to a more 'symbolic mode'. Tustin, in hypothesizing about the infancy of such children, described the processes by which a child's sucking of the inside of his cheek may become more and more deviant and perverse. Winnicott is clear that a transitional object may degenerate into something perverse, but Meltzer seems to suspect that the transitional object is itself fetishistic (Meltzer 1973). Meltzer's preference for making clear distinctions between the paranoid-schizoid position and the depressive position sometimes leads him to an either–or attitude which discounts the possibility of gradualism and transitional developments from one to the other. Yet Meltzer himself elsewhere points out that defence mechanisms may be modulating devices deployed for development (1975: 219).

Meltzer has an additional explanation for the obsessive repetitive behaviour in autism. He sees it as resulting from a process of 'dismantling the sensory apparatus into its component parts'. As a result, the senses attach themselves to the most stimulating object of the moment. 'The essential mode of activity is aimed at rendering an incipient experience meaningless by dismantling it to a state of simplicity below the level of "common sense" so that it cannot function as a "symbolic form" to contain emotional significance, but can only, in its various parts, find articulation of a random and mechanical sort' (1975: 217). Note the activity and intentionality in the notion of dismantling and rendering meaningless. I have certainly witnessed such active assaults on meaning by autistic children, but I would not feel this could be offered as the single explanation for their concreteness. It is my impression that their experience is also often 'unmantled'; sometimes some of the fragments have simply never been put together. (See Chapters 7 and 10 for a fuller discussion of the issues of deficit and defence.)

Meltzer has some interesting things to say about what he calls the 'autistic state proper' as opposed to the autistic residues. He

describes this as a state of withdrawal which interrupts the trans-
ferential object relations much as static on the radio interrupts, but
does not destroy the flow. Such interruptions, he says, are reversible,
and the living relationship can continue as though it had never been
interrupted. He describes how, if we cancel out the interruptions,
we may see something consecutive is happening, similar to the
timelapse photography of the blossoming of flowers (1975: 6).
This helps one understand the excessively delayed reactions and
touching recognitions these children are capable of. I still remember
my astonishment at Robbie's first comment on his return after the
ten-month break: 'Where's the ticket?' The purity, however, of these
apparent 'islets of ability' (Frith) are not, as Frith points out, a sign
of special ability. They are a sign of dysfunction, in the sense that
something *should* have happened to Robbie's memory. Powerful
flashbacks apart, the mind has to engage in processes of forgetting in
order for new and present experience to make its impact. Memories
need to take their proper place on the back-bench of the mind.
Robbie found it almost impossible to forget, and, unfortunately,
my early technique of continuing to try to understand persistent
material colluded with his addiction to the past.

The professional mnemonist studied by Luria also eventually ran
into the problem of being unable to forget and erase images he
no longer needed: great charts of numbers and sums from past
performances, from decades before, began to clog his mind. In his
concrete way, he tried to imagine himself erasing the blackboard;
he also tried writing the sums down and burning the notes. But
nothing worked until one day he discovered that a particular chart
of numbers was not turning up in his mind because *he didn't want
it to*. He said, 'Aha! That means if I don't want the chart to show
up it won't. And all it took was for me to realize this.' In Bunuel's
film *The Exterminating Angel*, the desperate starving guests believe
themselves to be imprisoned in the house where they have attended
a dinner party. Suddenly, after days of horror, they discover that all
they have to do if they wish to leave is ... leave! Similarly, and
equally slowly, Robbie and I came to learn that he *could* forget. He
could get rid of the apparently compulsive thoughts and sentences
that seemed to dominate and fill his mind. He could, that is, when he
wanted to and when he decided something else was worth putting
there. As he learned that he could exercise agency over his own
mind, be a subject rather than the helpless object of his thoughts,
and also as he began to achieve some differentiation between one

part of his mind and another (he had seemed to have very little ego), he often *chose* to indulge in his verbal rituals. But this was a very different activity from the past when they ruled him. Now he could choose to be sane, we could have whole sessions where he, somewhat slowly, could remain in full contact with me and himself throughout. But by now he had developed some sense of himself as possessing agency, potency and a will which he could exercise over his own thoughts. In a way, he seemed to experience his mind as possessing some muscularity and power and to be finally his own. It no longer had to be the flaccid, helpless and titillated medium for whatever thoughts happened to be passing through it at the time.

So far I have been trying to distinguish between motives for the rituals which involved attempts to manage anxiety or excitement and motives which were more clearly perverse or morbid. Yet, as in all real as opposed to ideal and theoretical situations, the motives were often very mixed, and it was sometimes difficult to tell, especially as Robbie's personality became richer and more complex, which was dominant and which was worth most discussion at any moment. For example, he would occasionally arrive in a clearly agitated state, telling me that someone at work had shouted at him. He would repeat this over and over. We had by now understood together for some years that he was not simply telling an upsetting and frightening story, he was also turned on in a perverse way by the experience and the idea of someone being angry with him. He was both frightened and excited, or, to be precise, he was frightened/excited. Sometimes he even had an erection as he repeated the story over and over. But it was not simply the content of the story or the idea that was disturbing and exciting him, it was also the way in which *he was living out this sado-masochistic phantasy in the telling of it to me.* He would be half glaring, a bit frightened of me, but also frenzied and thrilled by the way his repetitions were so cruelly penetrating into my mind. So it was necessary to show him that, although it was true that he was in part trying desperately to communicate his upset, he was not simply desperate, and he was by no means simply engaged in a communication. He was, instead, engaged in a highly perverted form of conversation designed both to excite and enrage the listener, so that he could get the irritability to begin all over again in someone else. If I missed the excitement and simply betrayed irritation, a highly sensual grin would show me I'd gone wrong and had played my part in the perverse game.

An object-relations perspective on the third symptom – where the observer uses both her feelingful perceptions of qualitative features of the ritualistic behaviour and also her counter-transference feelings and responses to the behaviour – means, I believe, that the symptom receives a fuller definition and a fuller description. I suspect that over the years of variations in the motives for, and mood of, Robbie's rituals I have seen examples of everything from Kanner's anxiously obsessive desire for sameness, to Wing's repetitive behaviour, to Meltzer's more active dismantling of meaning. At other times, I have seen Tustin's autistic object used to shut out meaning and life, and Joseph's addictive and perverted chuntering. We may need not one but several explanations for this symptom which is so threatening to normal psychological life and development.

TECHNICAL PROBLEMS IN THE TREATMENT OF STEREOTYPY: ROBBIE AT 31

The therapist of an autistic child who has developed rituals seems to be faced with two major technical problems: that of helping the child to give up his rituals and that of helping him to discover that life may be worthwhile without them. Of course, the situation is in fact far more complicated, because as the child becomes more alive the rituals themselves may be used in quite lively ways. So the problem becomes more one of helping him to learn to prefer interaction with a live object rather than with a totally controllable dead one. But this is very different from work with an obsessional neurotic patient who has at least a part of his personality that wishes to be free of his rituals. Many authors have noted the similarity between autistic repetitive behaviour and obsessional behaviour in neurotic patients. Freud referred to the repression and prohibition involved in obsessive-compulsive neurosis (1909). But, as Tustin has pointed out, a major problem with autism is that it is a relatively conflict-free state. Clearly, the obsessive-compulsive neurotic suffers; he complains about his symptoms. The autistic child seems at times to be thoroughly enjoying his symptoms and absolutely content, if not ecstatic. Meltzer has described their sensuality and 'the joy and triumph of possession' (1975: 10). The joy, of course, is by no means always innocent. Sometimes it is sadistic, but in any case it is invariably ego-syntonic. The autistic person may not complain, but his companions do. Tustin believes that the child has to experience firm restraint on his idiosyncratic activities to bring about the type of conflict and repression which is characteristic of normal healthy growth. She is therefore against abreaction and cathartic measures and warns that much individual psychotherapy with psychotic children has been too permissive and too passive (1981: 154). Sue Reid (personal communication) takes a similar view. Both argue that the restraint has to be carried out with skill and sensitivity. Tustin says that to stop these activities in a clumsy, insensitive way is as harmful as letting them continue – perhaps more so: 'The overriding aim should be to help the child feel "held" in firm and understanding hands so that inner structures can begin to develop' (1981: 155).

Barrows goes even further. She is influenced by Tustin's work, and believes that the Asperger's children she treats in California do have an organic deficit. There is, she says, a substantial difference between her approach and that of traditional non-directive play therapy:

> Whereas in the latter it is essential that the therapist take her cues from the child, the perseverative and non-relational aspects of the play of an Asperger's child demand that the therapist actively intervene to draw the child out. Often at the risk of what, in traditional therapy, would seem intrusive, I have had to structure my patient's play so as to introduce symbolic or reciprocal content where she would have persisted in ritualistic behaviour.
>
> (Barrows 1988: 149)

Since I have been treating Robbie for almost the whole of my working life as a psychotherapist, he has had to experience the whole gamut of my developing ideas. Although his intensive treatment did not start until he was 13, my work with him in the late 1960s and early 1970s was, I think, far too permissive and passive. Tustin's work on the autistic object had not been published nor had Joseph's on addictive chuntering. Later, the parallels between Tustin's young patients' use of toys and Robbie's use of repetitive stories became obvious. I began to understand the appropriateness of my counter-transference feelings of terrible impatience. I think what happened during those early years, when I was not permitting myself to use my counter-transference and was repressing or denying my boredom and resentment, was that my feelings sometimes erupted in a clumsy and hurtful way. I would suddenly, to my own surprise as well as his, raise my voice and tell him to stop talking about that or to stop rushing back and forth and to sit down. I now think that it is only rarely necessary actively to stop the patient. A vigilant use of the counter-transference, as well as of one's perceptions of what is going on in the patient, can usually ensure that the interpretation gets made early enough and firmly enough. Once the excitement has managed to escalate, it is much more difficult to get the patient back into contact, anyway.

But effective vigilance depends on how much work the therapist has done on processing the boredom and the feelings of distaste about the shallow thrills that the patient is indulging in. In the early years these were very private to Robbie, but, as his attachment to me and others grew, we became included in his phantasy life, so that he assumed, quite delusionally but fixedly, that I shared in the excitement of talking about what, to me, were the same old subjects but what, to him, were a form of mutual verbal masturbation. I had to learn not to repeat certain phrases of his and to make myself put things in a fresh way. (Such work demands constant supervision of one's own autistic laziness of mind.) At his most crazy moments it was sometimes better if I said nothing at all for a few minutes, for he heard my words, no matter how soberly they were spoken, as collusion and permission to go on. Yet sometimes, at those moments, he did seem to hear the silence. I also found that I never got away with the least trace of self- congratulatory eagerness in my voice – when, for example, I thought we were really on the edge of understanding something. That, too, would send him over the top. There were other problems to do with language and its usual capacity to carry implication. It was not enough, for example, to say to Robbie in one of his high states, 'I think you feel you are in bed with me today', although he clearly did feel just that. Unlike a sane person, he would hear that as a confirmation. So I had to turn the sentence round and say, 'It seems difficult for you to realize that I'm actually a few feet away from you over here on my chair simply talking to you and trying to understand you.' The temptation, as his licking gaze swept over me and his confidence in his delusions led him into ever more sensuous writhings, was to brush him off psychologically or, to be more honest, to scrape him off myself. (He rarely actually touched me but the intrusiveness of his gaze was so sensually unpleasant that he has, on at least two occasions, been attacked in public places by outraged strangers.) I had to do a great deal of work on myself not simply to reject him, either openly or subtly, but, instead, to try to get in touch with a part of him capable

214

of a close warm contact that was not so slippery and sensual. I also had to get myself to be capable of inviting such a part when there was often so little evidence of its existence.

With other autistic children of a different type, this evidence is not so hard to find. In Robbie's case, it really seemed as if a mind had to grow, and that I had to show him that a non-perverted form of pleasurable interaction with another person was a possibility. I also had to adjust my technique constantly to the level on which he was functioning at any given moment. When he was in a state of real and desperate confusion, and thus muddled about his 'I's and 'You's, it seemed better simply to do my best to understand. When he was in a calmer state, able to think, yet getting away with the old undifferentiated way of talking, it was important to help him to make differentiations. If he began the session by talking about something that had happened at 'this' house, it was necessary to show him his reluctance to bother to make the distinction between 'this' and 'that', between his house and mine. This casually neglectful attitude to thought was very different from the real confusions of identity and place that occurred more in the earlier phases of treatment. All these differentiations on my part helped, I think, to push Robbie back on his own resources and to give him a stronger and more focused sense of his own identity, and of the sense of his own bone and muscle that he spoke of so many years before. But this somewhat depriving element in the work had to be balanced with interpretations which not only were alert to the moments when he tried to be sane and to talk sanely with me in order to please me, but also noted the occasional moments when he himself enjoyed talking to me in an ordinary way. And, just as it was important to show him when he had clearly sensed my distaste for the perverted talk and my consequent dislike of him, it was also vital to show him that he felt I liked him much better when he made an effort to speak to me in a straightforward way. (There are some interesting parallels here between work with psychopathic or sexually abused children and autism.)

In his late 20s Robbie began to have moments when, instead of just parroting an old phrase, 'I want to grow and catch up', he showed real sadness and regret for his missed development and spoke of missing being a man. Naturally, this too got perverted, but more and more often the mood of regret was genuine. By now he was no longer an amoeboid single-celled psychological being; his mind was differentiated and had some structure. He had a sane self to struggle with the mad self. As his sane self gradually became able to take some pleasure in contact with a live mind, he became able tentatively at first to use his imagination and to be capable of the beginnings of symbolic activity, 'the other side of the coin of repetitive activity' that Frith speaks of. One of the consequences of his problem with symbol formation was that Robbie's grammar was very strange. He always spoke either in the present tense or the simple past. He had never used what in Latin languages would require the subjunctive mood – that is, he could never manage to describe, or probably even conceive of, hypothetical situations. He had rarely (except in the dramatic session described in Chapter 3) even said 'I want to have ...' and it was years before he could manage the future tense, because time simply was not differentiated out into a past, a present and a future. At first, there was only something like Kundera's dot, then, later, there was only the past pushing out the present and dragged remorselessly and relentlessly into every conversation. Finally, he became able to narrate a simple event, but I thought he would never manage to say 'I wish that I could' or 'I hope that I can' or 'I would like to'. One day in October at the age of 29 he suddenly managed it.

Around this time his mother told me that he had started calling her by her first name – a sort of playful trying on of his father's identity and an attempt to see his mother from his father's perspective. This 'binocular vision' (Bion 1950: 18–19) tends to be impossible for autistic people, and Reid has pointed out the importance of the development of a dual perspective and its implications for symbol development when it finally comes (personal communication). (See also Chapter 7 on Bruner's 'two-trackedness' and its link with the capacity to 'think in parentheses'.) One day Robbie began talking without waiting for me to ask him anything – an unusual start. He said, 'I'm *looking forward* to seeing Laurel and Hardy on the TV tonight' (my italics). He said he had seen a film about a man who had 'jumped in the river and been scared but had gone to hospital and been bandaged'. I said that he himself was a bit like the man, because he had 'taken the plunge' by starting talking first today; perhaps he'd been scared to do it but he felt that he and his words had arrived safely and he had managed to tell me some things.

At this moment some footsteps could be heard further up in my house (the consulting room is on the lower ground floor). Robbie went immediately into one of his stereotyped repetitive announcements, which consisted of the apparent confession, 'I've been running back and forth at home'. It is a complicated matter to explain this. The running back and forth was a very early autistic ritual of his. He would run back and forth shaking his hands as though to rid himself of something. I had not seen him do this for years and he had told me he no longer did it in public places. The problem, however, was that what replaced the running was a newer ritual: the confession itself. The confession had become a subtle way of achieving several purposes: sometimes it was designed to annoy the listener, presumably his parents who knew he had mostly given up the running long ago but would also have been alarmed to hear it had happened again, because on one occasion he had been arrested for behaving in this crazy way in the middle of the street. So no doubt he had managed to get a rise out of his parents on a few occasions. Sometimes it was a way of getting someone to pay attention to him when he actually needed some contact but neither knew how to get it in more normal ways, nor even really knew that this was what he wanted. But I felt on this occasion there was a bit more to it, in that it was probably directly related to the noise of the footsteps upstairs. So I said that I thought he was trying to annoy me with this statement but that actually *he* had been annoyed that someone upstairs was walking back and forth.

Here, then, is an example of a 'stereotypy', the apparently meaningless opposite of an object-related contact, being used in what I would maintain was an object-related way. First, it was, I think, responsive, however instantaneously and invisibly, to something other people were doing within his hearing; and, second, it was being used to produce some sort of effect on me and in me – that is, for purposes of projection and avoidance of anxiety. (In fact, I think it was nothing like so perverted a use of the ritualistic confessions as it had been in the past.)

Robbie seemed to attend quietly, and the confession didn't get repeated and did not escalate into one of his more excited outpourings. I asked what he was thinking and he said, 'I'm thinking of the stars in the evening' (I hadn't heard about this for years, not since the days of his terrible hallucination/nightmare of falling off a cliff into the evening). He went on: 'The sky . . . is dark . . . and the moon is lovely . . . I want to be up there . . . I want to be up here.' I suddenly realized how rare it was for him to say that he wanted to *be* somewhere else. There were no 'somewhere elses' when he was in his ecstatic states; he didn't have to want to be there, because he usually felt he already *was* there. But on this occasion, in spite of the confusional use of the word 'here', there was also a concept of a place where he wanted to be and where he felt he was not. Then he went on: 'I want to live . . . here.' I said that I thought he wanted to live here with me, and be able to go upstairs like a member of my family. He replied, happily but not excitedly, 'I want to live on the moon. It's bright there.' I said he seemed to be enjoying being able to talk about these feelings and ideas. I was struck by the way in which he seemed like a very young child enjoying experimenting with phantasy and enjoying the experience of sharing the phantasies with someone. I tried to show him that in a way he had got up on the moon just now, because he'd felt so free to use his imagination and was enjoying sharing it with me. He did not at this point get more excited. He agreed with me, sounding alert and interested, and then came the use of the conditional. He said: 'I'd like to fly up there in a plane – in a spaceship . . . I'd like to fly to Spain . . . and France.' At that point I made another transference interpretation, somehow feeling I should not, but not quite understanding why at that point. What I said was something about his wish to be with me at the weekend. He started to rise into a very high state, and I realized that there were two problems: first, he had heard this not as a description of a wish but as a sort of collusive confirmation and gratification of a wish. My interpretation should have included the understanding that he was aware that Spain was a place *elsewhere*, or that he knew he could *not* be with me at the weekend; alternatively, I could have enabled him to go on with the experience of exploring the places he would like to go in his imagination called 'Spain and France'.

Winnicott's stress on the importance of respecting the transitional space is relevant here. As his mood began to rise into a highly sensual and perverse state, I said quickly and soberly that he knew by now that he did not spend his weekends with me but that what he had just been doing here at this moment was enjoying talking with me and using his imagination. He calmed down, but without deflating into despair as he might have years before, and said, playfully but not crazily,'The policemen would arrest me! . . . I'd like it if they would fly after me!' I said he felt I'd had to police him then, but I was very struck by his use of the conditional and the sense of his being able to play with ideas and to inhabit a hypothetical world.

In a session later that year the old theme of falling emerged again but with a difference. He had started the session in a very mad state

– repeating one of the old refrains – but I had managed, with his help, to get him out of it. He then told me he'd seen a film about a man who had fallen down a pit. 'The man was not dead . . . he climbed back up on the rope.' He said this with unusual strength and determination in his voice, and I pointed out that perhaps he felt he was rather like the man, because in fact he had started the session down in the pit of mindlessness but he had managed to climb back up out of the madness and make contact with me, and perhaps he was proud of himself. (It had been unusual to hear strength in his voice, which even when sane usually had a light, thin, uncertain quality to it. He always seemed to be feeling his way. No single word sounded rooted, partly, I suppose, because he was never sure where his thoughts were coming from or where they were going. But this was different.) He agreed with me, and remained sane and talkative for the rest of the session.

Two years later, when Robbie was 31, the image of falling into perversion appeared again, but by now in a far more animated and feeling way, and it seemed he had not so far to fall. He had come late, but had managed by himself, without any pressure from me, not to go into a mad, agitated state about his lateness. Later, he announced proudly, 'I kept my mind clean, I told the dirty thoughts to get lost!' At the end of the session he exhaled and mused, 'There, I didn't slip over . . . into the gutter . . . into the *slippery gutter!*' He said this with real contempt and revulsion in his voice, and added 'I stayed alive!' It was interesting that he no longer seemed to have quite so far to fall, the problem was no longer despair and a headlong fall out of control, but a slip. I was struck even more by the animation in his voice and the fact that instead of having to parrot or even to use respectfully but emptily one of my metaphors, he was able to use his own.

What these last two sessions demonstrate, I think, is that there are signs of the establishment of some ego, some capacity to think for himself and even to think feelingly about the value of sanity. It would be difficult to claim that there was much evidence of that in Robbie's sessions in previous years. In those days, it seemed that it was up to me to carry the ego functions of judgement and discrimination, and also to do the necessary 'policing'. But now he seemed to have internalized some of this, originally in a rather pious way, but by that last session, he really gave the impression of speaking with his own voice on behalf of something which could finally be called his *self*.

A few months later, he surprised himself, I think, and astonished me by discovering that he could criticize me for endangering his still fragile mental balance. The session had started sane but about half-way through I had interpreted some eagerness of his, and had done so in what I suspected was a somewhat too eager tone: my voice had lifted a bit. He immediately started his unpleasant grinning and licking of his lips. Sometimes asking him what he is thinking helps to evoke a more reflecting part of him, but at other times it only exacerbates the situation. I decided to ask what was happening, and he replied, 'Ooh forget it ! . . . It's none of your business!' This is a phrase which he had used previously, not exactly in an echolalic manner, but in a parroty way and for self-scolding when he felt some inner figure was objecting to his intrusiveness. He had also sometimes used it in a very stereotyped and perverse manner. But it came out of his mouth with some feeling and a note of impatience. He stopped short, seeming to have surprised himself, as if considering the astonishing fact that he'd said it to me, not to himself. Then he seemed to register that it was actually appropriate to direct the phrase in my direction. He had been turning around on the couch and looking at me a great deal in this session in a clear and direct manner. He looked again, as though checking that the phrase fitted, and then repeated it, his voice gathering force, 'It's none of your business . . . it's . . . private!' Then he added persuasively, but kindly, 'You don't want to know.' Amazed by such a direct communication, and feeling that I had nearly weakened his resolve with my question, I agreed that he was right. Agreement over the simplest of things has often carried the risk of over-exciting him, and he started to giggle but calmed down, and began: 'When I was a little boy, Mrs James [a teacher he loved – now dead] and Mrs C' [the speech therapist] . . . [Here my heart sank because these figures play a major part in his ritualistic talk and, when they do, his voice usually takes on the singsong perverse quality. But I realized his tone was, indeed, rather moved and quiet.] He finished: 'They helped me . . . they asked me questions. They helped me to find out . . . things.'

What is interesting is not only that Robbie was relating to me as a real person in the session, but that he seemed now to have achieved some degree of identification with a sane discriminating figure who has feelings about what is worth knowing and what is not. He discovered that he could have the power to tell *me* what I should and shouldn't want to know.

220

The next day, I wanted to give him the dates of my Christmas holidays. I suspected that he was perhaps not concentrating fully but nor was he off on one of his highs, so I decided to try. In the distant past, of course, he could take in nothing like that, but in the middle years of his treatment, if he had failed to take something in, he would try to force me to give it to him again. He would make wild guesses which often forced people to correct him and thus repeat themselves. In other words, he made manipulative use of his mindlessness and passivity and I had had to watch this carefully. He would try and read the expression in my eyes to see if he had guessed right or wrong, and he was good at this. But this was dramatically different. He did repeat the dates correctly but in an absent-minded automatic way, and then he must have suddenly realized they had not gone in, because he shouted in panic, 'Help! I've dropped them! I'm falling off the cliff! I need help! I've let go of the rock! I'm falling on to the railway tracks! I've lost the dates. I'm ... it's ... I'm ... dangerous.' (He had lately started referring to danger, but was muddled about how to distinguish between the object or situation which was dangerous and the person who was in danger. But this was unimportant, compared to the fact that, I think for the first time ever, he had really cried for help and really understood something about the tragedy of his mindlessness and of the great chasms and canyons in which his thoughts could get irretrievably lost.) I said that he did feel in great danger when he didn't hang on to his sanity and memory and his contact with live people, and that he knew it was dangerous when he let this happen. I repeated the dates, and he, with his mind apparently back in place, worked out immediately how many sessions he would miss.

Robbie is now 31 years old, so this account of his shockingly long treatment and the beginnings of the growth of a mind is not a success story. Clinicians nowadays prefer to begin the treatment of autistic children in the pre-school years where possible, whereas Robbie's intensive treatment did not begin until he was 13. Although the diagnosis of his autism has been confirmed on many occasions, some of them quite recent, he started with much less mental equipment than the shell-type autistic children described by Tustin (1972). His passivity and amoeboid floppiness were so extreme that in a way I seemed to be starting from scratch in the attempt to help him become a person. As the book shows, I had much to learn about deficit. His parents, however, report that he is more alert and interested these days and positively pleasant to be with.

He has stoppped his insistent repetitive talk and has even shown some interest in them as people. He has joined a drama group, which is good for his new-found but still very childish ability to play with ideas. He has apparently played his parts with gusto and even contributed the occasional witty improvisation. He has shown, particularly in the last two years, some development of real initiative. He can now look after the family house on his own for the occasional weekend. Recently he was robbed on the street, and, instead of panicking helplessly, he went straight to the police and then dealt resourcefully with the consequent delays in an already complicated set of arrangements for that particular day. He came to his session, explaining perfectly coherently why he was late, and also why he had to leave early to go to a football match. When he left, he reminded me, politely but firmly, not to forget to ring his mother and explain why he might be a little late!

As for me, I have learned a lot by working with him, and I think that some of what I have learned has helped him, however belatedly, to begin to use his mind. It is a source of great sadness to me that I did not know at the beginning of Robbie's treatment what I came to understand later. Certainly, the lessons I have learned with him, and from the more modern developments in psychoanalytic work described in other chapters, have helped other younger autistic and borderline patients – my own and the patients of therapists whose work I have been privileged to supervise – to improve much more quickly. We all owe a great debt to Robbie's parents for their patience, tolerance, forgiveness and support.

APPENDIX 1

Brazelton says that the mothers seem to offer five kinds of experience to their infants in a period of interaction:

1. REDUCTION OF INTERFERING ACTIVITY

As in Wolff's study, the babies are not driven by bodily needs or bodily discomfort. For a period of interaction with their mothers to take place, the babies have been fed, changed, had enough sleep and passing upsets dealt with. Passing distractions or startles, too:

> 'When the infant demonstrates unexpected random behaviour, such as the jerk of a leg or an arm, the mother responds by *stroking or holding that extremity, or by making a directed use of that extremity to jog it gently up and down, thereby turning an interfering activity into one that serves their interaction. In these ways she might be seen to teach the infant how to suppress and channel his own behaviour into a communications system* [my italics].'

2. SETTING THE STAGE

> 'As part of containing behaviour, she might use a method that *orients him toward her. She can adjust his body to the midline so that he faces her, pulling up his sagging torso so that he is in an alert position, reclining at a 30° angle, but alert rather than relaxed. She can move her head so that she is in his direct line of vision, bobbing or making facial gestures to attract his attention. . . . When she pats or strokes him, she does so with a*

223

rhythm and an intensity designed to alert as well as soothe (e.g. there was a two-per-second rhythm which most mothers used for soothing AND alerting, and a slower rhythm for simple soothing). When he sags, her intensity and speed increase, or they decrease when he becomes overexcited. The part of his body that she touches also serves a double purpose – of soothing and alerting, for example, *as he quiets to her stroking his legs or abdomen, she moves her hands up to his chest and finally to his cheek in order to arouse his attention and focus it on her* [my italics].'

3. CREATING AN EXPECTANCY FOR INTERACTION

'Characteristic of communication, her behaviours have certain features: (a) RHYTHM AND INTENSITY – although they may start off explosively or slowly, they are quickly modulated to respond to the attention of the infant. Vocalizing, nodding, facial gestures, and patting, which starts off explosively or soothingly, are quickly geared to maintain the interaction. (b) AMPLITUDE is meshed in the same way. Large facial or arm gestures might initiate the sequence but are rapidly decreased in amplitude as his attention is caught. (c) DIRECTION. Since her effort is to *orient him to her face as the central focus, all these movements are reduced in amplitude and from the periphery inward in a way that will bring his focus to her face, using her movement to activate and then to siphon his attention into a central focus on her eyes and mouth.* (d) QUALITY is especially 'appropriate' to an interaction with an infant. Speech is simplified in rhythm and *pitched to gain and hold his attention*; for example, baby talk was high pitched, vowel-like, and interspersed with alerting consonants such as b, d, h, and tch. A mother's eyes and lips widen and close in rhythmic movements designed *alternately to alert and soothe her baby.* As he quiets, her vocalizations and facial movements become rhythmic and 'holding', and then speed up with more staccato and a faster pace. Her eyes alternately narrow and widen; bright and dull in a measure appropriate to his state. When he overreacts, her eyes take on a soothing look, becoming wider and brighter, to attract and 'hold' his attention [my italics].'

Brazelton goes on to describe how the mothers go about providing the fourth kind of experience, that is, INTENSIFICATION OF HIS ATTENTION. This is achieved by accelerating the interaction by, e.g., substituting one action for another, or adding them in sequences. He points out that a stimulus which may be accelerative at a certain point may serve to overload the baby at another.

The fifth kind of experience has to do with the kind of receptive sensitivity more familiar to psychoanalytic theorists. He calls it: ALLOWING FOR RECIPROCITY, i.e allowing the baby to digest and recover from the interaction, and also allowing him to reciprocate, and respond to her in his turn (Brazelton *et al.* 1974: 64–7).

APPENDIX 2

Klein's first mention of the 'manic position' is in the 'Contribution' paper (1935). After discussing the disparagement and contempt for the object characteristic of the manic defence, Klein says, 'Before I go on to make a few suggestions about the part which the paranoid, depressive and manic positions play in normal development, I shall speak about two dreams of a patient, which illustrate some of the points I have put forward in connection with the psychotic positions' (1935: 279). She goes on to talk about extremely pathological situations, but she does not return to the normal ones. Later, she says something very similar. 'Space does not permit me to deal here in detail with the ways in which the normal child works through the depressive and manic positions, which, in my view, make up a part of normal development'(p.284). She says she will confine herself to a few remarks of a general nature and then she goes on to describe her view of normal development, that at approximately 4 to 5 months of age the ego is made to realize that the loved object is the hated one. It comes to know its mother as a whole person and becomes identified with her as a whole, real and loved person. It is ther. that the depressive position comes to the fore and it is stimulated and reinforced by the loss of the loved object, which the baby experiences over and over again when the mother's breast is taken away from it. This loss reaches its climax during weaning. She stresses the difference between the normal baby in the depressive position and the adult melancholic, but also the similarities in terms of the problem of dealing with loss. Then she goes on to say that it is also at this early stage of development that the manic phantasies about controlling the breast and later the parents set in with all the characteristics of the manic position, and this is used to combat the depressive position. She indicates that the manic phantasies are defensive but also necessary (Klein 1935). Klein also makes an interesting comment on the importance of 'weaning to' alongside 'weaning from' (Klein 1936: 304).

226

BIBLIOGRAPHY

Abraham, K. (1927) *Selected Papers on Psycho-Analysis*, London: Maresfield Reprints (1979).

Alvarez, A. (1977) 'Problems of dependence and development in an excessively passive autistic boy', *J. Child Psychother.* 4.

—— (1980) 'Two regenerative situations in autism: reclamation and becoming vertebrate', *J. Child Psychother.* 6.

—— (1985) 'The problem of neutrality: some reflections on the psycho-analytic attitude in the treatment of borderline and psychotic children', *J. Child Psychother.* 11,1.

—— (1988) 'Beyond the unpleasure principle: some preconditions for thinking through play', *J. of Child Psychother.* 14,2.

—— (1989) 'Development toward the latency period: splitting and the need to forget in borderline children', *J. Child Psychother.* 15,2.

—— (1990a) 'Riparazione: alcuni precusori', *Prospettivi psicoanalitiche nel lavoro istituzionale* 8,3.

—— (1990b) 'The need to remember and the need to forget', in *The Consequences of Child Sexual Abuse*, Chapter 4, from ACPP Occasional Papers 3.

Balint, M. (1968) *The Basic Fault: Therapeutic Aspects of Regression*, London: Tavistock (1979).

Barker, P. (1983) *Basic Child Psychiatry*, London: Collins.

Baron-Cohen, S. (1988) 'Social and pragmatic deficits in autism: cognitive or affective?', *J. Aut. Devel. Dis.* 18,3.

Barrows, A. (1988) *Asperger's Syndrome: a Theoretical and Clinical Account*, unpublished doctoral dissertation, Wright Institute Graduate School of Psychology.

Barzun, J. (1987) *A Stroll with William James*, Chicago: Univ. of Chicago Press.

Bateson, G. (1955) 'A theory of play and fantasy', in Bruner, J.S., Jolly, A. and Sylva, K. (eds) *Play: Its Role in Development and Evolution*, Harmondsworth, Middx.: Penguin (1985).

Bentovim, A. (1979) 'Child development research findings and psycho-analytic theory: an integrative critique', in Shaffer, D. and Dunn, J. (eds) *The First Year of Life: Psychological and Medical Implications of Early Experience*, New York: Wiley.

Bettelheim, B. (1967) *The Empty Fortress*, New York: Free Press.

Bick, E. (1966) 'Infant observation in psychoanalytic training', *Int. J. Psycho-Anal.* 45.

—— (1968) 'The experience of the skin in early object-relations', *Int. J. Psycho-Anal.* 49.

Bion, W.R. (1950) 'The imaginary twin', in *Second Thoughts; Selected Papers on Psycho-Analysis*, London: Heinemann (1967).

—— (1957) 'Differentiation of the psychotic from the non-psychotic personalities', in *Second Thoughts: Selected Papers on Psycho-Analysis*, London: Heinemann (1967).

—— (1959) 'Attacks on linking', in *Second Thoughts: Selected Papers on Psycho-Analysis*, London: Heinemann (1967).

—— (1962) *Learning from Experience*, London: Heinemann.

—— (1963) *Elements of Psychoanalysis*, London: Heinemann.

—— (1965) *Transformations*, London: Heinemann.

—— (1957) 'On arrogance', in *Second Thoughts: Selected Papers on Psycho-Analysis*, London: Heinemann (1967).

—— (1967) 'A theory of thinking', in *Second Thoughts: Selected Papers on Psycho-Analysis*, London: Heinemann (1967).

——(1980) Discussion Group, London.

Bird, G, and Stokes, R. (1976) *The Fischer-Dieskau Book of Lieder*, London: Gollancz.

Bollas, C. (1989) *Forces of Destiny*, London: Free Association Books.

Bondioli, A., Achinto, F. and Savio, D. (1987) 'Intersubjective motivations and symbolic production: observations in a nursery school', Department of Philosophy, University of Pavia. *Scuola e Citta* 11.

Bower, T.G.R. (1974) *Development in Infancy*, San Francisco: W.H. Freeman.

Bowlby, J. (1969) *Attachment and Loss I*, London: Hogarth.

—— (1973) *Attachment and Loss III*, New York: Basic Books.

—— (1988) *A Secure Base: Clinical Applications of Attachment Theory*, London: Routledge.

Bradley, J. (1985) 'In search of pure stone: psychotherapy with a sexually assaulted boy', *J. Child Psychother.* 11,1.

Brazelton, T.B., Koslowski, B. and Main, M. (1974) 'The origins of reciprocity: the early mother–infant interaction', in Lewis, M. and Rosenblum, L.A. (eds) *The Effect of the Infant on its Caregivers*, London: Wiley Interscience.

Brenman Pick, I. (1985) 'Working through in the counter-transference', in Spillius, E. (ed.) *Melanie Klein Today, vol 2: Mainly Practice*, London: Routledge (1988).

Bruner, J.S. (1968) *Processes of Cognitive Growth: Infancy*, USA: Clark Univ. Press.

——(1986) *Actual Minds, Possible Worlds*, Cambridge, Mass.: Harvard Univ. Press.

Bruner, J.S., Jolly, A. and Sylva, K. (1976) *Play*, Harmondsworth, Middx: Penguin.

Byng-Hall, J. and Campbell, D. (1981) 'Resolving conflicts arising from distance-regulation: an integrative approach', *J. Marit. Fam. Ther.* 7.

Carpy, D. (1989) 'Tolerating the counter-transference: a mutative process', *Int. J. Psycho-Anal. 70.*

Casement, P. (1985) *On Learning from the Patient*, London: Tavistock.

Cassel, Z.K. and Sander, L.W. (1975) 'Neonatal recognition processes and attachment: the masking experiment', presented at the Society for Research in Child Development and cited in Klaus and Kennell (1982).

Chethik, M. and Fast, I. (1970) 'A function of fantasy in the borderline child', Amer. J. Orthopsychiat. 40.

Coltart, N. (1986) 'Slouching toward Bethlehem . . . or thinking the unthinkable in psychoanalysis', in Kohon, G. (ed.) *The British School of Psychoanalysis: The Independent Tradition*. London: Free Association Books.

Curcio, F. (1978) 'Sensorimotor functioning and communication in mute autistic children', J. Aut. Childhood Schiz. 8

Daws, D. (1989) *Through the Night: Helping Parents and Sleepless Infants*, London: Free Association Books.

Dawson, G. and Lewy, A. (1989a) 'Arousal, attention, and the socio-emotional impairments of individuals with Autism', in Dawson, G. (ed.) *Autism: Nature, Diagnosis, and Treatment*, New York: Guilford Press.

—— (1989b) 'Reciprocal subcortical-cortical influences in autism: the role of attentional mechanisms', in Dawson, G. (ed.) *Autism: Nature, Diagnosis and Treatment*, New York: Guilford Press.

Di Cagno, L., Lazzarini, A., Rissone, A. and Randaccio, S. (1984) *Il Neonato e il suo Mondo Relazionale*, Rome: Borla.

Dyke, S. (1985) Review of D.W. Winnicott's 'Deprivation and delinquency', *J. of Child Psychother.* ll,2.

Eisenberg, R. (1970) 'The organization of auditory behaviour', in Stone, J.L., Smith, H.T. and Murphy, L.B. (eds) *The Competent Infant*, London: Tavistock (1974).

Erikson, E.H. (1950) *Childhood and Society*. Harmondsworth, Middx: Pelican.

Fairbairn, W.R.D. (1952) *Psychoanalytic Studies of the Personality*, London: Routledge & Kegan Paul.

Fe D'Ostiani, E. (1980) 'An individual approach to psychotherapy with psychotic patients', *J. Child Psychother.* 6.

Fogel, A. (1976) 'Temporal organization in mother–infant face-to-face interaction', in Schaffer. H.R. (ed.) *Studies in Mother–Infant Interaction*, London: Academic Press.

Fordham, M. (1976) *The Self and Autism*, London: Heinemann.

Fraiberg, S. (1974) 'Blind infants and their mothers: an examination of the sign system', in Lewis, M. and Rosenblum, L.A. (eds) *The Effect of the Infant on its Caregiver*, New York: Wiley.

Freeman, N., Lloyd, S. and Sinha, C. (1980) 'Hide and seek in children's play', *New Scientist*, 30 Oct., 1225,88.

Freud, A. (1936) *The Ego and the Mechanisms of Defence*, London: Hogarth (1986).

—— (1980) *Normality and Pathology in Childhood*, London: Hogarth and the Inst. of Psycho-Anal.

Freud, S. (1895) 'Project for a scientific psychology', *Standard Edition* I, London: Hogarth (1966).

229

Freud, S. (1900) 'The interpretation of dreams', *S.E.* V (1966).
—— (1905a) 'Fragment of an analysis of a case of hysteria', *S.E.* VII.
—— (1905b) 'Three essays on the theory of sexuality', *S.E.* VII.
—— (1909) 'Notes upon a case of obsessional neurosis', *S.E.* X.
—— (1911a) 'Psychoanalytic notes on an autobiographical account of a case of paranoia', *S.E.* XII.
—— (1911b) 'Formulations on the two principles of mental functioning'. *S.E.* XII.
—— (1912) 'Papers on technique', *S.E.* XII.
—— (1914) 'Remembering, repeating and working-through', *S.E.* XII.
—— (1917) 'Mourning and melancholia', *S.E.* XIV.
—— (1920) 'Beyond the pleasure principle', *S.E.* XVIII.
Frith, U. (1989) *Autism: Explaining the Enigma*, Oxford: Blackwell.
Gillberg, C. (1990) 'Autism and pervasive developmental disorders', *J. Child Psychol. Psychiat.* 31,1.
Gleick, J. (1987) *Chaos*, London: Sphere Books.
Greenberg, J.R. and Mitchell, S.A. (1983) *Object Relations in Psychoanalytic Theory*, London: Harvard Univ. Press.
Grotstein, J. (1979) 'The psychoanalytic concept of the borderline organization', in LeBoit, J. and Capponi, A. (eds) *Advances in the Psychotherapy of the Borderline Patient*, London: Aronson.
—— (1981a) 'Wilfred R. Bion: The man, the psychoanalyst, the mystic. A perspective on his life and work', in *Do I Dare Disturb the Universe? A Memorial to Wilfred R. Bion*, Beverly Hills, CA: Caesura Press.
—— (1981b) *Splitting and Projective Identification*, London: Aronson.
—— (1983) Review of Tustin's *Autistic States in Children*, in *Internat. Rev. of Psycho-Anal.* 10.
Hartmann, E. (1984) *The Nightmare*, New York: Basic Books.
Hartmann, H. (1964) *Essays on Ego Psychology: Selected Problems in Psychoanalytic Theory*, New York: Int. Univ. Press (1981).
Hedges, L.E. (1983) *Listening Perspectives in Psychotherapy*, London: Aronson.
Heimann, P. (1952) 'Certain functions of introjection and projection in early infancy', in Klein, M. *et al. Developments in Psychoanalysis*, London: Hogarth.
Hinshelwood, R.D. (1989) *A Dictionary of Kleinian Thought*, London: Free Association Books.
Hobson, P. (1989) 'Beyond cognition: a theory of autism', in Dawson, G. (ed.) *Autism: Nature, Diagnosis and Treatment*, New York: Guilford.
—— (1990) 'On psychoanalytic approaches to autism', *Amer. J. Orthopsychiat.* 60,3.
Hocking, B. (1990) *Little Boy Lost*, London: Bloomsbury.
Hofstadter, D.R. (1981) *Gödel, Escher, Bach: An Eternal Golden Braid*, Harmondsworth, Middx: Penguin.
Howlin, P. and Rutter, M. (1987) *Treatment of Autistic Children*, Chichester: Wiley.
Hoxter, S. (1977) 'Play and communication', in Daws, D. and Boston, M. (eds) *The Child Psychotherapist and Problems of Young People*, London: Wildwood House.

Hunter, M. (1986) 'The monster and the ballet dancer', *J. Child Psychother.* 12,2.

Hutchinson, F.E. (ed.) (1953) *The Works of George Herbert*, London: Oxford Univ. Press.

Hutt, C. (1966) 'Exploration and play in children', in Bruner, J.S., Jolly, A. and Sylva, K. (eds) (1976) *Play: Its Role in Development and Evolution*, Harmondsworth, Middx: Penguin Books.

Isaacs, S. (1952) 'The nature and function of phantasy', in Klein, M. *et al. Developments in Psychoanalysis*, London: Hogarth.

Joseph, B. (1975) 'The patient who is difficult to reach', in Feldman, M. and Spillius, E. (eds) *Psychic Equilibrium and Psychic Change*, London: Tavistock/Routledge (1989).

—— (1978) 'Different types of anxiety and their handling in the clinical situation', in Feldman, M. and Spillius, E. (eds) *Psychic Equilibrium and Psychic Change*, London: Tavistock/Routledge (1989).

—— (1982) 'Addiction to near-death', in Feldman, M. and Spillius, E. (eds) *Psychic Equilibrium and Psychic Change*, London: Tavistock/Routledge (1989).

—— (1983) 'On understanding and not understanding: some technical issues', in Feldman, M. and Spillius, E. (eds) *Psychic Equilibrium and Psychic Change*, London: Tavistock/Routledge (1989).

—— (1986) 'Psychic change and the psychoanalytic process', in Feldman, M. and Spillius, E. (eds) *Psychic Equilibrium and Psychic Change*, London: Tavistock/Routledge (1989).

—— (1987) 'Projective identification: some clinical aspects', in Feldman, M. and Spillius, E. (eds) *Psychic Equilibrium and Psychic Change*, London: Tavistock/Routledge (1989).

Judd, D. (1989) *Give Sorrow Words: Working with a Dying Child*, London: Free Association Books.

Kanner, L. (1944) 'Early infantile autism', *J. Paediatrics 25,3*.

Kanter, J.S. (1984) 'Resocialization in schizophrenia: renegotiating the latency era', *Int. Rev. of Psycho-Anal.* 11,1.

Klaus, M.H. and Kennell, J.H. (1982) *Parent–Infant Bonding*, London: C. H. Mosby.

Klein, M. (1921) 'The development of a child', in *The Writings of Melanie Klein, Vol. 1*, London: Hogarth (1975).

—— (1932) 'The psycho-analysis of children' in *The Writings of Melanie Klein, Vol 2*, London: Hogarth (1975).

—— (1935) 'A contribution to the psychogenesis of manic-depressive states', in *The Writings of Melanie Klein, Vol. 1*.

—— (1936) 'Weaning', *The Writings of Melanie Klein, Vol. 1*.

—— (1937) 'Love, guilt and reparation', in *The Writings of Melanie Klein, Vol. 1*.

—— (1940) 'Mourning and its relation to manic-depressive states,' in *The Writings of Melanie Klein, Vol. 1*.

—— (1946) 'Notes on some schizoid mechanisms', in *The Writings of Melanie Klein, Vol 3*.

—— (1952) 'Some theoretical conclusions regarding the emotional life of the infant', in *The Writings of Melanie Klein, Vol 3*.

Klein, M. (1955) 'On identification', in *The Writings of Melanie Klein, Vol 3*.
—— (1961) *Narrative of a Child Analysis*, London: Hogarth.
Kleitman, N. (1963) *Sleep and Wakefulness*, Chicago: Univ. of Chicago Press.
Kohut, H. (1985) *The Analysis of the Self*, New York: Internat. Univ. Press.
Kolvin, I. *et al.* (1971) 'Studies in the childhood psychoses I to VI', *Brit. J. Psychiat.* 118.
Kundera, M. (1981) *The Book of Laughter and Forgetting*, Harmondsworth, Middx.: Penguin.
—— (1984) *The Unbearable Lightness of Being*, London: Faber.
—— (1986) Lecture at Mishkenot on receiving Jerusalem Prize for Literature on the Freedom of Mankind.
Kut Rosenfeld, S. and Sprince, M. (1963) 'An attempt to formulate the meaning of the concept "Borderline"', *Psychoanal. Study Child*, 18.
—— (1965) 'Some thoughts on the technical handling of borderline children', *Psychoanal. Study Child* 20.
Laplanche, J., and Pontalis, B. (1973) *The Language of Psychoanalysis*, London: Hogarth.
LeBoit, J. and Capponi, A. (1979) 'The technical problem with the borderline patient', in *Advances in the Psychotherapy of the Borderline Patient*, London: Aronson.
Leslie, A. M. (1987) 'Pretence and representation: the origins of "Theory of Mind"', *Psycholog. Rev.* 94.
Liley, A. W. (1972) 'The foetus as a personality', *Australian and New Zealand J. Psychiat.* 6.
Lowenfeld, M. (1935) *Play in Childhood*, London: Gollancz.
Luria, A. R. (1968) *The Mind of a Mnemonist*, New York: Basic Books.
Macfarlane, A. (1977) *The Psychology of Childbirth*, London: Fontana/Open Books.
Malcolm, R. (1986) 'Interpretation: the past in the present', in Spillius, E. (ed.) *Melanie Klein Today, Vol. 2: Mainly Practice*, London: Routledge (1988).
Mandelstam, N. (1970) *Hope Against Hope*, New York: Atheneum.
Meltzer, D. (1973) 'The origins of the fetishistic plaything of sexual perversions', in *Sexual States of Mind*, Strath Tay: Clunie.
—— (1975) *Explorations in Autism: a Psycho-Analytical Study*, Strath Tay: Clunie.
—— (1978) *The Kleinian Development. Part II. Richard Week-by-Week*, Strath Tay: Clunie.
Miller, L., Rustin, M., Rustin, M., and Shuttleworth, J. (1989) *Closely Observed Infants*, London: Duckworth.
Money-Kyrle, R. (1977) 'On being a psychoanalyst', in Meltzer, D. and O'Shaughnessy, E. (eds) *The Collected Papers of Roger Money-Kyrle*, Strath Tay: Clunie.
Muir, E. (1987) *Autobiography*, London: Hogarth.
Murray, L. (1991) 'The impact of postnatal depression on infant development', *J. Child Psychol. Psychiat.*
Murray, L. and Trevarthen, C. (1985) 'Emotional regulation of interactions

between two month olds and their mothers', in Filed, T. M. and Fox, N. (eds) *Social Perception in Infants*, New Jersey: Ablex.

Newson, J. (1977) 'An intersubjective approach to the systematic description of mother–infant interaction', in Schaffer, H.R. (ed.) *Studies in Mother–Infant Interaction*, London: Academic Press.

Ornstein, P.H. (1983) 'Discussion of papers by Drs. Goldberg, Stolorow and Wallerstein', in Lichtenberg, J.D. and Kaplan, S. (eds) *Reflections on Self Psychology*, London: Analytic Press.

O'Shaughnessy, E. (1964) 'The absent object', *J. Child Psychother.* 1,2.

—— (1989) 'The invisible Oedipus complex', in Steiner, J. (ed.) *The Oedipus Complex Today: Clinical Implications*, London: Karnac.

Papousek, H. and Papousek, M. (1976) 'Mothering and the cognitive head start: psychobiological considerations', in Schaffer, H.R. (ed.) *Studies in Mother–Infant Interaction*, London: Academic Press.

Piontelli, A. (1987) 'Infant observation from before birth', *Int. J. Psycho-Anal.* 68.

Pynoos, R. and Eth, S. (1985) *Post Traumatic Stress Disorder in Children*, Washington, DC: American Psychiatric Press.

Rayner, E. (1981) 'Infinite experiences, affects, and the characteristics of the unconscious', *Int. J. Psycho-Anal.* 62.

Reid, S. (1990) 'The importance of beauty in the psychoanalytic experience', *J. Child Psychother.* 16.

Robson, K. (1967) 'The role of eye-to-eye contact in maternal–infant attachment', *J. Child Psychol. Psychiat.* 8.

Rosenfeld, H. (1964) 'On the psychopathology of narcissism: a clinical approach', in *Psychotic States*, London: Hogarth (1965).

—— (1965) *Psychotic States: a Psycho-analytical Approach*, London: Hogarth.

—— (1972) 'A critical appreciation of James Strachey's paper on the Nature of the Therapeutic Action of Psychoanalysis', *Int. J. Psycho-Anal.* 53.

—— (1981) 'On the psychology and treatment of psychotic patients', in Grotstein, J. (ed.) *Do I Dare Disturb the Universe?*, Beverly Hills, CA: Caesura Press.

—— (1987) *Impasse and Interpretation*, London: Tavistock.

Rutter, M. (1981) *Maternal Deprivation Reassessed*, Harmondsworth, Middx.: Penguin.

—— (1983) 'Cognitive deficits in the pathogenesis of autism', *J. Child Psychol. Psychiat.* 24.

Sacks, O. (1973) *Awakenings*, London: Duckworth.

—— (1985) *The Man who Mistook his Wife for a Hat*, London: Picador.

Sandler, J. (1988) *Projection, Identification, Projective Identification*, London: Karnac.

Sandler, J. with Freud, A. (1985) *The Analysis of Defence*, New York: Int. Univ. Press.

Schaffer, H.R. (1977) 'Early interactive development', in Schaffer, H.R. (ed.) *Studies in Mother–Infant Interaction*, London: Academic Press.

Segal, H. (1950) 'Some aspects of the analysis of a schizophrenic', in *The Work of Hanna Segal*, New York: Aronson (1981).

Segal, H. (1957) 'Notes on symbol formation', in *The Work of Hanna Segal*, New York: Aronson (1981).

—— (1964) *Introduction to the Work of Melanie Klein*, London: Heinemann.

—— (1981) *The Work of Hanna Segal: A Kleinian Approach to Clinical Practice*, London: Aronson.

Sinason. V.E. (1986) 'Secondary mental handicap and its relationship to trauma', *Psychoanal. Psychother.* 2,2.

—— (1988) 'Smiling, swallowing, sickening and stupefying: the effect of abuse on the child', *Psychoanal. Psychother.* 3,2.

Spensley, S. (1985) 'Cognitive deficit, mindlessness and psychotic depression', *J. Child Psychother.* 11,1.

Spillius, E. (1988a) *Melanie Klein Today, Vol. 1*, London: Routledge.

—— (1988b) *Melanie Klein Today, Vol. 2: Mainly Practice*, London: Routledge.

Spitz, R.A. (1946)'Anaclitic depression', *Psychoanal. Study Child* 2.

Steiner, J. (1979) 'The border between the paranoid-schizoid and the depressive positions in the borderline patient', *Brit. J. Med. Psychol.* 52.

—— (1991) 'A psychotic organization of the personality', *Int. J. Psycho-Anal.* 72

Stern, D. (1974) 'Mother and infant at play: the dyadic interaction involving facial, vocal and gaze behaviours', in Lewis, M. and Rosenblum. L.A. (eds) *The Effect of the Infant on its Caregiver*, New York: Wiley.

—— (1977) 'Missteps in the dance', in *The first Relationship: Infant and Mother*, Cambridge, Mass.: Harvard Univ. Press.

—— (1983) 'The early development of schemas of Self, Other and Self with Other', in Lichtenberg, J.D. and Kaplan, S. (eds) *Reflections on Self Psychology*, Hillsdale, NJ: Erlbaum.

—— (1985) *The Interpersonal World of the Infant*, New York: Basic Books.

Stern, D. and Gibbon, J. (1978) 'Temporal expectancies of social behavior in mother–infant play', in Thoman, E.B. (ed.) *Origins of the Infant's Social Responsiveness*, Hillsdale, NJ: Erlbaum.

Stolorow, R.D., Brandchaft, B. and Atwood, G.E. (1987) *Psychoanalytic Treatment: An Intersubjective Approach*, Hillsdale, NJ: Analytic Press.

Stolorow, R.D. and Lachmann, F.M. (1980) *Psychoanalysis of Developmental Arrests*, Madison, Conn.:Int. Univ. Press.

Storr, A. (1983) *Jung: Selected Writings*, London: Fontana, 1986.

Strachey, J. (1934) 'The nature of the therapeutic action of psychoanalysis', *Int. J. Psycho-Anal.* 15.

Sullivan. H.S. (1953) *The Interpersonal Theory of Psychiatry*, New York: Norton.

Symington, N. (1980) 'The response aroused by the psychopath', *Int. Rev. Psycho-Anal.* 7.

—— (1986) 'The analyst's act of freedom as agent of therapeutic change', in Kohon, G. (ed.) *The British School of Psychoanalysis: The Independent Tradition*, London: Free Association Books.

Trevarthen, C. (1974) 'Conversations with a two-month old', *New Scientist* 2 May.

Trevarthen, C. (1977) 'Descriptive analyses of infant communicative behavior', in Schaffer, H.R. (ed.) *Studies in Mother–Infant Interaction*, London: Academic Press.

—— (1978) 'Modes of perceiving and codes of acting', in Pick, H.J. (ed.) *Psychological Modes of Perceiving and Processing Information*, Hillsdale, NJ: Erlbaum.

—— (1984) 'Emotions in infancy: regulators of contacts and relationships with persons', in Scherer, K. and Ekman, P. (eds) *Approaches to Emotion*, Hillsdale, NJ: Erlbaum.

—— (1986) 'Development of intersubjective motor control in infants', in Wade, M.G. and Whiting, H.G.A. (eds.) *Motor Development in Children: Aspects of Coordination and Control*, Dordrecht: Martinus Nijhof.

Trevarthen, C. and Hubley, P. (1978) 'Secondary intersubjectivity: confidence, confiding and acts of meaning in the first year', in Lock, A. (ed.) *Action, Gesture and Symbol: The Emergence of Language*, London: Academic Press.

Trevarthen, C. and Logotheti, K. (1989) 'Child and culture: genesis of co-operative knowing', in Gellatly, P., Rogers, D. and Sloboda, J.A. (eds.) *Cognition and Social Worlds*, Oxford: Clarendon Press.

Trevarthen, C. and Marwick (1986) 'Signs of motivation for speech in infants, and the nature of a mother's support for development of language', in Lindblom, B. and Zetterstrom, R. (eds) *Precursors of Early Speech*, Basingstoke, Hants: Macmillan.

Tustin, F. (1972) *Autism and Childhood Psychosis*, London: Hogarth.

—— (1980) 'Autistic objects', *Int. Rev. Psycho-Anal. 7*.

—— (1981) *Autistic States in Children*, London: Routledge & Kegan Paul.

—— (1986) *Autistic Barriers in Neurotic Patients*, London: Karnac.

—— (1990) *The Protective Shell in Children and Adults*, London: Karnac.

Urwin, C. (1987) 'Developmental psychology and psychoanalysis: splitting the difference', in Richards, M. and Light, P. (eds) *Children of Social Worlds*. Cambridge: Polity.

Vygotsky, L. (1978) *Mind in Society: the Development of Higher Psychological Processes*, London: Harvard Univ. Press.

Wallerstein, R.S. (1983) 'Self psychology and "Classical" psychoanalysis – the nature of their relationship', in Lichtenberg, J.D. and Kaplan, S. (eds) *Reflections on Self Psychology*, London: Analytic Press.

Wells, H.G. (1985) *Christina Alberta's Father*, London: Hogarth.

White, A. (1979) *Beyond the Glass*, London: Virago.

Wing, L. and Gould, J. (1979) 'Severe impairments of social interaction and associated abnormalities in children: epidemiology and classification', *J. Aut. Devel. Dis. 9*.

Winnicott, D. (1935) 'The manic defence', in *Collected Papers. Through Paediatrics to Psycho-analysis*, London: Tavistock (1958).

—— (1951) 'Transitional objects and transitional phenomena', in *Collected Papers: Through Paediatrics to Psycho-analysis*, London: Tavistock (1958).

—— (1958) *Collected Papers: Through Paediatrics to Psycho-analysis*, London: Tavistock.

Winnicott, D. (1960) 'The theory of the parent–infant relationship', in *The Maturational Processes and the Facilitating Environment*, London: Hogarth (1965).

—— (1965) *The Maturational Processes and the Facilitating Environment*, London: Hogarth.

—— (1971) *Playing and Reality*, London: Tavistock.

Wolff, P.H. (1965) 'The development of attention in young infants', in Stone, L.J., Smith, H.T. and Murphy, L.B. (eds) *The Competent Infant: Research and Commentary*, London: Tavistock (1974).

Wollheim. R. (1971) *Freud*, London: Fontana Modern Masters.

—— (1984) *The Thread of Life*, Cambridge: Cambridge Univ. Press.

Woolridge, M.W. (1986) 'The "anatomy" of infant sucking', *Midwifery* 2.

NAME INDEX

Abraham, K. 115
Achinto, F. 179
Adler, A. 15
Alan 156–9
Alessandro 85, 89
Alice 120, 121
Andrew 122, 123, 125, 126
Asperger 204, 213
Atwood, G.E. 202

Bach, J.S. 11, 143
Baron–Cohen, S. 193–7
Barrows, A. 213
Barzun, Jacques 42
Bateson, Gregory 58
Beckett, S. 168
Bentovim, A. 71
Bick, Esther 62, 197
Bion, Wilfred 1, 3, 4, 6, 9, 25, 26,
    46, 53, 54, 56, 57, 58, 60, 63, 66,
    73, 75–7, 86, 88, 92–5, 100, 106,
    113, 116, 117, 130, 154, 165, 169,
    176, 177, 179, 180, 191, 193, 197,
    198, 199
Blanco, Ignacio Matte 3
Bollas, C. 197
Bondioli, A. 179
Borderline Workshop 109
Bower, T.G.R. 74, 80, 96
Bowlby, J. 82, 117
Brandchaft, B. 202
Brazelton, T.B. 67, 68, 69, 72, 84,
    99, 100, 146, 197, 198, 223
Brendel, Alfred 60

Bruner, Jerome 93, 95, 96, 97,
    107, 117, 170

Capponi, A. 109
Carol 180, 181
Catherine 161
Chethik, M. 109
Cindy 98–103, 106
Clara 111, 112
Coltart, N. 85
Cordelia 51, 54
Cousteau, Jacques 42
Curcio, F. 203

Danny 181
Dawson, G. 192, 204–6, 209

Escher, M.C. 10, 143

Fairbairn, W.R.D. 2, 116
Fast, I. 109
Fordham, Michael 165
Freud, Anna 5, 113, 117, 130;
    clinic 109
Freud, S. 1, 2, 5, 7, 9, 10, 15, 43,
    53, 54, 62, 63, 74, 92, 115, 119,
    128, 154, 165, 166, 169, 170,
    173, 212
Frith, Uta 188–90, 192–4, 197, 203,
    206, 208, 209, 210, 216

Giannotti, A. 185
Gillberg, C. 186

SUBJECT INDEX

absence, notion of 64, 170
abstract representations 74
abuse *see* sexual abuse
accessibility 77, 79
activation, level of 76
affects: categorical 75; deficits in
    197, 201; vitality 75; *see also*
    emotions
agency, sense of 117
aggression 139
agitation 124
alarm, arousal of 56–8, 60, 85
alertness, infant 9, 63, 66; maternal
    role in 67, 68, 84, 197, 224
alimentary model 78, 79
aliveness, expression of 131
alpha function of mind 75–6,
    88–91
alternation 95, 97
alternative object 197
anorexia 90
anticipatory identification 175, 183
anxiety 5, 72, 76, 139; avoidance of
    217; depressive 116; overcoming
    121; persecutory 118; relief
    from 119
apathy 127, 186
arousal: inability to modulate
    204–7; infant 61
arrogance 5, 19, 130
articulated link, with reality 26, 27
ascensive feelings 131, 132
attention: abnormalities of 205;
    eliciting 203, 206; intensification

of 225; shared 203; span
    67, 68, 73
attraction 84, 206
autism 14, 23, 40, 81, 83, 122, 124,
    136, 138, 149, 156, 199, 200;
    aetiology of 82, 184, 185–8, 191,
    200; affective theory of 196;
    amoeboid type 190; awakening
    from 163; beginnings of 31,
    57; behavioural description
    of 200, 201; causation of 184,
    186; cognitive theory of 196;
    entangling type 190; higher-level
    204; improvements in 133;
    organicist theory of 184, 192–6,
    200, 206, 213; psychoanalytic
    theory of 184; psychological
    features of 188–91, 199;
    shell-type 189, 190, 194, 221;
    study of 198; sub-types of 189;
    treatment of 21, 35, 184
autistic: objects 43, 44, 167, 193,
    197, 212, 213; residues 209; *see
    also* transitional objects
avoidance 189
awakening 29–32, 50–1, 55, 65

backbone, as a metaphor 45–9, 52,
    215; *see also* firmness
balance: between illusion and
    disillusion 169; mental 220
beauty, appreciation of 121
benign circles 144, 147, 187; *see
    also* vicious circles

240

thought disorder *see* thinking
defect
thoughtfulness, teaching of 7
time: preoccupation with 36;
-scale, absence of 29, 93, 97, 98
transference 2, 51, 54, 55, 79, 84,
102, 109, 110, 123, 126, 202, 210,
218; narcissistic 108, 110, 111
transformation 4, 53, 76, 78,
105, 197
transition, difficulties with 42, 177
transitional: identifications 179;
level 168; objects 43, 44, 167,
209; space, respecting 218
translating function 3, 4, 88
trauma 151, 154
triumph 134
two-trackedness 101, 106, 107
typogenetics 143–4

unassociated thoughts 95
unconscious 6

understanding, seeking of, by
infants 9
unfolding *see* translating
unintegration 94
unlinked thoughts 95
unmasking trend 153

vegetative hold, on life 41
vicious circles, in infant–mother
behaviour 72, 187

wakefulness from choice 66
well, as a symbol 21, 22, 30, 34,
54, 55, 84, 127
withdrawal states 13, 14–25,
34, 35, 45, 80, 189, 190, 195,
200, 201; deliberate use of
39; in infants 61, 65, 72, 73;
maternal 72

zone of proximal development
180